Eighty Acres

Eighty Acres

Elegy for a Family Farm

Ronald Jager

With a Foreword by
Donald Hall

BEACON PRESS · BOSTON

Beacon Press
25 Beacon Street
Boston, Massachusetts 02108-2800

Beacon Press books
are published under the auspices of
the Unitarian Universalist Association of Congregations.

97 96 95 94 93 92   8 7 6 5 4

Text design by Christine Leonard Raquepaw

Library of Congress Cataloging-in-Publication Data

Jager, Ronald.
  Eighty acres : elegy for a family farm / Ronald Jager.
    p. cm.
  ISBN 0-8070-7044-0 (cloth)
  ISBN 0-8070-7045-9 (paper)
  1. Farm life—Michigan—Missaukee County. 2. Missaukee
County (Mich.)—Social life and customs. 3. Jager, Ronald—
Childhood and youth. 4. Missaukee County (Mich.)— Biogra-
phy. I. Title. II. Title: 80 acres.
F572.M65J34   1990
977.4'66'009734—dc20   90-52583
                                                  CIP

To the memory of
Jess Jager (1901–1987) and
Kate Schepers Jager (1902–1983)

And for my wife, Grace,
who first suggested it
and always encouraged it
and finally named it

Contents

There is something appealing about a miniature universe. I think of the landscapes people assemble to run model trains through, where the scale of locomotive and car permits a cosmos: tiny roads with tiny barriers that rise and fall, little houses with doors that open and lights that go on and off, mirror-fragments for ponds, small pupils carrying microscopic lunchbags into infinitesimal schoolhouses. Some books provide this Terrarium Effect, not because they are small, but because the scale and distance of retrospect combine to make an angle of vision: the wrong end of the telescope. In *Eighty Acres*, the boundaries of 257 pages imagine a system, and Ronald Jager makes—by memory, by judgment, and by good sentences—a performable world. As we read this book, we run trains through it.

The author lives in the town of Washington, New Hampshire, and has earlier written philosophy; he was a professor of philosophy at Yale, best known for work on Bertrand Russell. After quitting academia in his forties, he wrote (in collaboration with his wife) histories of his state and his town. Now, in *Eighty Acres*, he has returned to an earlier landscape, telling us about growing up as a farm boy in western Michigan. When I read Ronald Jager, I become aware of strange overlaps and oppositions—in his experience and in mine—which add curiosity to pleasure as I read. While Jager as a child hayed and picked berries in western Michigan, I did the same (a more elderly child) on a New Hampshire farm. But I lived this life—horse and buggy, antique farm implements—only in July and August, for when summer ended I returned to suburban Connecticut. Ronald Jager's early life was integral; mine was bifurcated into summer and winter, country and suburb, old time and new. My suburb thrived outside New Haven, where Jager later taught at Yale, but by the time Ronald Jager arrived in Connecticut I had departed from New England—to spend seventeen years in the State of Michigan. My Michigan was academic Ann Arbor— where (among others) I taught the children of Dutch farmers, mostly transfers from Calvin College. By 1990, both of us have the good luck to live in New Hampshire writing books.

Until Jager went to Calvin College, he expected to become a farmer like his father; he had no thought of professorships or philosophical doctorates. While *Eighty Acres* recounts only his early life, of course the man in his fifties writes about one world through the spyglass of another. Jager tells his rural childhood with warmth and intimacy, with an affectionate irony—and from long retrospect. Jager is separated from his childhood not only by decades. Although his prose never makes academic noises, his rural childhood sees itself through the spectacles of a man who has survived graduate study at Harvard and teaching at Yale. The separateness of culture is inevitable; and after all, if Jager had remained to farm his land, he would have found exile willy-nilly. The machines and banks of agribusiness would have altered his farm—and his mind— as much as reading Kant did.

The reader profits: for exiles write the best books about home. Without separation, there is no vacancy to fill; we make wealth out of poverty; we rush to fill what history has emptied. But I want to ask: Why *must* we write about lost worlds? *Nostalgia* is the word by which people dismiss recollections or praises of times gone by. Heaven knows, we may grant that nostalgia is frequently a device for idiots and salesmen. Looking at television ads for GM, for sweet wine, for insurance, for hardware stores, and for beer, one might understand that United States was a rural country.

The semi-smart response to dumb nostalgia is to dismiss *all* recollection as equally contemptible. But no two things are ever quite the same. There is nostalgia and nostalgia—and nostalgia. If I caesar all nostalgia into three parts, it is to toss two parts into the town dump. First, I toss out the manipulation of stereotypes to sell products; second, I toss the merely universal result of aging, our sentimental equation whereby *I get feebler every day* translates into *The world gets worse every day.* This second, personal, and un-historical nostalgia is universal; smart folks must remain alert not to succumb to it.

But the past (by the magic of tautology) is no longer present. Useful nostalgia acknowledges the pastness of the past, its irrecoverability, and attempts preservation (not quite restitution or reconstitution) by images that conserve. Such an exercise is indeed *conservative,* but it does not imply political conservatism. (Usually preservation is anathema to political conservatives who are radicals of Modernity and Progress: archons of agribusiness, Attilas of development.) Our reminiscence helps us remind ourselves—lest we inhabit a shallow present—that things *really* disappear. What's gone is gone, all right; by memory we keep its ghost around, not merely to look at but also to think with. The past criticizes the present; this criticism may help to construct a future. If we don't keep the past around—in museums and theme parks, in poems and stories—we can't use it.

Some people have suggested that, if disappearances are perpetual, maybe they are always the same. The implication has its truth: I love a passage found in Eastman's 1900 *History of Andover, New Hampshire,* where an old man laments the passing of the teams of horses that used to haul freight, O teamsters of yore, along the turnpikes of olden time. The old fellow allows as how your Modern Inventions, like railroad trains, are mighty and utilitarian, all right all right . . . but oh, how he regrets those beautiful teams of horses! I try to remember his elegy whenever I weep to regret 1943, huge freight trains rolling with war material north to Canadian ports, a hundred cars long, O cabooses of yore; whenever I ululate over the ghost trains that never roll on the grown-over track unblowing their rusted whistles.

Yes: men and women die, buildings rot or burn; especially technologies (horse teams and locomotives) vanish. We preserve them in photographs or other visual bodiments, but we preserve them best in language—*Gilgamesh*. Homer, Virgil, and Sarah Orne Jewett. The word's power describes, and even *inscribes*—by rhythm, image, and metaphor—the tone and feel of a lapsed moment. And the dried pellet blooms into full flower with the reader's willing damp participation. Maybe most reminiscence is merely archival, decently preserving for descendants the name of a creek and a great-grandmother, rotation of the crops and the seasons, but when a writer like Ronald Jager does it, we are allowed to rehearse inside our own bodies and minds an articulated instant of the never-experienced past. We enter the spirit of a Dutch farm family in western Michigan, we smell horses and outhouses, we remember pregnancies and berrypicking, cats and dogs and churches; we walk into a dead kitchen and sit down.

We need *Eighty Acres* not for mourning so much as for knowing. We need its preserved world and we need also to judge that world. *Eighty Acres* allows its attractions full speech—and sentimentalizes nothing. We feel Jager's affection for family life, yet we understand also his criticism of passivity and narrowness. We enjoy his small universe intact and whole, with its smells and comforts, its fatty diet and its security, enacted before us like a village behind glass, small trains running through it. Always the author's affection tempers itself by the light wash of an adult and responsible irony—thoroughly gentle, loving, and uncompromised. Always the train works its lifelike circle, and its whistle hoots out loud in the circle of the dream.

Donald Hall

Preface

When we walked barefoot through the puddles in the driveway, it was nice to feel the mud between our toes. I haven't done that in some time, but I remember what it's like and where it was.

In Missaukee County, Michigan, there was a rectangle of straight and grassy fencerows enclosing eighty acres; and upon those acres, a woodlot, a swamp, a dozen fields, a few undistinguished buildings. South of the barn were the pastures and a pond; east of the house and to the north, the orchard and the garden; westward stretched the long curves of the driveway, sometimes muddy, otherwise just a pair of gentle sandy ruts pointing to the gravel road. The Depression and World War II were in the air, and so was the harsh squeak of the neighbor's rusty windmill, twisting, twisting to catch the fickle wind.

There we, a family of seven, worked hard, played hard, felt the pungency of farm life. It will be a part of us all forever.

My aim in this book is documentary: to capture and exhibit the experience of being young and on a farm—work and whimsy, warts and all. I have a point of view: from rural New England, forty and more years later, I review the fields and farmyards of Michigan, my native state. Old New England, whose history is etched into the rocky, wrinkled face of its landscape, secretes robust memories—its own or anybody's who falls under its sway. I've been under its sway for decades now, but each year when I return to Michigan, deeper memories from a vanished world rise from their slumber and tramp across the horizon. They come from the days when experience first slipped into the memory whole and undigested. Parochial episodes some of them certainly are—though valid, I hope, for the quality of their insignificance—and seen as through the other end of a telescope, sharp and clear and far away, within the compass of quite another world.

If my early experiences are rooted in the soil of rural life, they are now linked in recollection with that most curious flowering of American iconography: the Family Farm. Like many icons, this one too has a presence and an authority that are nearly inscrutable. I'm not trying to explain it, just offering an example. There are hundreds and thousands of such examples, and every one is different and every one is the same. I mean my example to be realistic, and if it's symbolic as well, that's fine.

In our part of Michigan the saga of the Family Farm had a certain short and mythic symmetry: a beginning, a middle, and an end. Ours was an immigrant community, composed among pine stumps, and in its original form it lasted little more than fifty years. Because my brothers and sister and I happened to enter the drama near the middle, the scenes I've gathered carry the plot from the thirties through the forties. In about 1950, the Michigan enactment of the Family Farm (and not only Michigan's) began to wind down very swiftly, then fade into the background. There wasn't a conclusive moment for that mode of farming, but there was an ending nevertheless, and new beginnings of still-uncertain destiny.

That sounds more grave than I want it to be, for I didn't set out to be solemn. In fact, initial seed for this book was casually sown a decade ago, when my young son would scramble onto my knee after dinner and demand yet another story about "when you were a little boy." Later, some of the episodes that got caught in the planning for this book were probably ones that echoed in memory more clearly because I was watching him grow up and was making the inevitable comparisons.

Thus variously stimulated, I set out in high spirits to document, by recall and by example, the texture of American rural family life in my locale at about the time of World War II, its peculiar tang and resilience, as revealed in scenes and circumstances recollected. It's the humor and banality of farm life, its sport and charm, its callousness and quirkiness as well as its deep coherence that I sought to depict. I'm aware of the elegiac tendency of this tale, and of our inextinguishable national romance with the idea of the Family Farm. I began writing somewhere in the middle of this book— among the crows and the huckleberry pie, or thereabouts—and plowed cheerfully toward both ends, convinced, as I still am, that if I was scrupulous enough, rightly cultivating the bare facts, then the meaning, if such there be, would sprout and flourish by itself.

I hope, therefore, that I have drawn attention to some of the tenuous and expressive lines that join two very different orders of reality: the vivid experience of living within a farm family and the abstract idea of the Family Farm.

Eighty Acres

❧ 1 ❧

Landscape for Figures

Michigan is the low-lying bed of an ancient sea. New Hampshire is a thin layer of soil halfheartedly covering a large and obtrusive chunk of granite. The granite is even older than the sea.

Whenever I reflect on the wide and spare landscapes of Michigan, I can't help comparing them with the near and jagged horizons of my part of New Hampshire. Ever and again when I return to Michigan, the first and overwhelming fact that strikes me, intimating a presence more than visual, is the persistent flatness of that land. From the wrist where I enter the state, I drive for three or four hours to my destination at the second knuckle of the ring finger, and I hardly find a wrinkle. The scenes that unroll are smooth and fair, and there are no surprises.

So I hunt for the venerable things, and for such decorum as they suggest: old farm windmills, everlastingly charming and scenic and often askew, some of them just spinning freely in the wind, year after year, long since unconnected to the water pumps that now lie rusting at their feet; pine-stump fences, still bristling and durable, linking generations of farmers to last century's waves of lumbermen; groves and farm woodlots with sharp boundaries set a hundred years ago; farmhouses of fieldstone here and there, many neglected now but maybe next century's historic homesteads; and long, bright fields of crops, sometimes flanked with somber swaths of fallow farmland.

The inherited rural composure of these regions, though scattered and hidden, is still apparent to attentive eyes and is punctuated now by the incessant clusters of farm silos, which have their own more modern and ambivalent decorum. But whenever there is a city in the offing beside the flattened highway, the world's highest, gaudiest billboards raise an indecorous clamor to the skies. I do not know why. Does terrain that is not doing much for itself invite someone to do something to it? At any rate, the statements made on this landscape are artifacts, man's idiom, not nature's. In two hundred miles I have barely climbed two hundred feet, and I can pick out small objects, groves or windmills, from miles away. Everything is on view. Again and again my attention runs out of favorite objects and keeps reverting to the flatness of the land and the expanse of the sky. Here is a landscape with scattered memories and few secrets.

I drop off the long horizontal curves of the interstate to cut through a string of crossroad towns: zig north, zag west, zig north again, another zag west. Spilling out of every town, suburbia trickles along the edges of the two-lane road—houses parked in a row where the potato patch used to be. The story of America. Almost certainly I shall spot an old two-handled horse-drawn walking plow, parked on a flat rock or on a little concrete pedestal in the center of someone's lawn. The plow's moldboard, once steel gray and glistening from the soil, might now be painted silo blue, its handles barn red, white petunias flowering at its feet. I have to re-spect a landscape so candid as this, but I incline also to sympathy for the plow, for a retirement so conspicuous as that.

Back on the level interstate, aiming again toward a certain well-known eighty acres, I put aside the modern story of the land and lapse into a favorite background fable. Ages and ages ago, as this future farmland oozed upward from the bed of a dying sea, a giant rolling pin swept across it, squeezing the moisture to the sandy edges of great lakes of fresh water. The lakes today shape the Michigan profile as they do because aeons and aeons earlier, when God formed the world, He rested His hand gently here, and as He lifted it the moist primordial soil clung with suction to its Creator, reluctant to leave the hand that formed it, then dropped into its present shape.

My fable is too extravagant even for Michigan friends. Flat? Michigan? Heaven's own handiwork?

If the flatness of most of the state's lower peninsula strikes me forcefully now, it may also be because it escaped my attention for the first twenty-five years that I looked at it. Our eighty acres in Missaukee County, though perfectly rectangular like every other, seemed neither predictable nor flat. Every farm I knew had its own small, rolling hills, its peculiar gullies and ruts and wet spots, its own swales and slopes. Close up, the texture of every farm was its very own, unique, like the face of a friend. Same pattern, different fabric. Yet, altogether, they seemed to unfold monotonously at a steady pace all the way to the wide, encircling lakes. All there was, wherever one went, was another farm and more flatland.

Time has wiped away what was once the inevitability of the Michigan terrain and invested it with meanings, and possibilities of meaning, I did not know it had. Familiar things: openness and freedom; a tractable landscape; nature easily subdued and rationalized; a past that is short, and worn rarely and lightly and uneasily; horizons for the mind and eye that are far away and unobstructed; fields and fencerows and roadways that are square and straight and absolutely predictable; a sense of space if not of place; a physical environment where the hand of man is in the foreground and the hand of God is now only in the background. The land's story is a wide-open book.

Michigan was mostly virgin pine wilderness when surveyors went to work on it, drawing brisk sets of perpendicular parallel lines. Voilà! A checkerboard descended upon the forest primeval. Dozens and dozens of neat squares, dozens of townships, every one six miles on a side, each one numbered if not already named, and each divisible into exactly thirty-six neat square-mile sections, each section of 640 acres being numbered, using the same formula in every township and starting in the northeast corner. How casually, and definitively, was the Michigan wilderness demystified! Today I am driving toward a certain rectangle of land, one already pinpointed by a unique description, very cold and precise, 150 years ago, when this land was still unbroken pine: "S 1/2 NW 1/4, Sect. 15, Township 21 North, Range 7 West." That's the south half of the northwest quarter of a square-mile section in a certain township. That's exactly eighty acres.

These townships of thirty-six sections have exact but arbitrary bounds: natural and geological boundaries they did not offer, political boundaries they never acquired, so emotional boundaries they do not have. How unlike New England! In Michigan, the background echoes are not the pulse of history or the strife of politics but only the murmuring pines and the hemlocks. Although our eighty acres was in what the map called Riverside Township, that wasn't where we were "from" and it was never part of a postal address. (In rural New England you are definitely "from" your town, and even your country home or farm invariably defines itself by the town it is within.) In most of rural Michigan you aren't "from" anywhere, and the farms do not fall "within" towns. Michigan rural folk just live in places like "west of town," "south of Vogel," "toward Lake City," and so on. The township is just a square, boring background fact.

When Michigan wanted counties, it was easy to create them: large, square blocks of townships, sixteen whenever possible. Most of lower Michigan today—counties, townships, sections, farms— is an ordered patchwork of squares threaded together by straight roads and fencerows. Jetting 30,000 feet above it, you can count the crossroads as they flip past the edge of the plane's wing, one about every six seconds; and you can calculate your speed, about 600 miles per hour. Down there, there are few ambiguities about boundary lines and there is seldom a boundary dispute. Rural sociology is just that much simpler, local history that much sparer.

The historical line goes straight back to the Land Ordinance of 1785, in which the Continental Congress stipulated that the Northwest Territory would be surveyed in six-mile squares. Not seven or five. Six. The fathers were founding a world in which you could play square with your friends, square off with your adversaries, and square up with your debtors. Today I drive around our local town, McBain, and its environs, and I see again that every building, house or barn, farm or village, stands square with the world, the only exceptions being the compliant structures huddled along the northwest-running railroad track. I am more aware than ever that a person could live on that plotted, checkered countryside for half a lifetime without noticing how relentlessly rational it was.

Or what a succinct metaphor it is.

The landscape insinuates its way into your sense of what is real—becomes, in fact, itself a locus and medium of values, no less powerful because expressed in the language of figures. Our eighty acres was a rectangle, or two forty-acre squares, set in the very center of an immeasurable sphere, and the Michigan we lived in was a place that valued square meals, square deals, square fields, corn planted on the square, square sections, square townships; and a good furrow was always plowed square with the fencerow. In contrast, the paisley-shaped towns of New England, gerrymandered and wrapped around one another like fish in a pail, are exhibiting their own history too—a history that seeps into everything, blurring straight lines and cutting corners. True, many New England towns tried to start out more or less six miles square (which is where Congress got the idea for the Northwest Territory), but the land—to say nothing of politics—was utterly recalcitrant. Not so Michigan, whose history was still uncluttered and whose pliant terrain yielded and was squared away without a murmur.

As it yielded, the land also came to echo the figurative language of the Bible. The New Jerusalem, the symbolic City of God portrayed in Revelation, has foundations laid in heaven and is "four-square," equal in length and breadth and height, perfect in spiritual substance and visible form. Square is perfection—order, domestication, peace. From atmosphere and environment we absorbed the play of such imagery: landscapes of value and fact, spiritual and physical, shaping one another's contours.

In my early twenties, I left Michigan to teach in Iowa for a year, and I learned there that indeed most of Michigan is hilly. But I write now from New England, which has been home for thirty years. If Iowa temporarily confirmed for me that Michigan is wrinkled, the perspective from New England has flattened it forever.

The two regions offer sharply contrasting specimens of the historic encounter of man and nature—or, rather, of farmer and field. Unlike my native Michigan, with its accessible environment, the geography of New England is inhibited and inhibiting, never banal, stubbornly resistant to human will, and nearly everywhere a physical obstacle that one submits to with humility or surmounts with pride. Although there are few or no wolverines left in the Wolverine State, the granite is inexhaustible in the Granite State.

But New England is also weighted down with its cultural traditions and artifacts, its slowly accumulated sense of place, time, and precedent. The stone walls of generations of yeomen lie heavy across the land, ushering memories of ancient struggle with a landscape along winding roads toward village greens where Revolutionary soldiers once tramped. Here American settlers first carved farms from what they called a "howling wilderness"; here they subdued to fields the implausibly rocky surfaces of the Granite State, building homesteads designed to last forever; and from here their descendants, in the latter half of the nineteenth century, being devoted to farming and to livelihood and not to antiquities, fled in droves—left these ancestral homes for Iowa, where the soil was rumored to be everywhere level and a yard deep, and for Michigan, where a good man could earn a dollar a day and buy good land for a dollar an acre.

My ancestors did not come to Michigan from New England; they came from the northern provinces of the Netherlands.

The day they left the Old Country, they became one and all "Hollanders." They had been farm laborers there and, late in the nineteenth century, they came to seek a better life in the land of opportunity. And they found it. They had the wit not to stop off in New England, though the agricultural offices of Vermont and New Hampshire were then advertising in northern European periodicals that farms were available and cheap in New England. My ancestors would have heeded rather the counsel of their pastor, so they headed straight for Michigan, where someone they knew already had connections. That was about 1900.

It took the Hollanders a generation or so to get around to thanking America for the opportunity, for they had not come to become Americans; they had come as colonists. They found Michigan lands nearly timbered off, level, and marked out in accord with the rational preferences of God, nature, and the government. That represented the kind of discipline these Hollanders could appreciate. They set up their colony and did what they could to ignore the Americans who had surveyed, timbered, or homesteaded the land —after buying the best of it from them. By the time I came along, in the early thirties, the non-Dutch residents of the community were referred to, without a hint of irony, as "Americans" or "outsiders," those terms being synonymous. The land of opportunity had delivered what it had promised: the opportunity to be what you were. This is what they were: Dutch, Calvinist, very well instructed in religion, hardworking, independent, apolitical, and dedicated to the production of large, stable families to be nurtured within the fold of the church.

On the whole, it worked out. By 1930 the colony of Hollanders in and around Missaukee County numbered approximately six hundred families and fifteen churches and two Reformed denominations. (Families, churches, and denominations were the relevant units of social accounting.) The Dutch yeomen and women had established an agricultural society that was remarkably stable and predictable for the entire first half of the twentieth century, despite war and depression and war again.

During the ascendancy of this small sector of Michigan agriculture, almost all of New England's farm communities were sliding downhill, a decline already well under way in the last quarter of the nineteenth century, when Missaukee County was first being cleared of its pine trees and the first prospecting Hollanders were starting to sift the soil in the clearings. They saw that the land was flat and the soil sandy, as in the old country; therefore it must be good. Actually, it was rather poor. But their religion told them that if they worked hard, it might improve. They did and it did.

The poets have suspected that intimations from our landscapes work upon our spirits unobserved and only later seep into consciousness. At any rate, it is by ruminating among the landscapes of New England that I have come to repossess a sense of the Michigan countryside that I imbibed as a youth but knew too intimately to understand. It's always possible, of course, that over the shoulder the old landscape appears flatter and squarer than it is, and its furrows straighter, just as it certainly once appeared hillier, the grass taller, the thunder louder, the music sweeter, than it really was.

2

Following Furrows

I started plowing at about age four, but I was not a prodigy, just a fanatic.

In my earliest recollections I am following my father as he is plowing—tramping patiently behind him, furrow after furrow after furrow, hour after hour after hour. Monotonous and repetitive as it was, somehow it gave me an intimate share in my father's wondrous operations, whose scope and grandeur mesmerized me, drawing me on, mile after mile. Perhaps a normal kid would have used his creative imagination in a sandbox; but I had a congenial sandbox substitute in the back forty that required no brains at all: just follow the furrows.

What lingers in memory is the keen, sensuous delight of cool and shiny furrow bottoms under the soles of bare feet, flat and firm as a linoleum floor, perfect pathways, straight and narrow, no more than a foot wide; the reassuring sound of the horses' steady tramp, tramp—the faint squish and squeak of their leather harnesses, and the soft, bell-like tinkle of the dangling links of the harness tugs; the calm, unbroken guttural hum of the plowshare as it effortlessly lifted the sod, turned it gracefully along the moldboard, and buried it facedown in long, elegant strips; the excitement of turning the corner at the end of the field, where I had to scramble out of the way so we could make a new furrow to follow. I could not get enough of it.

Occasionally my father would stop to rest the horses, and I would sit on the sod with my feet in the furrow to watch him. He would yank the plow out of the soil and tip it sideways, reach into the front pocket of his bib overalls for his jackknife, and go to work on the plow's moldboard (the curved face that slid beneath the sod and turned it), picking at the rust spots so that the soil could shine the entire surface to a sparkling steel gray. Far behind us the furrows stretched back, almost to the end of a four-year-old's world— or at least way back to the chokecherry trees. We drank in the smell of the fresh earth and were then cheerfully under way again. What my parents reported in later years (and I forgot) was that I zealously fought off all attempts to make me stop and rest. Once the undertaking had begun, I would not leave it; my protests were so unreasoning that they would relent and let me go until the field or the day was done—or until I was, and dropped.

Eventually, my parents did make me give up plowing and sent me off to kindergarten. They could not have known then that in the long run it would probably be school, in one form or another, that would redirect my peasant impulse. Although the single-mindedness of a four-year-old is a passing thing, and mine too gave way to more erratic forms of amusement, I have from those earliest days retained an affinity for the farm and farming; and even the drudgery of many chores, which I later discovered and exaggerated and learned to loathe with all the righteous vigor of youth, did not incline me to thoughts of escape. And years later, when I plowed by myself—not with horses, which I seldom had a chance to do since my father reserved that for himself, but with the neighbor's tractor—I still found the task absorbing, still found the long, smooth furrows seductive. All farmers love the plow.

But they don't plow every field each year. We plowed only the fields that had a sod and were to be planted to row crops, such as corn or potatoes. Fall plowing helped to keep the quack grass at bay the next year, but we paid something for that in winter erosion of the bare soil. We also gained something by making lighter the next spring's work load, which was generally too heavy for comfort. Fall plowing was the last work of the season, and my father did it in November after the potatoes were packed away in the cellar, after the corn was husked and the sugar beets were sold, and just before the ground froze and the snow came and it was time to think about winter woodcutting.

The straight furrows of those Missaukee County farms were connected with larger fields of enterprise, with patterns apparently written in the stars, written in the air, written in the minds of all the future farmers in the community. The main pattern was this:

When a young man had worked as a day laborer long enough to have saved a down payment, he bought a farm (eighty acres was pretty standard) and married, and the couple promptly started a family. Both knew then that they would spend the next twenty-five years trying to "get ahead," on a path already well laid out. Financially, the young farm family had three challenges: cash flow, overhead, and capital expenses, which boiled down to grocery money, taxes and interest on the mortgage, and machinery. They tried to meet the weekly grocery bills, which grew as the family grew, with the regular sale of eggs and milk or cream, hoping for a little extra to buy clothes, gasoline, and a few incidentals. For taxes, mortgage interest, and capital expenses—which always assumed exactly that order of priority—every farmer relied on one or more cash crops: potatoes, beans, and sugar beets were the most common. Only if the cash crops were unusually good could the farmer consider a serious capital purchase, such as a new team of horses. The other field crops—hay, corn, wheat, oats—were consumed by the livestock and were thereby funneled into the cash flow.

If things went as expected, the couple eventually "got ahead" and in thirty years or so had paid off the mortgage and had begun to save for retirement. What differentiated farmers at this point was probably not cash in the bank, for nobody had much, but the condition of the farm—its buildings, tools, fields, and livestock—and thus its market value. At about age sixty or sixty-five the couple sold the farm, usually to a son or son-in-law, moved to a small house in town, and lived out their days from the interest and the mortgage payments, just as their parents had done.

Such was the prevailing conception of human society in the community I grew up in. Although it was not a pattern first devised in Missaukee County, when it was planted there, just before the turn of the twentieth century, it took root and grew. Uncounted communities had done it before, and uncounted writers had rung the changes on the basic themes of American agrarian culture: villages and small diversified farms, lands owned by the freemen who tilled them, noble yeomen close to neighbors, close to nature, close to God; a self-sustaining society of family farms—the foundation of freedom and democracy. Wasn't there a fable of husbandry somewhere in the air to that effect?

There was indeed. But it would have sounded very strange to the ears of these Missaukee County farmers. Did these Hollanders know that—if the ancients are to be believed—there is a special grace that flows from the well-tended soil to the soul of the tiller? This was mainly a community of immigrants; they had built their barns, enlarged their families, and tilled their fields long, long before they began to pick up on the astonishing political folklore that in America, the foreign country where they toiled, civic virtue itself was supposedly drawn from the family farm. They didn't know that a hundred years before they got here, the precedents had been worked out both in theory and in practice, with copious classical allusions; that Thomas Jefferson had declared that "those who labor in the earth are the chosen people of God." To those of English descent in this community, such talk would have sounded merely strange. To the Dutch it would have sounded positively pagan—as new ideas often did. Had the same Jefferson affirmed that "the small landowners are the most precious part of a state?" Who, *us?* Precious to God, yes; but they scarcely considered themselves part of a state at all. They were merely doing what came to hand.

The Hollanders of this community and their ancestors had been menial laborers across the sea; their experience was meager and their models were few. Their ideology was Dutch Calvinism, not literary agrarianism, and if they were reenacting the American rural dream, they were certainly not stimulated by ideas in the air but by raw materials on the earth. What they brought to the conveniently cutover flatlands of Michigan was a little piece of the Netherlands, church and all, and they simply parked it among the stumps and went to work, their rural pieties being structured by the Old Country and the Old Testament, not at all by the pastoral rhetoric of the American gentry.

In the Netherlands they had not been landowners, so they had to fashion a new mode from scratch, and what they designed, almost casually, was an agriculture that appeared to be as workable as it was simple. Like hundreds of little cultures before them, the Hollanders reinvented the American family farm.

For all its storied simplicity through the years, the family farm involves, and conceals, complex economic orders. The system we knew relied upon a fine-spun network of interdependent strands: look closely and you see that everything seems to depend on everything else. Perhaps the type of mixed farming practiced in our region was not so much an option chosen as a set of corollaries that flowed naturally from already-given premises.

One man and two horses or a small tractor could handle up to eighty acres, which set a natural limit to farm size. Crop diversification, based on the farm's needs and the market's demands, put everything into a modest scale: ten acres of any one row crop was a lot. Moreover, the soil itself, not especially fertile, required crop rotation, and that alone imposed variety in field crops. The soil also required manure, so the farm required livestock. Diversification was also a financial necessity, a hedge against failures: the potatoes might be blighted one year, but the bean crop could probably be depended upon; milk prices might drop, but egg prices would hold; if not, we could sell some chickens, feed the grain to the cows, and sell cream. Thus all the major demands of the system— cash flow, feeding the family on a regular basis, built-in insurance against hard times, predictability, and the need for the farm to pay for itself steadily over the course of three decades or less—were exactly geared to the rhythms and variables of small-time mixed farming.

No wonder all the farms shaped up in remarkably similar ways: a half-dozen standard field crops, some wasteland in pasture, at least two cash crops, six to ten cows, a team of horses, a hundred chickens, some pigs, an orchard, a garden, a woodlot. On every farm every one of those elements was tied to each of the others, some very tightly, some less so. We hauled the hay that fed the cows that fertilized the fields that grew the grain that thickened the milk that fattened the pigs that supplied the bacon that fed the family that hauled the hay. I suppose all this made hauling hay and spreading manure significant; I don't recall that it made them fun.

Tightly integrated as it was, the economic network had some slack, room for innovation. If we tugged on the webbing at one spot, adjustments fell into place all along the line. One neighbor would try sheep for a few years and cut down on milk cows; another chose to sell milk instead of cream, and therefore to feed grain and grass instead of skim milk to the pigs and calves. After a few years of severe potato blight, some farmers dropped potatoes and put in sugar beets instead. That affected six acres but not the crop rotation. Nobody did anything radical, such as selling all the cows to raise only sugar beets, for that would be ruinous to the soil, create an unmanageable seasonal work schedule, make the farm vulnerable to crop failure, and dry up the regular cash flow. No one around us was incautious; the incautious ones didn't stick around.

But there were dozens of interstices in the network where a

farmer could exercise his whims or improvise. Just after the war, we found that there was a market for strawberries and that we were good at raising them. Within a few years we had a thriving little garden industry, bartering berries at stores, selling them at the door and even on a pick-your-own basis, unheard of at the time. When string beans came along we developed a new August cash crop—and a new way for the kids to earn good money to buy new clothes for school. We picked beans by the pailful, up to two hundred pounds a day apiece, and sold them by the bagful at the outlet that a distant canning factory had opened in nearby McBain. Later, when we found that the woodlot was full of potential potato crates, we readily taught ourselves how to extract and sell them. It proved to be good Saturday work in the winter.

Did anyone fully appreciate how much the whole system leaned upon the competence and versatility of the women? Not likely. Women managed incredibly labor-intensive households, often without electricity and with water that had to be carried in from the outdoor pump, and they were expected to stand in readiness as extra farmhands when special needs arose. All farm women had some experience milking cows or driving a team or tractor, and some few did it regularly for months at a stretch. Some could handle a pitchfork on a hay load side by side with men. Although I never saw my mother harness a horse, I knew she could do it, for she had done it often as a teenager. (That was something *her* immigrant mother was embarrassed never to have learned, for her family had been too poor to own a horse when she was a girl in the Netherlands; but in America, this fabled land of opportunity, my grandmother had daughters who could harness their own horse to their own surrey.) So, yes, the women worked extremely hard; and most of them accepted it as part of the good life.

We were interdependent with the neighbors, and not just for emergencies, for no farmer had all the tools he required, nor all the manpower or horsepower. Haying, threshing, butchering, operating the buzz saw to cut logs into stove-length wood, filling the silo—for these, neighbors traded time with one another. An unwritten rule was that common tools and machines were seldom lent out, but the services of an implement with team and driver were sometimes bartered. Dad regularly bindered the grain of one neighbor and got paid for it by the use of that neighbor's horse to help our horses pull the binder to cut first our grain and then another neighbor's grain—for which Dad was paid three dollars per acre. Thus were economy and farm ecology in some kind of intricate balance, a complex organic system.

Complex, yes, but somewhat in the way that, for example, the underlying grammar of the English language is complex. On the face of it the economy appeared straightforward, like an English sentence: it was always quite apparent what needed to be done. Intuitively, everyone gets the hang of the language simply by using it; analytically, hardly anyone grasps it. Though our farm system was intricate, we didn't have to contemplate its inner logic; analysis was for another generation.

The use we made of the woodlot (to us always "the woods") illustrates the connectedness of things, for it was literally the storehouse of the farm-supply system: fuel and lumber, certainly, but a great deal more too, tangible and intangible. Indeed, whenever possible, Dad didn't buy the things the farm needed—he grew them: sleigh runners, wagon tongues, rafters, tool handles, hen roosts, ladders, fence posts, and a dozen other such things, not to mention maple syrup and spring flowers or brush piles for rabbits or browse for deer or shade for cattle or a playground for kids or a quiet destination for a Sunday afternoon walk. The woods was an intricate part of the logic of the whole family-farm scheme. And when I see that the woods my father used for sixty years is in better condition today than when he bought it, I am reminded that farming is nurture and culture, not mining.

The entire system was firm enough, well enough tried and proven, to sustain its own moral expectations. Individuals were directly assessed as lazy, hardworking, slovenly, ambitious, selfish, honest, or kindly without much extenuating to-do. Getting ahead in this world was bluntly attributable to hard work or long hours, and failures were laid to very specifiable causes: natural disasters such as sickness or fire, or lack of willpower or gumption. The system itself was never on trial; it was as much a given as the wind and the weather.

My parents were born in 1901 and 1902 on farms about seven miles from each other. The farm they lived on for 55 years, after they married, in 1927, is also within seven miles of both of their birthplaces. That, then, is where they spent their lives, except that Dad passed a few years of his youth in Kalamazoo, and in their early twenties both my parents worked for a few winters in Grand Rapids. But it is fair to say that their lives were rooted very firmly in the soil into which their immigrant parents had been transplanted. Their parents had been uprooted, and their children would wander; they stayed put. That pattern holds true for almost all the families I knew as I was growing up. Whereas my parents settled a few miles from where they were born, among neighbors and relatives who had also been born and settled there, their children—my siblings and I—have settled in Washington, D.C., Ontario, New Hampshire, Michigan, and Arizona. Theirs, not ours, was the stable and predictable generation; and they, not their parents or their children, lived in a world that seemed predictable.

It was the Depression of the thirties that put the sharpest kink in the whole system; but even that did not break it, did not dislodge its basic assumptions. The burden of the Depression was mainly mental, not physical. There was food and shelter for everybody. Even the poorest had bread as well as meat and potatoes and a warm home, all of it derived directly from the land and from the labors of their hands. My parents always put cream in their coffee, and we always had butter on the table—though we were carefully taught to spread it thinly. Everybody had butter, but nobody had money.

The debt on the farm was the heaviest burden: scraping together the interest payment or pleading for more time was a major agony. Sell a cow to pay the taxes? And sell the hay the cow might eat to pay the interest? Then how would we buy groceries next month? There were neighbors who foreclosed on neighbors and even parents who foreclosed on sons—not always (I understood later) because they were vindictive or without sympathy, but partly because the entire community, confronted with the desperate circumstances of the Depression, simply lacked the moral imagination to figure out what to do. In the face of the totally abnormal, they fell back on legality.

My parents were fortunate. Although for years they paid nothing on the principal and sometimes paid the interest late or not at all, they knew they had a safety net, for the mortgage was held by my father's mother. During later, more prosperous war years, my mother confided to me that her worst dread during the previous ten years had been that she and Dad might never pay for the farm at all, might die leaving that debt to their children. Failure. She could speak of it to me only when it began to appear that that dark shadow might someday be lifted—as it was.

The war economy of the forties straightened out the Depression kink and actually reinforced the old system. After the war, normal patterns returned, though the pace quickened, and many farmers, my parents included, finally pulled out of debt within about five years of the war's end. The world was in tune again and would go on as before. I presumed that the peasant passions I had nurtured behind the plow before I was five would eventually find their natural outlet—on this farm or some other, bigger and better. And when we read in the Bible that "while the earth remaineth, seedtime and harvest, and cold and heat, and summer and winter, and day and night shall not cease," the vision summoned was of groups of small family farms vibrating to their annual rhythms on flat

Michigan landscapes. We would always follow the same furrows. Those were the eternal verities.

Or so it was easy to suppose.

In fact, nobody appeared to have any idea at all of what really lay in the next furrow beyond the turn at midcentury. Agribusiness was not yet a fact, and nowhere within earshot was it even a word; consequently, very few or none were the farmers who suspected that it would so soon drive an entirely new kind of furrow straight across the face of rural history.

Figures on a Landscape

There was a man in our church named John Smith, who had a brother also named John Smith. How queer, we children thought. We had been taught to share things, all right, but sharing names in the family seemed to be carrying it a bit far.

The Smith parents had dealt with the matter simply by calling them Big John and Little John. The one we knew was Big John, who was only about five feet six, but his brother Little John was somewhat taller. They pronounced their name the Dutch way—Smit—since a native Dutch tongue finds the sound *th* unsayable. It's a pretty common Dutch surname, and in fact they also had a grandfather with the same name—John Smith. It seemed to run in the family.

It did indeed. Among some Hollanders tradition decreed that the eldest son be named for his paternal grandfather, and the next son for his maternal grandfather, a custom sometimes so strong that violating it would have opened a family war. The grandfathers of the young brothers Smith happened both to be named John, so that settled that. Middle names might have provided a way around the problem, but I doubt that anybody saw it as a problem. Anyway, nobody had middle names in my parents' generation, for theirs was a spare economy, free of luxury and ostentation. Names were recycled, not squandered where they were not needed.

When my parents took up the naming of children, the old tradition was still alive but more relaxed, so they found a compromise: sons would be named for grandfathers but not called by that inherited name, and they would be given a middle name to use as their very own. (In the immigrant generation's eyes, the conferring of middle names was a secular concession to Americanism.) Accordingly, my older brother was named George Marvin for Grandpa George Jager, and, as the next son, I was duly named Albert Ronald for Grandpa Albert Schepers. An obscure element in this tradition, a source of some ambivalence, held that there was also to be a special bond between grandparent and namesake, but my brother and I were early deprived of the overt burden of that luxury by the untimely death of both grandfathers. I never met either, but one of them cast a spell upon me nevertheless.

In our culture, family lore handed from one generation to the next was sparse, highly selective, and purposive; therefore, what my mother told me about her father had my moral education clearly in view. Grandpa Albert Schepers, who immigrated to this country with a wife and three children in the year 1900, was a man of many passions, likable, a devoted father, capable of great warmth and affection, but also possessed of a legendary, sometimes self-destructive stubbornness. If one must have intimate connections with that sort of man, it is doubtless easier to confront him aloft in an ancestral tree, where he may be an object of curiosity, than, for example, next door as a neighbor, where he might be a subject of controversy. Periodically, Grandpa Albert had had his problems with the neighbors.

Time was when he had been a favorite in the community of Hollanders, a founder and pillar of the local West Branch Christian Reformed Church, an elder in its ruling body, or consistory. But one year—it was about 1915—he was not voted back into office, and he blamed another elder, his neighbor and friend, for voting against him. True or not, warm friendship turned to warm enmity, which soon disturbed the peace of the whole church. When the pastor made a call to try to patch things up, Grandpa, who happened to be haying at the time, chased him off the premises with a pitchfork. Here was something to set the tongues awag! In a biblical community such as that, Grandpa's extraordinary gesture gave him instant notoriety; it was approximately the moral and religious equivalent of stoning the prophets.

As prescribed by the rules of the church, the consistory initiated censorship. The first step was simply that the pastor made an impersonal public announcement, soliciting prayers for an erring member of the congregation. Within the very stiff formality of the church services of that time, and within a culture where the church was the only significant social organization, one to which all immigrant families belonged and in which every member had known everyone else for years, that announcement was a terrifying reproach in its own right. My mother, a girl of about thirteen, was encircled after the service by her friends, jabbering the news: "We gotta pray for your pa, don't we?" This humiliation, together with the episodes that preceded and followed, devastated her—as was evident to me both from the tale itself and from the pain of her retelling it, a generation later.

My grandfather was not a man to be humbled by a few prayers; and he was not only unrepentant, he was defiant. Of course, it was unthinkable to stay home from church, but it was eloquent to go conspicuously to another church of a different denomination. That would show them! So a scenario unfolded: each Sunday, Grandma and her children twice walked two miles to the West Branch Christian Reformed Church, and Grandpa took the horse and buggy six miles to the Falmouth Reformed Church. He had found a potent weapon: he could nurse his grudge and his religion at the same time. For years, while his family and friends ached for him, he kept warm his quarrel with the neighbor and the pastor and the church. "Oh, what peace we often forfeit / Oh, what needless pains we bear" was my mother's summary, quoting a hymn they often sang, one that I suppose he too sang, alienated, alone, and in another town. It was the great grief of my mother's youth.

He held out through seven years and ten thousand family prayers. The old pastor died and a new one came and gently, patiently intervened, and eventually the old man mellowed. Grandpa confessed his fault and was reconciled to his neighbors, family, church, and God. The whole community rejoiced, marveling at what an extraordinary miracle it was. But the experience had seared the edges of my mother's memory, leaving scars of hypersensitivity. Had something been deficient in her father's upbringing? Some weed, perhaps, sowed by the devil in his soul that had not been discovered and uprooted at a young and tender age? It was a thing to watch out for.

Now and then my mother's scars became inflamed. There were times when she gazed at me when I was at a young and tender age, and she saw her father—saw his affections and personality and passions, saw him in my reddish hair and fiery temper. Name, hair, looks, temperament—of course she glowed with pride; of course she cringed with apprehension. Didn't she hear every week in church from the Old Testament that the sins of the fathers might be visited upon "the third and fourth generation"? Whatever that meant precisely, it sounded like a solemn warning. No doubt all children throw a tantrum now and then, but mine were regularly regarded in the special light of my name and looks and ancestry, and it wasn't unusual for a blast of willfulness from me to send my mother careening back to the fields of pain in her own youth. At those times she could not suppress what was for me her ultimate reproach.

"Just like my pa!" she would mutter through clenched teeth.

Always those four words! How I loathed them! How helpless I was against the stigma, for I then possessed only the most fragmentary facts and images of an obscure grandfather, a distant, brooding figure, obviously gravely flawed. Once I fought back, storming and shouting, denouncing the old villain whom I had never seen and who shadowed my steps. "I'm sick and tired of hearing about your stupid old man every time I . . ."—and by this time I had overdone it and was slamming doors and stamping out.

My tirade was precisely the kind of performance that was the root of my mother's concern in the first place, but I was unaware of that; nor was I aware that, on her side, that hated sentence was perhaps not always a rebuke but sometimes a gasp of wonder at the mysteries and continuities of life. We had copious raw materials here—grandfather, superconscientious mother, namesake son—for creating a full-blown specter. But we didn't; it was aborted early and faded away. My mother was alert enough to hear through the storm a small voice pleading for release from a certain insidiousness, and she dropped that hated reproach from her repertoire. One day she unfolded for me the full story of the preacher and the pitchfork and its melancholy aftermath; but she also introduced me to other, more favorable streaks in that complex grandfatherly figure. Perhaps in this way she was also able to still the dark whispers from her own past. For my part, I never again doubted that the inner life of the earlier generation's communities was often more serene from a distance than on closer inspection.

Generally, it was my mother, as keeper and interpreter of family lore, who cultivated the conversations through which we children sifted our experience and assimilated it. My father embodied his values in actions and demeanor, seldom in speech—except indirectly in his ready, dry, and ironic wit. (Later in life his conversation was often loaded with whimsy and banter, the sign of a man at peace.) On day-to-day matters Mother was far more forthright, occasionally very blunt or peppery with friend and stranger alike. She let her concerns show by her outspokenness; he, by his silences.

Since Mother was more likely than Dad to explain the rationale of an event or a decision, we had a better shot at having a policy discussion with her. Not that we got very far. But once in a while she joined a conspiracy to get Dad to back off from the negative limb he had crawled out on. Dad sometimes found it easy to say no first and think later, and he was not graceful at manipulating the social machinery for a change of mind. He sought to avoid precedents of any kind, since he knew they could make life complicated. Usually he pronounced no as "Not just yet," and yes as "We'll see once."

"Never mind what others say," my father would declare, predictably as sundown, responding to our preoccupation with peer-group attitudes. We got the message: of the two contexts from which the younger generation might take its sense of direction, home and companions, the home always had exclusive dominance, not probably or usually but always and absolutely. We lived by certain certainties: our diet had all the nutrition necessary—secure love of parents, trustworthy community of relatives and neighbors, church and school on an even keel, God in his heaven, prayers and a portion of the Bible with every meal, and never a meal missed for want of supply or attention—but not a lot of spice or emotional seasoning beyond that. The world we encountered made sense, for its policies and practices were not casually adrift but usually predictable and principled, although sometimes a little lopsided.

Parents of that culture were fastidious, and ours had a sense of propriety excessively well developed in certain directions. Dad was not beyond taking up a pencil to strike out an offensive word in a book he was reading. (In recent years, retired from farming and carpentry to gardening, he enjoyed James Herriot's books, but he stopped midway through one volume. Too much profanity, he said.) Other attitudes were in line with that approach. Pregnancy, to take one example, was discussed only if unavoidable, and then in the most oblique way possible. In those days storks were still rumored in Michigan, and sex was not mentioned, for the subject did not really exist at all. Still, for all their reticence, for all their strict and abstemious consciousness, my parents were not negative. Both lacked the judgmental and censorious elements of an otherwise Calvinist puritan temperament.

"It's just a stage" was my mother's favorite all-explanatory proposition for handling unsettling phenomena. How exasperatingly dismissive and empty we found it—and eventually how memorable! Time came when it appeared more wise than banal. My mother had never heard of Arnold Gesell, but she would have understood him instantly. We youngsters would rush in to report with alarm that baby Carl was eating grass again, just as he had the day before. Was he somehow weird? "It's just a stage," my mother would say calmly, as she roughly wiped the green juice and the bright grin from his chin. Sure enough, the next week Carl was off grass and complacently eating mud.

In today's jargon I suppose we were ethnics, since our parents could speak a foreign language; indeed, they sometimes talked familiarly of places in the Old Country, places they had never seen but that had been enshrined in their thoughts by their immigrant parents. Probably we met other criteria for ethnicity too, for in the public schools we sometimes ran into the jeer "Dutchman, Dutchman, belly fulla straw. All you can say is Haw Haw Haw." In the older immigrant families, many adults made little effort to learn English and felt no need to. One of my grandmothers, who came to Michigan in 1900, when she was in her thirties, and lived there forty years, never spoke or understood English; so we children never had a conversation with her, though she often lived in our home when she was a widow. My older sister, Gladys, developed a kind of private "Dutchlish" with Grandma through which they seemed to communicate rather well; but to mere boys this lingo was inscrutable and was probably meant to be.

My father was a competent farmer but not among the best. He sought solvency, not excellence, and making money held no charm for him at all. "Love of money is the root of all kinds of evil," says the Bible, and he believed that and lived by it, though he didn't preach it, for it seemed too obvious to need much repeating. Bigger, Faster, Stronger, Cheaper, More Scientific, More Modern, Quicker, Sooner—all the little tin gods of the rural countryside could not awaken his awe. He set very modest goals, achieved them, and achieved something else of immeasurable value, namely, contentment. Even efficiency did not weigh heavily with him: often, I think, he would just as soon work a little harder with a dull hoe as sharpen it. He was far too content, we children often thought, eager juveniles full of fantasies of bigger, better, faster things. We had the notion that we had to be "progressive" to be respectable, and I knew from the time I could say the words that I wanted to be a Scientific and Progressive Farmer.

"Dad, why don't we get a tractor next year? Then we could rent Grandma's Forty or maybe some of Mynie's land."

"Not just yet."

It was exasperating. It was also just enigmatic enough not to completely quash our hopes. We had had the same exchange the previous year. We would have it again the next year. And the next. We never got a tractor; we never even came close. Part of the truth—which we could not have imagined to be true—was that Dad simply would not have enjoyed learning to operate one. Not enjoy driving a tractor? Surely parents were beyond the pale of the young wisdom of their own offspring!

In our community, mores were carefully arranged and well understood—even where they were whimsical or worse. For example: men smoked and women did not; boys tried it out on the sly, and girls (presumably) didn't even try it. This was a matter of mores misunderstood as morals; health and social courtesies were not part of the equation.

Alcohol was a much more complex matter. My mother had a view that was stern and simple: all alcohol was bad, period. The subject was therefore undiscussable, there being essentially nothing to discuss. My father had a more complex stance, namely, that it might be permissible for a grown man to have a beer on a hot summer day—such, at least, was the report of my elder siblings. I picked up on this because it seemed to reveal a philosophical difference between our parents, a point to be savored, for there were not many of them to contemplate. I checked out my father's position directly; sure enough, he declined to affirm that it was always automatically wrong for a man to drink beer. (I did not venture a question about women drinking beer; I think the idea would not have occurred to him.) However, Dad did not personally manage to live down to his liberal principles, saying simply that he did not like beer. His official opinion on the matter made it easier, however, for us children to accept without judgment the fact that an uncle or neighbor might have a few beers cooling in the bottom of the stock tank. I doubt that my parents discussed their differing opinions very much, for in practice they came down to the same thing.

If my father was a teetotaler without emotional baggage, my mother's views had a more specific and illuminating origin. The Dutch immigrant colony from which they sprang had passed through a predictable phase wherein a cultural cleavage developed between the immigrant generation and their American-born bilingual children, the elders dwelling in an alien land whose language they did not speak and whose mores and folkways they did not approve. But they had not come from the Netherlands as teetotalers (Dutch Calvinists have long been among the world's best brewers), and it was easy for the younger generation, seeking forms of rebelliousness against their parents' quaint European ways, to drift to the available pre-Prohibition forms of excess. Drinking became part of the routine of growing up and having a job.

There was enough visible overindulgence in the rural communities of my mother's youth to make the appeal of the temperance movement compelling among high-minded young people. Not from her parents but from her elementary-school teacher my mother and her friends learned to stand erect, point to their toes, and recite, "These are little Temperance feet, / And you'll never find them / Walking in a beer saloon / Dragging me behind them." A strong teacher with clear convictions about these things often set patterns of mind that lasted a lifetime. My mother did not try to compel us to adopt her views, but she took care to explain them to us and to embellish them with a few graphic tales of humiliating public drunkenness. (Years later I discovered that my wife's mother, reared in Wisconsin in a very similar Dutch community, had views exactly like my mother's, and that she had learned them from the same kind of teacher in the same kind of school.)

One day a visiting relative brought some homemade plum wine to our home. Well, at least he *said* it was wine, and probably it had fermented. I clearly recall seeing a plum in the jar, though it is a little late to make a point of that now. Of course, my mother was apprehensive, though I think not about the plum. They were bringing *wine* into her kitchen? Or was this stuff, being homemade, really wine? Was drinking it permissible under these unclear circumstances?

"I don't know, Jess," said Mother.

"We could try it once," said Dad.

Game spirit that she was, Mother tried it, and discovered to her chagrin that the winey plum juice had an attractive taste. She liked it! That left her with a problem almost theological in scope: Was it indeed true that all *real* alcoholic beverages—unlike this mere juice—were bad-tasting, requiring a kind of perversion of palate if not of morals even to like them? (A good theory, which I think had served her well.) Or were alcoholic beverages really after all good-tasting—like, for example, this plum wine—requiring continuous exertions of virtue and self-discipline to resist them? (Not a bad theory either, now that she thought of it.) Clearly, my mother had a conundrum on her hands. Which of the opposing theories would she go for?

If I have forgotten the precise resolution of her perplexity, I can surmise the one that falls within the spirits of the occasion. My mother was fair-minded: if there were two sides to a question, or two contradictory theories both pointing toward the same pre-selected conclusion, she was happy to embrace them both. So, very well, alcohol, being the concoction of the devil, had a very insidious taste, terrible but attractive; you had to be corrupt to like it, but you also had to be virtuous to resist it. The splendid illogic of that resolution was of the kind that pleased Dad immensely. She had two opinions, so he didn't need to have any at all, and the fact that he would rather enjoy this than judge it said a great deal about them both.

So Dad smiled and offered no comment on the plum wine except that it was tart, which you could take any way you wanted to. He offered me no wine, either. Good thing: I knew that the merest teaspoonful of that stuff—whether tart, terrible, or delicious— might turn me instantly into a staggering drunk.

It is true that there was sometimes heavy weather over light issues in our household. But the weather had been stormier in the previous generation. Compared with theirs, our own youth was a breeze.

Fragments from the Chevrolet Era

The horse-and-buggy era ended one spring day when I was three years old. For my father the switch to an automobile was a major psychological move; he had not learned to drive in his youth, and in his mid-thirties he bought a car with decidedly mixed feelings. The mixture involved enthusiasm, obligation, and foreboding— especially foreboding.

And, sure enough, within the first year he was in an accident.

One Sunday afternoon, driving out of the churchyard, he was struck by a passing vehicle, resulting in no injury but considerable damage to his car. I was absent from church that afternoon—had probably faked an ailment of some sort—and when the family arrived home with the neighbors and reported that they had had a "crash" and that the car was "broke" and would take some time to "fix," I had to imagine the scene.

The car, I supposed, had shattered on impact like a glass tumbler that crashes to the floor; that is how things "broke." No doubt small and medium-size pieces of car had been scattered all about the roadway and on the grassy banks, and the occupants had found themselves suddenly in the open air, the car about them having vanished into shapeless bits like broken crystal. The task at hand, as I vividly imagined it, was for someone to collect those myriad pieces, as one would a jigsaw puzzle, and reassemble a car from them. It was with this image of things in mind that I offered the savage opinion that I hoped the man who had done it had wrecked his wheels as (so I thought) he drove mercilessly over the scattered shards of our car. Nobody could assure me that that had been his fate. Clearly, there was no justice.

When the car came back, a few weeks later, I looked for but could not find the breaks and crack marks, the seams where they had put the jigsaw car back together. Clearly, there was skill. At any rate, that reassembled 1927 Chevrolet was replaced a few years later by a more modern 1932 Chevrolet.

We drove a Chevy because my parents voted Republican; Democrats drove Fords. That is how I then assembled that part of my social world from the fragments that came to hand. The seams show in a fabrication like that, but I didn't see them then.

Fragments. The memory keeps but a piecemeal diary during the early years—disconnected bits, inconsequentialities.

The Gnostics of old believed that the soul is born in the child at the age of seven. The summer of 1940, when I was seven, recedes as background for one collection of fragmentary events, all gathered around one extraordinary event: our family took a long automobile trip to visit relatives in a far city. It took place over a July weekend and was fondly known thereafter in family lore as "the Trip," notable not only for its highlights but also for the fact that it took place at all. Indeed, for the most part the Trip comes back to me now abstractly, as Event, outlined in memory by the glow of a few shining episodes. It was our journey into the wide world.

We were returning a visit to the families of my father's four brothers—who lived in Imlay City, Michigan—one or more of whom visited us every year. Evidently the visits were not always announced beforehand to us of the younger set, for I know that I sometimes awoke during a summer night to discover a third person in the bed with Nelvin and me, one who invariably claimed, under sleepy interrogation, to be a cousin. Lying there in the dark, we were not in a position to dispute this: we had slews of cousins, and this might be one we hadn't recently seen or felt close to, so we withheld judgment until daylight. It usually turned out to be an Imlay City cousin who came supplied with more of the same, and an uncle and aunt to match.

Thus my uncles' families traveled, but my father was committed to not traveling anywhere, if it could be avoided. There was some basis for his attitude, but rank stubbornness exaggerated it. Because of his early accident and his inexperience, he was still not comfortable with driving, with the idea and the mechanics of it, and he hated the thought of traffic and traffic lights, dreaded the thought of "car trouble" in strange places, and dreaded too, I think, the idea of driving a long distance in a car packed with noisy kids. Moreover, like many others of his generation, he was not yet reconciled to the idea of driving for recreation. Necessities such as going to church and town and to the nearby neighbors and relatives made sense to him; "chasing all the way across the state," as he often put it, did not. So we did not venture far from home. And when my father got stuck in this kind of conservative reasoning and posturing, it sometimes required all the conspiratorial ingenuity of mother and children to release him from it.

Underneath, what bothered my father about this proposed Trip was the very idea of being away from the farm, away from everything that depended on him. Since he had bought the farm, in 1925, he had done the chores and milked the cows twice every day for fifteen years, an unbroken sequence of nearly eleven thousand milkings, part of his covenant with his farm. Just drive away from that commitment for a weekend lark? How easy it was for him to resist the family clamor for a trip—despite all the sweet reasonableness we children fancied we mustered in the cause.

My father caved in when my mother pointed out that his reasoning didn't wash with the relatives anymore: they had mustered the unanswerable logic that he could knock off four brotherly visits with one long, daring drive. The dark news on the world scene had its effect, too. In the summer of 1940 Hitler's minions overran Europe, including the Netherlands, where we had relatives. Maybe one ought to visit relatives here while our part of the world still held—no telling what the situation might be next year. Thus abetted by logic and by Hitler, my father made one exception to his principles.

The facts are straightforward enough.

Origin: McBain, Michigan

Destination: Imlay City, Michigan

Distance: 175 miles

Date: July 1940

Schedule: Leave Friday, return Tuesday

Means: 1932 Chevrolet

Expenses: Several dollars for gas; no other costs

Farm Chores: To be done by Ben Baas

Personae: Father, Mother, Marvin (12), Gladys (9), Ronald (7), Nelvin (6)

Umm . . . it does seem just a bit meager at this remove. Time and distance lend perspective? Only sometimes true. They may also destroy perspective, piling clutter in front of the significant milestones. As a family we all sensed that the Trip was somehow for us a social watershed: we broke out of the sphere of our normal movement, a twenty-mile radius, and went forth to see the world. To hear us from the younger generation report it, everybody else went on trips; well, now so did we. And the Imlay City trip, as symbol and as fact, was forever *the* journey against which all subsequent trips were measured.

As was to be expected, there were family protocols. Children, with all their clamorous vested interests, were not invited into the planning. After parents had made the decision, my mother parceled out the plans to the children in strategic portions, and in accordance with the standing order of merit for children, namely, the scale of our ages. Marvin knew of the projected trip for a month, Gladys for several weeks, and I for only a few days. Nelvin learned the full truth only on the morning of our departure.

However, during the last weeks, Nelvin and I each had an associated "secret," a kind of partial truth leading up to the big truth of the Trip. My secret was just that next Friday we were all going to the town of Marion, eight miles away. This secret piece of the total truth kept me tractable for the week, I presume, and in an appropriate state of expectancy. (Our parents introduced us to as much reality as they thought we could bear.) But when I discovered on the day of departure that Nelvin's secret had been that we were going to Marion "and then somewhere east," I was annoyed that his secret had been better than mine! No fair! The protocols hadn't been strictly observed: I was older than he; my secret should have been better than his.

I content myself at this late date with the following explanation of this apparent lapse in parental justice. Our parents doled out these partial truths, cut into emotionally manageable portions and served up as secrets, as benign forms of discipline and reward. The secret was conceived so that it could be upgraded if the occasion warranted; thus, not just to Marion but now "to Marion and then somewhere east." My theory is that Nelvin's secret had been upgraded from its original form and mine had not. But why? Shall we suppose that he needed an additional bribe or promise at some point to keep him in line, whereas I didn't? Why not suppose that? The other possibility—that he had somehow earned the favor of a better secret and I had not—I dismiss out of hand; and the idea that our parents may simply have been lax about the matter is too farfetched to contemplate.

Friday came. With the foregoing metaphysical ripples behind us, we set out: six of us in the '32 Chevy. In the backseat, Marvin sat at the left window, Gladys at the right window, the privileged positions, and Nelvin and I sat between them, he at my left next to Marvin. For eight years, that was the only arrangement we four ever had in that car, no variation being allowed by us or by our parents. Consequently, there was never a quarrel about who was to sit where or whose turn it was for what. There were no turns; there was a scale of value. That scale was determined by our relative ages, which had been determined by God, and it was not for us to question it. In our world it was as obvious as daylight that the older child deserved the better seat; morality was firmly founded on the nature of things.

In today's jargon, we lived in a structured home. Experience and impulse were fragmentary, centrifugal; policy kept things together. Arrangements were often made more or less automatically by reference to some simplifying principle such as age, sex, precedent, biblical maxim, cost, time. I think my parents abhorred decision making by default or haphazardness; they believed that Christian parents had family policies, and they worked very conscientiously at developing them. Most policies, even the eccentric or serenely wacky ones, were not oppressive, and those that did not serve justice, such as car seating arrangements, at least served decorum, a high value in its own right.

The interior of a '32 Chevy is only slightly larger than that of a Model A Ford. A spare tire is mounted on the rear of the car, and there is no trunk. Where put the luggage for six people for five days? We traveled light. There was just one suitcase, all we owned, and it rode aboard the left front fender; the lunch basket was tied to the other fender. Everything in balance. Thus we set out, heading south into terra incognita.

Marvin had studied a map and described our route, assuring us that there would be marvelous sights and, indeed, that much of the trip would be over paved roads. Although we lived only seven miles from a paved road, we didn't often get to travel on it. Now we learned that we could select a paved route taking us through the edge of a National Forest Reservation. With one voice we voted for the National Forest route, and readied ourselves for the first grand vista, the wonders of the wilderness. (Actually, the vote was five to zero, with Dad abstaining, as was his wont.) Visions of giant trees leapt to our minds—at least to some of our minds—for our conceptions of such matters were easily arranged. This was the arrangement: in our own woods there were some large trees; then, there were *county* parks with larger trees; next, there were *state* forests with still larger trees; finally, there were *national* forests with the largest trees of all. Simple as that. Since we lived in an ordered world, where age and size coincided exactly with merit, we drew the available conclusion, each of us forming a mental picture of what lay before us. Gigantic firs and sequoia-like monarchs of the national forest: they would soar up at the edge of the roadside and tower in majesty above us, leaning against the sky, plumes and profiles befitting the location and occasion. National Forest trees.

The trees did not rise to the occasion. The view offered to us of this region was of cutover pine barrens growing up to scrub oak, trees scrawnier than those in our own woods, stumps like those on the neighbors' farms but smaller. This was a *national* forest? It was more like an assault on our patriotism.

Later in the day there were compensations for the forest failure, sights not to be anticipated. Near Midland we came upon an airplane parked next to the road, and we could not have been more astonished if we had found a submarine parked in our farm pond. The thing was unworldly. Since I had never been to an airport or close to an airplane, I hadn't realized that airplanes—it was probably a Piper Cub—were so *big*. But sure enough, it was a real airplane with real wings and a propeller, and it was right there, almost close enough to touch. Could we stop, we pleaded in chorus from the backseat, and look more closely at this wonder? As we anticipated, Dad thought we'd better not. The trip itself involved precedents enough; no point in courting complications; we were in strange territory; who knew what lay ahead? "There's a lot more to see farther down the road," he said. I know now that whatever reasons he gave or withheld, Dad was thinking that he had promises to keep and miles to go before he'd sleep. We roared on past the sitting plane at nearly thirty miles per hour.

None of the other roadside scenery measured up to the airplane, but there was competition: the bridge in Bay City that tipped up to let boats through on the river below ("Will it tip up when we are on it?"); the factory in Flint that was half a mile long ("Is this the world's biggest building?"); the black family we saw in Saginaw ("Do they *live* in Michigan?"). Marvin had picked a good route and Dad had been right: there were more exotic things to see in one day than we normally saw in a whole year.

And Imlay City, when we got there late in the afternoon, did not disappoint us, even though it was but a small one-stop-sign town with an ambitious name. Just as he had told us, one uncle had a muck farm where the soil was as level as a table, as black as coal, and completely free of stones. Our aunts kept interesting homes, and each of them had a different smell—or did, until my father and Dutch uncles settled down with cigars, after which they all smelled the same: to me, the wonderful aroma of guests. One of my aunts' homes had "running water," meaning indoor plumbing—a curiosity to us children, a luxury my mother dreamed of, an extravagance that did not really appeal to my father. Our cousins, innumerable and very worldly-wise, talked knowingly of a place called Detroit, an important but distant suburb of Imlay City, as I got the picture.

Sunday we attended the Imlay City Christian Reformed Church. Till that day the summer weather had been extremely dry, but a sudden rainstorm struck during the worship service and fell upon a roof whose wooden shingles were shrunken and dilapidated. Rainwater trickled in through the church ceiling in a dozen places; water spattered in the aisles, fell on pews, and ran across the backs of seats as people tried hard to concentrate on the three points of the sermon and pretend that nothing unusual was going on.

Some pious souls, maintaining their poise, slid forward in their wet pews and perched on the dry front edge of the seat, solemn eyes and face still on the minister. In our pew my mother followed the example of others and tried casually to dam the flow with handkerchiefs, but I saw her frail silk dam wilt in the thin stream and collapse, and then I saw the tiny rivulet head for us youngsters, who had been permitted with a sidelong glance and a slight nod to slide to the other end of the pew. The scene in the sanctuary took on an Alice-in-Wonderland cast, curiouser and curiouser; for these Hollanders were a hardy lot, calm and stubborn, and governed, today at least, by a silent covenant: Don't just *do* something, sit there! Like family life itself, worship too had its protocols, not lightly abandoned; and it belongs to the ancestral soul of the Dutch that no water problem will faze them. But it was hard to concentrate on the higher things, hard to squelch the urge to snicker out loud, a thing simply never done in church and certainly not in somebody else's church. Was this weird sideshow really hilarious, and was that a faint smile on Mom's face? Or was it just awful, a massive catastrophe, and was that a faint frown on Dad's face? We children sat convulsed, eyes darting everywhere, alarm and hilarity at war within us. What in heaven's name was going on?

The loyal congregation was being randomly baptized, that's

what; and some worshipers, caught in a direct drip, calmly left their seats and stood at attention in dry corners of the church, leaving their families to dam the pews and cope, or dodge the rain and sing, or just praise the Lord and pass the handkerchiefs. Evidently, the service would carry on, come hellfire or high water. The entire church scene was one of subdued and solemn chaos, the worship service proceeding, merely destroyed but not interrupted.

The excursion to Imlay City lies at the edge of memory, near the beginning of self, sparkling like glassy fragments in the bright sun, ever larger, as Event, than any sum of its remembered parts. It was the only overnight trip we ever took as a family and became, therefore, a pivotal reference point in household lore. If the experience was a slim basis on which to rest our view of the larger world, it is also possible that we might have traveled more while experiencing less.

My idea of what we had achieved was nearly shattered when we returned to school in September and Nelvin and I reported on our life and times to our respective classes. I supposed I would easily top everybody in my grade, and when my turn came I could afford to be summary and succinct.

"We went on a trip—way to Imlay City," I said, and paused for effect.

There was no effect. My classmates simply looked at me. Where's that? What's that? The second-grade class at McBain Rural Agricultural School was definitely not impressed. Evidently, they had never heard of Imlay City.

Never heard of it? I had known about Imlay City all my life and now I had been there. Who were these punks?

Over in the first grade, Nelvin fared much better. He didn't try to sum up the one seamless Event. He was only six years old and he put no soul into his report—just tossed out a few glittering fragments. "We took a trip," he said, "to see an airplane on the ground and a bridge up in the air and a church that leaked, too."

The kids thought he'd had a great summer. And they were right, too.

Songs of Innocence, Songs of Experience

Today I am watching a year-old child entertain himself. Gently, very gently, without the slightest flicker of malice, he pours handfuls of sand on a woolly caterpillar. The more the woolly bear squirms to climb out from under the downpour, the more it pours down upon it. And the noisier is the child's glee. There are worlds in grains of sand; the poets have said so.

Somewhere, far away, images stir. Two familiar kittens uncoil, emerge from remote shadows, and stalk across my memory.

One summer day when I was about six and Nelvin was five, we killed a little gray kitten. We did it by casually torturing it to death.

We began by just playing roughly, then by worrying and assaulting the hapless thing, somewhat as we had seen its own mother do with many a mouse and gopher. We poked and slapped at the kitten with sticks—gently, so as not to destroy it, just slow it up a bit. We jabbed it with a pole when it crawled into the lilac bush, and slapped it and jabbed it when it tried to get out. Then we poured sand over it and dug it up immediately. We did all the normal and subtle things that, for example, a year-old child might do to a caterpillar. Finally, after we had buried it and worried it and poked it some more, the forlorn little kitten just lay still. To our complete surprise, the thing was dead. Our fun stopped.

This appalling behavior was briskly set in its proper light by our mother when she learned of it. I don't know how she found out. We didn't have the wit to hide the evidence by burying the kitten; anyway, we had no experience at burying dead kittens, so that wouldn't have occurred to us. Perhaps we just left the body where it last fell in the garden path, expecting that the matter, if it came up at all, would be charged to the dog's account. What I do recall with a clear, pure light is my mother's response, a tongue-lashing of extraordinary eloquence and force. I see the little gray and lifeless fluff of kitten lying there at our feet and my mother towering over us, pouring reproach and shame and guilt upon us, burying us alive in it, as we had buried the kitten in the sand. Her final withering blast was that we had behaved like "wicked children."

We deserved what we got, and I got most of it, for I was older by a year and a half and had been presumed to know better. My mother, as I learned later, had been too overcome by our bizarre behavior to spank us. After our chastisement she had gone into the house and wept that children of her own flesh and blood should be capable of such unfeeling and wicked behavior, and she prayed that God would convict us of our sin and that we would repent and be forgiven.

In a sense we had not known what we were doing. But suppose we had been interrupted; asked what we were up to, would we have sung songs of innocence? "Oh, nothin', just torturing this little kitten to death, why?" However that may be, *wicked* had not yet become the empty and banal expletive of youth that it is today; it was a biblical term, heavy with Old Testament solemnity. And here we were, lads of six and five in the middle of the twentieth century, and duly certified as wicked by our own mother—who was in a good position to know. My punishment was heavy: it was that I would intermittently remember that burst of wickedness for nearly half a century.

I know that the little kitten was gray and that the deed was black, but this must not be taken to mean that I never tried to kill a cat again. But the next time I knew somewhat better what I was doing and did it under some duress, trying hard not to be wicked but to be noble. It was a juvenile nobility: misguided, misapplied, and ending in comedy or catastrophe, depending on one's degree of detachment.

There were always several cats on our farm, and frequently there was a superfluous batch of kittens. There was no market for kittens. We had to accept the harsh truth about what happened: my father put them into an old burlap bag—known as a gunnysack—along with a large rock for ballast, and dropped them gently into the water hole. We never observed this, but we knew. Did our knowing incline us to insensitivity toward that little gray kitten?

When I was about ten, it chanced that I laid successful claim to a kitten as my own special pet. Rover, our exuberant beagle, was very fond of teasing kittens, stalking them, running them down, upsetting them, feigning to chew on their ears and tails, rolling them over until they were dizzy, and pestering them until they jumped up on a beam and spat down on him. Although the kittens seemed to court this casual persecution as much as they fled it, it seemed to me to be much too rough and I would regularly rescue the most victimized kitten from Rover's aggressive affections. A bond grew between us and she became my kitten.

Of course, my kitten hung around the barn with the other cats, living mostly on mice, for the standard farm view of the time, fully shared by my father, was that dogs and cats did not belong in houses. Rarely, a cat was brought into the attic or basement on temporary special assignment—destroy all mice in the region—

and then returned to the yard. My father's idea was that we needed just enough cats on the premises to maintain an ecologically balanced mouse-to-cat ratio without having explicitly to feed the cats.

Cats did not have names, but this was not an oversight; it had to do with the metaphysics of cats. We tried Tabby on one cat, almost succeeding, and ShakeTail worked pretty well on another, but the general pattern was that cat names didn't stick. In this, the cats were something like cows, on which we also pinned names that didn't stay (is it because you don't often address a cow to its face?), and different from dogs and horses, to whom names stuck without effort. But try to name a chicken? That idea seemed ludicrous on the face of it. So cats were the only creatures that seemed both to require naming and to resist it. Years later, reading T. S. Eliot, I realized that we had stumbled upon a significant cultural issue, the naming and addressing of cats. My father, who had not read Eliot, dealt with the matter not by disapproving of naming—he would not squander his disapproval on a thing of that kind—but by just not submitting to the felt absurdity of cooperating with it. So most of the names fell off like dead leaves. Thus I had a good cat but the cat had no name. No matter; nothing against the cat.

The root of my father's philosophy was that cats and dogs were not really pets: they were elements in a local economy, like chickens, only more versatile and interesting. Moreover, he believed that cats had been designed to be self-sufficient, clothed and fed by the God who created them, like the birds of the air. Whatever food they got from us was to be considered gravy, though in fact it was really thin stuff. Twice daily at milking time they got foam, which we flipped off the top of the milk pail onto a little pile of clean straw. Skim milk diluted with air bubbles, more attractive than nutritious, disguised as whipped cream—it is to cats what cotton candy is to kids. The cats wisely lapped it up in a hurry, having learned that otherwise it would simply vanish into thin air. However, all our cats thrived cheerfully on the diet of gophers, mice, and cotton candy. I sneaked some real milk to my kitten when no one was looking, but I have never owned up to it until now. As it turned out, she became a most successful scavenger—which was, indeed, her undoing. The real drama was not in how she lived but in the way she died.

When my cat was about a year old, my brother Marvin, about fifteen at the time, was in the rabbit business—a sideline hobby I was therefore destined to take up in a few years, at about the time he would graduate from Advanced Rabbit to Introductory Chicken. His rabbits had extraordinary talents for digging their way out of the pens he had built for them, and there were usually several pairs of white renegade rabbits at large on the premises, living in sin, bearing their young in burrows of their own digging, ganging up on the dogs and cats and foxes and other predators in the environment. But we were not jaded, and we rather enjoyed the sight of a family of white rabbits on the front lawn.

One family of rabbits living just southwest of the house near the lilac bush seemed to suffer a population implosion: starting with seven white bunnies the day they first came up for air, their number diminished day by day: six, five, and then four. Had some fox developed a keen taste for very tender white rabbit and ventured upon our yard? Three, two. It was on the day the countdown reached two that the bitter truth came out. Behold—here was my very own cat stepping jauntily across the lawn with very incriminating evidence in her teeth, namely, a badly mangled, mostly dead, little white rabbit. The conclusion was hard to evade: Ronald's cat had been eating Marvin's rabbits. Here were grounds for a holy war within the family.

But war did not break out, and the negotiations that averted it were so automatic or swift or painful or whatever, that I do not remember the details, only the upshot. My cat was summarily tried and convicted on five counts of rabbit slaughter, and I was deployed to carry out the sentence: death by drowning.

There was probably some confusion as to whether I was being disciplined or the cat was, or neither; or whether we were just protecting future generations of rabbits. What was clear was slightly more abstract: there had been a serious breach, and it was time to close ranks swiftly around the relevant values, no questions asked. That was how things worked. Probably no alternative sentence was seriously contemplated; mitigating circumstances, there were none. No doubt I believed that I had a manly duty to perform, that it was a measure of my maturity as an eleven-year-old to carry it out without flinching, strenuous rite though it be. Thus fortified with high sentiment, the only refuge available, we lowered ourselves to the task at hand.

The procedure had its own protocol: cat and rock went into an old gunnysack, which my father tied with twine. Then he helped me hoist the burden over my shoulder. With body and mind more or less poised, or at least under a controlled wobble, I strode off alone to the water hole—strode off, in fact, toward disaster. I removed my shoes, rolled up my pant legs, waded in to my knees, took a firm two-handed grip on the gunnysack, and swung it to and fro so as to toss it far out into the depths. Back and forth I swung it, and then with a final vigorous heave I let go. Goodbye pet!

But the rock was too heavy and the gunnysack too old. I heard a ripping sound just as the burden left my hands and before it disappeared into the dark waters. The weight of the rock tore open the sack; the rock plunged to the bottom and the bag shot to the surface. I watched amazed as the bag began to move, sink, surface, and then jerk about in a frenzied way. Suddenly a cat bobbed up near the bag and began swimming with strong strokes, cutting rapid circles around the gunnysack. The hole left by the departing rock had let the cat out of the bag. Hello tiger!

I knew immediately—or thought I did—what I had to do, namely, finish the task I had undertaken. No doubt the emotions of the moment were in a precarious balance, and unfortunately my instinct for duty seized the upper hand. Without stopping to think, I splashed out to the scene of action, grabbed the cat (no longer my cat) with both hands, and tried desperately to push her back underwater. She would have none of it. I couldn't hold her. We struggled there in the water, cat and frantic master-turned-executioner, for a dramatic minute or two that seemed an hour, and then in desperation the cat turned on me as I tried in my blind panic to grab her once more. With wide-open jaws and a quick twist of her head, she laid open a long gash on my left wrist, whereupon blood poured out, mixed quickly with water, and ran to my fingertips and then to my elbow. For one whose fragile and utterly misapplied nobility was already taxed beyond limits, this was quite overwhelming. All my reserves and defenses collapsed completely, and I was reduced to the child I was as I cried out in confusion and frustration, in fear and pain.

It was high time for me to do something reasonable for a change, and I did. I fled. Dropping my superheated conscience in the pond, I went pell-mell for the barn, where I found Dad and stammered out a version of what had happened—totally incoherent, but graphic and well illustrated with blood and tears. My more generalized message was that all the rabbits in the world could be eaten alive for all I cared, that I would have nothing to do with protecting any of them. After he had calmed me down and sent me to the house, he went off to finish my job. Undoubtedly, the job had to be finished, for the break in diplomatic relations between cat and me was beyond repair, as he well understood. Meanwhile, my mother was soon able to show me that the slash in my wrist was more bloody than serious and, in fact, that when bandaged it did not even hurt very much.

Cat episode number one, the affair of the little gray kitten, left a sore but unambiguous legacy. Our deed was unconscionable. Cat episode number two, on the other hand, is harder to assess. There were wrongs, all right. I carried conscientiousness straight to disaster. In our inexperience we may have imposed the wrong sentence, or sent in too innocent an executioner, or chosen a flawed means, or just had bad luck. Or all of those. A case may be made for each; but no case was ever made. Our family councils were not normally a format for pondering our vexations or for putting our regrets in order. We stuffed the raw data into the archives, never intending that anyone would open the file to pass judgment. "Charge it up to experience," said Dad, thereby closing a difficult case in his characteristically calm way and implying that there was, however mysteriously, some latent value in it.

❧ 6 ❧

Enlarging the Family

"Boy, oh boy! Are you ever getting fat, Mother!"

I was nine years old. On this July Monday morning, wash day, I was standing on one side of the mechanical, hand-operated washer, my mother opposite me, her stomach protruding over the tub rather too conspicuously for my taste. I had noticed it before and I didn't like it a bit. This morning it seemed particularly grotesque, and I just blurted out my feelings.

"Shall I tell you a very important secret, Ronny?" Secrets were a vital bit of social currency among siblings. I was always on the lookout for a good one, and my mother's solemn tone, almost a whisper, suggested that this might be one worth having.

"The doctor has told us that we are going to have a new baby in the family."

"Really?"

"Sometime this fall."

"Really? Really? Mom! Really? Is that *really* true? Oh, Mother!"

I simply could not assimilate such extraordinary, such overwhelmingly exciting news. Only in other families, I imagined, did such momentous things happen; it couldn't *really* be happening to us!

"Remember, it's a secret," she cautioned when I had calmed down. "You are not to talk about it." I understood: some news was too hallowed to be violated with juvenile chitchat.

Waiting for October . . . the long summer months stretched themselves out under a cloud of extravagant discretion. In a household with four children (eight, nine, eleven, and fourteen) and a very pregnant mother, we did not once discuss the coming baby. Three times a day we six assembled around the kitchen table at mealtime. Plenty of opportunity there to talk about it; but we did not. None of us children knew just how much the others knew. My parents had no established idiom for bandying about such a topic in front of us, and if they mentioned it in our hearing they slipped into Dutch, the language of ancestral pieties.

My mother had a strong sense of humor—to laugh came easily—but no jesting about pregnancy or childbirth ever escaped her. Only at the very end of the summer did I hear her make a rare and furtive reference to "when the stork comes this fall," and that was no joke. That was candor. In that time and place it was a woman's privilege to share her solemn secret with those she chose, in the way she chose, something today's gabby culture generally denies her. The ambiguous ceremonies of "confinement" were part of that process. My mother stopped going to church about the time I learned the secret, stopped going anywhere. Stopped being presentable? Large families were admired, and a pregnant woman in public was unseemly? Thus was pregnancy honored. Honored by consignment to privacy.

Let anthropologists decipher these rites of reticence and ambivalence, for surely they were wise, absurd, ironic . . . inscrutable. This much I see: a birth in the family was not primarily a family event but a woman's event, intensely personal, bound by ties of sentiment and spirituality first of all to her unique sense of self-hood. And I see many elements blended there, including a puritanical view of sex and a woman's sense of self-protection in case of disaster. Something at the still center of the family was sacrosanct, best honored in the silences of a mother's heart.

For a child of the time the message was clear: to be casual or jocular about childbirth would be profane, would desecrate the mystique. Where emotional discourse was spare in any case, it was natural to feel that a new baby in the family would be a wonder beyond words. In fact, most of the language allied with the stirrings of the inner life had been conscripted for religious rhetoric, so it was not hard to think of new babies as heaven-sent.

I did not marvel then at the curtain of mystery and silence drawn across the coming event. Yet, if joy expressed and shared is simply better than joy suppressed—as I believe it is—then we missed something valuable as a family that year, even though the secretiveness of summer led to an autumn of unsuppressed joy.

Summer ended with the first Sunday in September.

My mother told us children that she was not feeling well, and Dad stayed home from church with her in the afternoon. When we came home, Nelvin and I were given permission to go to Aunt Ada's and play with our cousin Bob. "Maybe you can even stay for supper—if you keep out of mischief there. We'll see once," said Dad.

So we kept out of mischief. Following cow paths out to the back pasture, we three went to explore some of our favorite swamps. We took Bob's bike with us, pushing it along the cow path, until we realized that it was a big truck, requiring three tough drivers. We drove the truck-bike carefully straight through the largest swamp—a lot of work, since we had to build the road as we went, fighting off cruel attackers all the way—and came out on the cow-path-highway on the far side of the mountains and dangerous wilderness. About to be ambushed, we circled back through a desert-hayfield where fierce beasts of prey lay in wait for us in the jungle-fencerows. We shot them. It was a very successful trip, yielding tons of gold and heroics to match. Supper at headquarters with Uncle Angus and Aunt Ada was okay, though the fried potatoes were not like Mother's. Then we went out to defend our forts and castles by climbing to our posts high in the apple trees. When we came back to the house for more cookies, Aunt Ada was gone but nobody said where. So it had been a normal Sunday afternoon: we had not only kept out of mischief but kept all our adversaries out of it, too.

Meanwhile, chore time had come to our place: Dad and Marvin were milking the cows, and Gladys was posted in the house. She was worried. It had not escaped her that throughout the afternoon Dad and Mother had conversed almost wholly in Dutch—not a good sign. Presently Mother told Gladys to call Dad and then she herself retired to the bedroom. Dad finished milking the cow he was on, then put down his pail and walked to the house. All afternoon he had tried to call Dr. Masselink but could not reach him, and now it appeared too late for that. So he telephoned Aunt Ada.

Aunt Ada started out for our place at a sedate trot. Now, farm women did not jog down country roads in those days, and the sight of her doing so was enough to bring the first car that came by to a quick stop.

"I'm racing the stork," said Aunt Ada.

"Then get in here, lady," said the driver, doing a brisk U-turn through the ditch.

The homestretch lay directly before them. The Model A Ford with Aunt Ada aboard and a stork with the usual shipment aboard were both now flapping full tilt toward our house. The stork was ahead. Matter of fact, the stork had taken this route several times before, he knew the territory, and he had formed the habit of doing it faster every time he came. This time, in fact, he was in such a helter-skelter rush (he may have overheard all the Dutch being spoken) that he didn't follow standard transmittal procedures. He had the right address but made the wrong presentation.

My father, just in from the stable, was a step or two ahead of the other contestants. That's when he discovered that it was to be an awkward arrival, that a stork in a hurry apparently doesn't bother with the normal protocols of delivery: this time the portion of the package that traditionally warns "This side UP for delivery" was on the bottom. Accordingly, on this blessed occasion when my parents were alone and about to enlarge their family, they had a "breech presentation" on their hands. My father didn't know the name for this arrangement, but he recognized it when he saw it. He had delivered calves like this, so he had an idea what to do. He washed his hands and said a quick prayer and then helped my mother deliver their son. Sunny-side up.

In fairly short order he had the impatient infant, battered but breathing and still attached, safely deposited on his mother's breast, and he could attend to his next duties: first, to welcome Aunt Ada (who had lost the race) to the postpartum ceremonies, and then to hurry to the stable to share the news with his kids and finish the milking. Gladys, who was eleven at the time, was just returning from the stable with a milk pail when Dad went out to tell her that she had a baby brother. She sat right down where she was, next to the pump, milk pail at her side, and wailed—not with tears of joy. Already afflicted with the blessing of three brothers, she had had her heart set on a baby sister. Dad took her by the hand into the house, believing that a glimpse of the living, breathing baby boy would revive her spirits and relieve all her anxieties, as it had his own. But when she saw the squirming baby, pasty-faced, wrinkled and still unwashed and the wrong kind, and saw her mother, wan and pained and tearful and smiling, she was repulsed by the whole baffling spectacle and wanted only to escape as quickly as possible. She begged for permission to run immediately to Aunt Ada's house, where she knew she could share and sort out her mixed-up feelings with cousin Mic. So she set out on a sprint down the road whence Aunt Ada had just come.

Meanwhile, Nelvin and Cousin Bob and I were heroically defending the tree-forts along the driveway at Uncle Angus and Aunt Ada's place. At dusk we had just slain our last enemies when Gladys hurried into the yard, a herald now from a very different order of unreality. She paused when she saw us, looked at Nelvin and me, and then spoke very evenly:

"Do you boys know you have a baby brother at home?"

We dropped our swords and guns and jaws at this fantastic statement, delivered in this do-you-know-your-face-is-dirty tone of voice. I had been told, well, October, and this was early September. I had suspected nothing. Nelvin had been told nothing. How could we credit such a report?

"What? What? What?" Nelvin and I kept up the chorus, and she just repeated her statement: "You got a baby brother."

"I'm going home," I said.

"No, you can't," she said. "Us kids hafta stay here overnight, and Aunt Ada is gonna stay at our place."

"Who said?"

"Dad did."

"What's the baby like?"

"Just a baby. It's a boy."

"Where is it?"

"Where's what?"

"Where's the *baby?*"

"Aunt Ada has it."

"What's she doin' with it?"

"Washin' it, I guess."

"*What?* What's that for?"

"I don't *know.* Where's Mic?"

Down the road and across the field, home was only three-quarters of a mile away. There was, allegedly, a baby brother there. And she said I had to stay *here?* I didn't even consider staying; I only considered strategy. Within half an hour Nelvin and Bob were playing with trucks, and Gladys was jabbering girl talk with Mic about names for boy babies. Uncle Angus was reading the *Michigan Farmer.*

Unobserved, I casually eased out the door, bolted down the driveway, and headed for home.

The night was now dark, but I could easily pick up the straight white streak of gravel road, which I knew like the back of my hand: up one hill, down the other side, over the bridge, and then up the slope toward the grove. Arriving at the corner of our farm, I felt in the damp grass and thistles for the woven-wire fence, squeezed under it, and struck out diagonally across the pasture. The kerosene-lighted window of the house showed up in the distance, and I made straight for it, oblivious until nearly too late that the horses were pasturing there that night. I came within inches of running pell-mell into old Cob, our big, clumsy workhorse, as big as the slaughtered wild beasts of the afternoon and black as the night. He was as startled as I was by our sudden meeting, and he thundered off in one direction and I in another. For just that one night I was at least as fleet on my feet as was Cob.

Then I was at the door of our house. Pushing it open, shaking with exhaustion and anticipation and a hundred nameless joys and dreads, I stood there stock-still in the doorway, panting, panting. The pause was just long enough to make an engraving in my memory, a picture still green and golden. In the center of the kitchen, a lamp on the table at her side, sat Aunt Ada, and in her left hand lay the tiniest baby I had ever seen. Into his tiny mouth she was spooning black coffee, a heart stimulant, and he was spraying it back out at her to the best of his very tiny ability, and she was grinning at the baby. Portrait of rural midwifery at its high point. For my part, I had thought that babies were rosy and plump and smooth; this one looked crinkled and scrawny and had blotches of blood matting its so-called hair.

"Is that the baby? Is it okay?"

Aunt Ada said it was just fine. "He's beautiful," she said.

"Yeaaah," I sighed, thinking that it was very beautiful and very homely, too.

Then she let me come right up to it and touch its hand, which was almost too tiny to be real. It might come off. But it was real. The whole baby was really real. And this one was in our very own family. I spoke in whispers, afraid, perhaps, that I would wake up.

I stood beside my mother's bed the next morning and she reached out her hand and took mine in her own. The baby was squeaking in a box beside her bed, a cardboard box that had once contained a dozen mason jars and was now recycled as a crib. She looked very happy and very tired. The baby looked very disgusted and was making faces at life. My mother did not chide me for coming home against instructions, she only asked me why I had done so. I could not say why, and she smiled again and said it was okay. She asked me if I was glad to have a baby in the family, but I was far, far too glad to have any words for that. So I said something else.

"It's awful little, isn't it?"

"The baby was born early," she said, "about a month. But it will be all right."

"I like the baby," I said. "I wanna help take care of it."

"You may."

Within days the baby would stop being an "it" and become a "he," and within weeks the clamor for baby-sitting privileges would begin among us siblings, but for now all was hushed and subdued—as if the spell were fragile still and might be broken at any moment.

My mother said she wanted me to take a note with the news to the Baases, our near neighbors. Dad wrote the note, something like: "Baby boy moved in with us unexpectedly last night. Kate and little chap doing good."

I took the note to the Baas family, running all the way. Mrs. Baas was busy with the washing, but she dried her hands as I came in and took the note that I handed over with as much ceremony and pride as I could muster. She read it and shouted aloud, calling to all the family members and spreading the news. It was inexpressibly good to see that they were all excited and showed it; and immediately it dawned on me that I was going to get a lot of social mileage out of this baby. There was but one little darkish cloud, and I thought I ought to be candid about it while on neutral territory. So I let the Baas family in on a concern that I hadn't dared to express fully at home.

"He weighs only six and a half pounds," I said, awkward and embarrassed about this dismal part of the news.

"That's not bad," said Ben.

"That's real good," said Johanna.

"He'll grow real fast," said Margaret.

Such a relief! Nothing to be ashamed of, after all! Nobody at school would ridicule us for having a baby brother too small to be respectable.

Childhood has its own anxieties, its own ecstasies. Across the fields through the tall grass I raced home, the morning sun in my face. Our baby was perfect, and he was even the right size. Tomorrow I would start the fourth grade, and if Nelvin didn't beat me to it I could tell the teacher and everybody about the new baby.

Pollywogs and Apples

Many a spring we gathered great gobs of pollywogs and put them into a glass mason jar and fed them cornmeal—which they did not like and would not eat. They all died. After that we forgot them. After that they stank. Then my mother threw them out, and we waited until the next year to do it again. It's hard to remember why we did this.

Cornmeal *looked* like pollywog food—to us but not to the wogs. Rotting grass, stinking of decay, would have been much better, but how were we to know? We were too preoccupied with our science to make observations on our data. With our exercise we were probably running a casual test on the rumor, tediously repeated by teachers and other adults, that pollywogs turned into frogs. It seemed an implausible idea on the face of it and it didn't fit our evidence or our experiment, so we never verified it. I recall that I toyed with a better theory: pollywogs that weren't caught just disappeared, probably melted like ice or went out as air bubbles; we often saw the bubbles in the pond near the pollywogs. Frogs, on the other hand, were evidently just generated full-size by rotten leaves and grass and junk in the waters of the pond.

Our all-purpose farm pond, or water hole, lay behind the barn, far enough away to be clear of the worst contamination. It was ever a favorite resort of horses and cows and kids, and home to all manner of interesting creatures: sometimes muskrat and mallard; at all times frogs and flowering weeds, water striders and mosquito larvae and pollywogs. And its shorelines were the summer-long stalking grounds for the extravagantly dignified great blue heron. Almost as memorable as the pollywogs were the vast floating armadas of water beetles, gliding from the shore in great black, shimmering sheets as we approached.

There is a difference, not everywhere acknowledged, between a water hole and a pond. We had both, depending on the season. It was mainly a matter of size, which varied tremendously: from as much as six or seven acres in March and April to an acre or two in tadpole time to a frugal half-acre in frog time to an eighth of an acre or just a mud flat in late September. The pond of early spring declined into the water hole of late summer. As the water sank through the sandy soil and the pond shrank through the summer and the cattle monopolized it more as their watering hole and cooling-off spot, we kids tended to back off, recognizing that although the pond had been ours the water hole was theirs.

During the spring thaw the pond was in its glory, being fed, briefly and wildly, through a small and narrow ravine—or rather, the Ravine, as we always knew it, never once thinking of it as small—that drained twenty acres of neighboring swampland. Our pond was the dead-end destiny of that water, and the official herald of spring was always the cry "Ravine's flowing!" The lure of running water, forever associated in our young minds with the Ravine, drew us inexorably to that spot after school, there to build dikes and dams, and throw rocks at the boiling water. Although copious brooks trickle from every springtime pore in the New England countryside, that is not so in the midwestern plains, where the level, sandy soil seems to suck the water in. A roaring ravine was special, and we knew it: few of our friends had flowing water nearby, even in springtime, and no one had a ravine, much less a Ravine like this, whose hum and burble we could hear a quarter mile away. It never failed to get us in its grip, both for its own charm and for the way it swiftly transformed a small and slushy winter water hole into a magnificent six-acre spring pond. Not for us the poverty of town kids condemned to build their dams in street gutters.

The pond was where we learned to swim; and a slow and arduous business it was, being entirely self-taught. With no guidance whatever, we had to reinvent the art from the beginning, for we were not often in water with children who could swim. Very few from our parents' generation had ever learned how, and my parents seldom showed up at the pond, much less at the water hole. They had nothing to teach us about swimming, except "Be careful." As youngsters our swimming trunks were worn-out or outgrown bib overalls cut off above the knees. Recycling worn-out clothes was a standard policy, but not every application of the policy was as stylish as this.

We had surmised that there were two ways to learn to swim. The first and most direct way was to wade out to hip-deep water, lift our feet, and flail about with arms and legs as furiously as possible, hoping to keep our feet out of the muck and our head out of the water. This method is presumably very ancient, since it is absolutely impossible to imagine anything more primitive. Nevertheless, we proceeded to reinvent the method and to apply it assiduously. Results were meager. Summer after summer, swimming seemed to me a thing impossible to learn. Why, I sometimes wondered in those early days, would anyone really *want* to swim? Flying, for example, would be considerably easier.

Fortunately, there was another method, indirect and more sedate in its approach, requiring the use of a large log. Long before we had learned to swim, we had mastered the technique of traveling around the pond by "swimming" with hands (or chest or chin) on a large floating log, feet churning up a storm for propulsion. We had the idea that our feet had to be kept *above* the water, pounding the surface, lest they sink and pull us under. The transition from "swimming" to swimming was harder than it appeared: releasing hands and pumping furiously so as to keep our head up was the more difficult just because we had learned to be completely dependent upon the log. Moreover, it is not easy to swim trying to keep most of the body safely exposed to the air. Eventually, our stubbornness prevailed over our wretched techniques and we cautiously abandoned the idea that we had to swim *on* the water, like a log, noticing that we could swim *in* the water, like a muskrat; and we did all learn to swim. Upon careful reflection on our two methods and their associated theories, I find that I cannot recommend either.

Our point of entry to the pond was the sandiest edge, but it is doubtful anyone would have been so sanguine as to think of that area as a beach. It was, in fact, the place where the cows and horses drank daily, but it was attractive enough to suit our taste, which was, fortunately, well underdeveloped. Frequently, to clear our spot for the day, we lifted a crisp, sunbaked cow-pie from the sand and tossed it aside. If we got a pie that was done to a turn, with no soggy undercrust, we could sometimes make it sail like a

Frisbee. Unfortunately, we did not then know that a Frisbee craze was in the offing and that American civilization would soon demand that the Frisbee be patented and marketed in quantity. True, ours was a fragile sort of toy, to be tossed with care and caught with trepidation, but it was surely history's first and best Frisbee, free and disposable, recyclable, biodegradable, environmentally sound, a natural product. The legend that the Frisbee was invented at Yale with a pie plate isn't true; it was invented in the sands of unremembered barnyards, with a pie.

There was a household rule that we not go in the water alone—one of those rules that we unaccountably observed. Not that any of us, barely afloat "swimmers" that we were, would have been of much assistance to anyone in distress. But nothing of the kind was ever required, not even on the day when Nelvin was sure he was drowning.

He and I were about seven and eight, too young to have made any headway as swimmers, and we had been puttering about at water's edge. Our mother was in the house and well aware that we were both at the pond, when Nelvin suddenly burst in upon her with terror all over his face.

"How long after you fall in the water do you drown?" he demanded.

When one of two boys returns from a pond alone on a dead trot with fear in his eyes and that question on his lips, it does not take a mother long to reach the dreadful conclusion.

"Oh, it's Ronny!" she screamed, nearly upsetting Nelvin as she dashed for the door.

Out the door and down toward the pond she sped, shouting for reinforcements, certain as she was that Ronny was lying facedown in the bottom of the pond and that Nelvin had escaped to report it. Nelvin was even more alarmed and outraged by this reaction, and he yelled for his mother's attention—which was hard to get because she was already past the lilac bushes, nearing the barn at full throttle, heading for the pond. She had nearly reached the straightaway between the elms when who should saunter into view but

Ronny himself, perfectly safe and nearly dry, handsomely attired in sawed-off bib overalls, and the proud captor of five—count 'em, Mom, five—squiggly pollywogs, and happy to have an audience to explain how he had caught them. Nice of Mother to come way out here to see them. Could he have some cornmeal?

Meanwhile, back at the house Nelvin was in a state of panic, aggravated by parental indifference. He had heard it said once upon a time that, well, no, you don't always drown *immediately* if your head accidentally goes under and you get water into your mouth and nose; so his present problem was, then how long *afterward* might you drown? He had slipped in accidentally in pursuit of a pollywog, had gotten his head wet and his mouth full, and, without telling me his worry, had sped off to the house to find out if he might drown. He'd had a terrible accident, for heaven's sake, and it just might be fatal; would someone please tell him if so, and when? His own mother had ignored him and callously raced out of the house instead. Surely the situation *was* alarming; didn't anyone care that he might drown at any moment, standing right there alone in the middle of the kitchen, howling for help? He followed her out of the house back toward the pond, afraid he might drown before he got there. That would serve them right.

He didn't drown. There had been a failure of communication somewhere. But it was Nelvin and not I who had to be rescued after all, and Mother did it by patiently explaining the facts of life and death by drowning, convincing him that he would survive. I gave Nelvin one of my pollywogs, now installed in a mason jar. He got a little one, which was not very lively. On the trip from the pond in my cupped hands it had gotten its head above water and taken in a gulp of air, and it looked as if it might expire at any moment.

Nearly all the farmers who tamed Missaukee County between the years 1880 and 1920 had planted fruit orchards on their farms. The first farmers did this, a legacy for generations to come, as automatically as they built barns and preserved woodlots, and all the orchards we ever saw were carefully planted in straight rows—"on the square." Yet very few of them were well tended by the next generation of farmers, most of whom knew little about the care of fruit trees. Many orchards had become decrepit or sickly or worse well before the middle of the twentieth century: most of the plum and pear trees were dead and unreplaced, the apple trees unpruned, unkempt. If all the original orchards in the community had been tended even as well as ours, which set a fairly low standard, we might not have had so many customers for free apples as we did. My father at least hacked off—when he got around to it—what appeared to be surplus branches; but I think most farmers did nothing at all to their orchards, and their unpruned trees strangled themselves, eventually fruited poorly, and began to die early. By mid-century most of the orchards in the community had been cut down.

Ours was an unusually large, well-planned, and diverse orchard, which thrived under our program of benign neglect and minimal upkeep, repaying us a hundredfold for every bit of attention it got. Originally forty-five in number and planted square with the world, the trees had lost a dozen or so from their ranks when we of the younger generation came upon the scene. The orchard was a playground for children, a tree climber's paradise, and a good place for youth to find and bury treasure. We got to know most of the trees intimately, almost personally, not just the taste of their fruit and the spectacle and fragrance of their blossoms but the skeleton and texture of the trees themselves, their individual contours, their worn and weak spots, their clumsy, wide-open, beckoning arms, their rough resistance to our climbing and embrace. By much experience we came to know and enjoy the strenuous contortions demanded of us by some trees for getting to certain of their far-flung branches to inspect the robins' nests, or to reach our secret and windblown retreats where we hid from one another and fashioned heroic tales about giants of the forest who might have waylaid us had we not gotten them first.

My sister, Gladys, by turns little lady and vigorous tomboy, explained to me one summer day that I was old enough to build a genuine tree house—so of course she was—and that this was the time to do it. With her sense of purpose and my flush of pride, and with some rickety old boards and rusty nails and much labor, we actually managed to build two ramshackle floorlike structures in opposite arms of one of the largest apple trees. Then we worked out a domestic system whereby she and I could retire to our respective so-called houses out on the high branches and direct Nelvin on the ground below to shunt back and forth between us with important mail. The mail included secret documents, money, and dynamite. All the mail was shrewdly disguised and hidden (Gladys patiently explained) inside these little green apples, which we gathered through the windows of our lofty lairs and sent down to Nelvin in buckets on long pieces of string. At first he proved very deficient in appreciation of such arrangements and of the honor of couriership. He also had a wayward yen to get out of the postal service entirely and into the building trades. Those defects of character had to be curbed, and, in accordance with the chain of command, I was detached to explain matters to him. With some difficulty we eventually taught him the relevant version of the family code: the younger have no rights whatever except by sufferance from the older. Without such a code at our command he might have proved intractable and spoiled our day.

All around us wondrous varieties of apples ripened in sequence from midsummer onward: first Yellow Transparent, Early Harvester, Red Astrachan; then Duchess, Wealthy, and Winesap. After that came Snow Apple, Maiden Blush, Ben Davis, and Grimes Golden, followed by Wolf River and Russet. Last of all was the great and unforgettable Pewaukee, our principal winter apple. There were also various sweet apples and crabs, and some other nameless varieties, uninteresting to us but no doubt put in originally as cider apples. Of some varieties we had several trees: Duchess and Transparent had four apiece, and each tree had its own special nuance of tang and flavor. Even within a given variety we had our favorite trees, even our favorite sunny sides of favorite trees. Much experience did not jade but rather refined our taste in apples.

We harvested apples by the dozens of bushels and typically had far more than we could possibly handle. We ate apples daily from late summer to late fall, baked and pied and sauced and dried and also put into apple duff. We canned apple sauce (rather, my mother did, as the rest of us pared and peeled), a hundred quarts a year sometimes. We gave away apples, to relatives and neighbors first, and then to peddlers and salesmen and anyone else who turned up at our door. We fed apples to the pigs, bushels and bushels. And we let apples rot in the sun, layers and layers of them, turning to a soft brown mush whose sweet vinegar was gratefully spirited away by the wasps and the bees—we were careful where we stepped with bare feet. And some years there was a cold spring in which the blossoms froze and not an apple appeared in the orchard. "That's farming," said Dad. "You never know."

Drying apples is a method of preserving that goes back thousands of years to the misty origins of agriculture itself; and yet today the method appears to be at risk, almost a dying art. The technique is utterly simple, merely time-consuming; consequently, we produced bags and bags of dried apples every year. Cored, peeled, and thinly sliced, the apples are spread on a large framed screen (a window screen will do, but quarter inch galvanized hardware cloth is better) and hung from the ceiling above the stove. They need only dry warmth and ventilation. In a few days the apple slices are tough and leathery, and they are then put into thin cloth bags (not tight containers, lest they mold) and hung in the pantry. They will last for years, to be chewed as snacks or soaked in water and then cooked into sauce or pie. Dried apples have a special sweet and dark brown flavor, not often appreciated by children but beloved by most civilized adults—a taste as ancient as civilization itself.

One classic use of apples was denied us. We never made cider, and there wasn't a cider press in the community. Instead, there was a set of enticing rumors about the good old days when farmers made cider by the barrel; but by the Depression years that had become a lost art in our community, like the pruning of the apple tree itself. Perhaps the mentality that led to Prohibition was the worm in the apple that had discredited cider and cider making, soft and hard. We suspected that we were being deprived of something good, and we were right.

It was a June evening and I was about ten. At my feet next to the porch my eye caught an unusual small plant, not more than five inches high. It was the merest seedling, but my father identified it as a young apple tree. Immediately I adopted it. I would transplant the seedling and care for it as my own little tree, and it would thrive under my care, and when I was a man and farmed this farm it would bear good apples for me. Dad proposed a spot between the driveway and the garden, and that very evening he dug up the sod for me, and I, all tenderness and attention, planted the little tree there. Throughout the summer, whenever I remembered to, I pumped some water and took it to my tree.

My own tree—but that was not a new idea for us. All the children had a tree or two in the yard, most of them box elders, but now I had an apple tree as well. Our innocence about fruit trees was our good fortune, for I did not know then that all the trees in our orchard had been nursery grafted, and that grafts, as true clones, reproduce the parent tree exactly whereas apple trees grown from seeds are often barren or bear only inferior fruit. Although this was well known thousands of years ago, it was not known to me (or to the Johnny Appleseed of legend); and if my father knew it, he kept his own counsel, not disturbing my optimism.

I took a boy's care of my tree, alternating negligence and tenderness. Against the odds, it thrived. I cheered it on as it slowly prospered in the face of the quack grass that strove to suppress it, and eventually prevailed even against the regular predations of Pearl, one of our workhorses, who was fanatically partial to its taste and made a beeline for it to snatch a branch whenever she got a chance.

Came the years when my tree had a few blossoms but no fruit, and later came disquieting news from a high school textbook: apple seed trees often revert to a prehistoric crabbed and wizened apple. Had I only known. Still, it was a nice tree and I was fond of it, so I tried to prune it by the book; at least it would look good, there by the driveway. Then I went off to college and forgot about it.

My back was hardly turned when the tree began to bear—slowly at first, then more generously, then extravagantly—tasty and versatile apples, good for eating and for sauce, superb for drying, and usually more free of insects and diseases than those from any tree in the orchard. And ever since—for thirty-five years now—the tree has regularly poured down its nearly flawless bounty, usually surpassing in production every veteran tree in the orchard: twenty bushels is nothing for that tree. Yearly, another generation of relatives and neighbors comes and helps to shake the branches and bear the surplus fruit away.

I had foreseen it all. This perpetual bounty is what I had fully expected during all those early years when I didn't know what I was doing; had I had even a little learning in these matters, I would not have bothered to plant or tend the tree. It was nurtured on blind faith, and the harvest that was all but impossible becomes now all but inevitable.

The tale keeps twisting. Scions from that maverick Michigan apple tree, which I grafted to my wild trees in New Hampshire, seem intent on having the last word: a decade of my best care of them has resulted in just two little apples, and both fell to the ground wizened and unripe, and both had a flavor at once tart and insipid. If irony has a taste, I suppose it is the taste of those little New Hampshire apples, the distant fruit of my tree in Michigan. Grateful as I am for that exotic tree, I've never understood it at all. The theory seems plain enough; only the facts are confusing. Then again, I've had to deal with some strange theories and facts about pollywogs and frogs, too.

The Hoekzemas Are Coming

On our lean social calendar the news that the Hoekzemas were coming was the biggest news there was.

The Hoekzema family arrived from Grand Rapids in a big, gleaming, wedge-shaped Hudson, dark blue, the glory of the road. Nobody around McBain had a car like that, a car children didn't lay a hand on, for Al Hoekzema had made it clear that he wanted no little fingerprints on it. A car too precious to touch? I got the impression that my mother saw something vaguely idolatrous in this. "I think he even puts wax on it," she once whispered to me, hinting of decadence. She was very fond of Al, but once in a while, if pretension or ambition got too conspicuous, she called him a big shot. My, but I thought big shots were interesting!

The sight of that big blue Hudson turning off the dusty road into our long driveway invariably sent our spirits soaring. The car glided to our door with its marvelous intimations of distant places, prosperity, cities, success, cigars, "boughten" bread, oranges, bananas, exotic things—everything our daily routines didn't suggest. Its arrival also meant company, kids to play with, and holidays. At the time, there were just three official holidays in our year, namely, the Fourth of July afternoon; Thanksgiving Day, starting with dinner at noon; and Christmas, starting on Christmas Eve after chores. It was the Hoekzemas who then put Memorial Day—everyone called it Decoration Day—on the holiday calendar by their visits. They also created ad hoc summer holidays by dropping in on a Saturday morning and staying for the weekend.

Our families formed reverse images of each other. We were a farm family of six, later seven. The Hoekzemas were a city family of six. We were poor; they were not. We rode in a 1932 Chevy; they traveled first in a Terraplane, then in a 1940 Hudson, and then in a 1942 Hudson De Lux. Yet in their own way they were about as sophisticated and worldly as we were; we occupied opposite sides of the same social coin.

My mother and Mrs. Hoekzema (Jennie to us) had been factory girls and boardinghouse friends in Grand Rapids. My mother had then returned to the countryside to marry a farmer, but Jennie had found a rising young urban businessman: Al Hoekzema was a self-employed interior painter. "Painting and Decorating" was what it said on his pickup truck, and that gave his profession some class— or was meant to. Al had always been keen on class. As a lad of sixteen he had jumped ship in New York from the Dutch navy to seek his fortune in the land of promise. He found it or made it. His fortune consisted of a modest house in Grand Rapids, a family with a wife who spoke English without a Dutch accent, a small business and a big car, and friends in the country to whom he could afford to play Dutch uncle. Al had a formidable Dutch accent and smoked formidable Dutch cigars, and both he and Jennie had large and generous Dutch hearts. The bond between our families was warm and deep.

The family farm is an enduring tenet of our national theology, and a little-noticed reason for that is this: a farm makes instant experts of us all. Survey a small farm scene—anyone can do it—and you see immediately what needs doing. A fence is rickety and a gate sags, a tree limb has fallen and a wall needs support, a pen needs repair, a field needs cutting, a roof wants a patch, and a hinge is loose. A half hour's survey, and any amateur is expert enough to produce a farmer's agenda for a week. Of course it may not be the relevant agenda, for the real priorities are dictated by rhythms unseen by the casual eye.

"Jess, that house would look a lot better if it was painted."

"Yeah, I know, Al. But when do I get the time?"

"Heck, I betcha me and Claus could do it in a coupla days."

"Paint that whole thing?"

"You get the rest of the siding on, and some weekend me and Claus will slip up here and slap on a few buckets of paint."

"Well, let's see once what Kate says."

My father had built the house with his father in 1919, not knowing that he would later buy the farm and live there the rest of his life. He and his father had also built the south wing of the barn. Neither building had seen any paint; and now, fifteen or more years later, the east side of the house still wore tar paper. My mother thought Al's paint plan was terrific.

"Jess, what you should have is a *real* lawn mower."

"I like my four-legged lawn mowers," said my father. "What's more real than that?"

In those early days our lawn mower was a young heifer tethered to a heavy old iron wagon wheel. As necessary, Dad could roll the wheel to greener pastures under the clothesline. It was a simple and efficient system: it got the grass clipped and the heifer fed and it saved the pastures for the milk cows. Al knew he could improve on it.

When the Hoekzemas arrived on Memorial Day, Al would usually go to the car's trunk and proudly lift out an enormous Florida watermelon. But he had a knack for implausible surprises and on one occasion he announced that he had a present for Marvin; then he pulled from the trunk a creature such as we had met only in books. It was a little bearded billy goat kid, and Al beamed with pride as he handed it over to Marvin.

"There, boy, a nice lawn mower. Have fun," said Al.

"Oh, oh, Al!" said Mom.

"Boy, oh boy!" said Marvin.

"Baa baa," said the little goat.

"Well Gek!" said Dad, which is half Dutch for "This may be nutty!"

As usual, Dad was right. The goat was charming at first and was duly tethered to an old buggy wheel on the edge of the yard; and from that moment on he recycled everything within reach. But there was no way he could keep up with the quack grass under the clothesline—and especially with such delicacies as cardboard, rope, tin cans, clothespins, old harness straps, and now and then a sock from the clothesline to round out his diet. Well nourished, he very soon became a full-size billy goat—became, in fact, a very, very smelly pet, to put the matter mildly. My mother thought the situation was abominable, and she made the reasonable suggestion that the goat be banished and that Dad handle the grass with a scythe; she would handle Al. The next Memorial Day we got a watermelon again.

Al Hoekzema had worked in the tulip beds in the Netherlands as a boy, and consequently as an adult he took himself to be well equipped to give my father advice on how to farm in Michigan. They were splendid opposites: my father was tall and lean and abstemious; Al was short and stout and extravagant. If my father had never handled a paintbrush, as I think he had not, Al had never harnessed a horse, but I don't think he would have admitted it. Perhaps they got on so well partly because Al kept earning his right to share his opinions. One weekend in the late thirties, Al and Claus slipped up to our house and slapped on a few buckets of paint, and it *was* a great improvement, just as he'd said. And the year after the billy goat episode he brought us another improvement: a mechanical lawn mower. It was old and dull and hard to use—less interesting than a goat—and none of us ever had much affection for it, but we did the job with it. In fact, we were one of the first in the neighborhood to cut our lawn with a mower instead of with a scythe or with livestock. City friends were easing us into the world of high-tech farming.

As the years went by and Al became an even better authority on farming, there was a lot that he thought could be torn down or built up or converted or transformed. My father always listened tolerantly to his counsel, but there was no way he could accommodate it, for Al did not merely dabble in details, he had his eyes on the grand design. Did Dad have a grand design? He was mainly trying to make do by trying to do what had to be done. For Al a farm was an arena for the free play of fancy: we should have more cows and fewer chickens or fewer chickens and more cows; we should have sheep; we should get a new horse or buy more land or we should paint the barn or raise more hogs. The drift was, we should be more progressive; for example, we should just sell the horses and get a tractor.

Now there was an idea! For my brothers and me, farm boys catching snatches of all this strategic conversation, it was the pitch for a tractor that lent credibility to the rest. Here was a man who clearly knew what he was talking about, and we devoutly hoped Dad would listen. What we boys saw in a tractor was precisely what Al Hoekzema saw in it, though neither of us could name it. A tractor was a symbol, the countryman's equivalent of a Hudson De Lux.

My father was not ready for a farm deluxe. But that did not keep him from enjoying the transcendental vision of country affairs that he saw reflected in his friend's mind.

The old buggy had been retired from its regular job some years earlier when we got a car, but it had not yet been turned out to pasture. There really wasn't much use for it anymore, no market for it, and not even a good place to store it. It stood in the barn for some years, waiting, waiting . . . The truth was that it was just in the way. Not *much* use for the buggy? It was apparent that there was *no* use for it. It got parked in the barnyard, but out-of-doors it aged quickly.

What to do in the thirties with an old buggy not yet worn out? If that was a melancholy question for our parents, it was a blessing for their offspring. One day, as if with a wave of a wand, the old useless buggy had been transformed into an exotic toy. Thereafter, a pre-dictable question popped out as soon as the big Hudson from Grand Rapids opened its doors.

"Can we play with the buggy, Uncle Jess?"

"Well, we'll see once." That was how Dad said yes.

Now eight Hoekzema-Jager kids drag the venerable buggy down the lane and across the field to a pasture hilltop. There we lift the shafts high in the air, and then with shouts of triumph we all pile in and push off. Pell-mell, we ride our chariot open-throttle to the bottom of the hill, eight tongues in full cry. Then again. And again. Young as we are, we know at such times that we have found the meaning of life, and it is no wonder to us that the Hoekzema youngsters cherish the visits to our farm. If you can ride a new Hudson De Lux to the countryside and ride an old buggy down the pasture hills, what more is there to ask of life?

In those days every farm had a natural gymnasium—one that re-quired no planning, no capital outlay, no upkeep, no rules that didn't evolve organically, and no supervision. Ours was especially alive with activity when the Hoekzema kids were with us, they as-suring us that there were no such wondrous places in the city. The specifications for a first-class old-style gymnasium are worth record-ing: There must be rough walls to climb, with knotholed boards unevenly spaced for toeholds, and exposed beams and braces for wall scaling. There should be high, open beams to hang a swing from and to creep or shuffle daringly across, crunching the dried sparrow droppings; also lofts and secret rafter triangles to resort to for hide-and-seek, and haymows of several sizes to romp and wrestle in and slide out of, and straw piles to burrow in; also hay ropes to climb to the rafters on to get a crazy sensation in your groin from, and another rope to swing from and burn your hands with when you slide down too fast; and old ladders, wooden and wobbly, to get to remoter mows. An attached granary, with bins of oats, wheat, and rye—good to stamp around in with bare feet—is desirable but optional; also a large and variously scattered assortment of grain bags, cats, old boxes of forgotten uses, sacks of ground grain, live sparrows, crates, forks, a bag of oyster shells, some corncobs, kittens, and similar things. Last, pad the floor thickly, very thickly, with chaff, remembering that the exuberant youngster who leaps from the wall beam may overjump the pile of hay. That is the basic gymnasium, upon which science and technology cannot improve, the locus on every farm of countless hours of undirected sport. When not in use it may also serve the farm as a barn.

When I was ten and Nelvin was nine we got a comparative look at city life. Our families swapped two children for a week: Betty Jo and Hermina Hoekzema came to our farm, and Nelvin and I went to Grand Rapids. That memorable week makes it easy to pinpoint our first encounters with urban exotica: an ice cream soda at Joppy's, an elevator at Herpolsheimers, an Egyptian mummy at the Grand Rapids museum, even an airport. Sonny Hoekzema, somewhat junior to Nelvin and me, was our streetwise host for that week, and we even got a chance to coast down sidewalks on his bike. We had not been on a bike before, so we were not able to balance and pedal it. We had the skills to pilot an old buggy down a rough hill in the pasture and to scale a high beam on the barn wall, but not to propel a bicycle along a city street.

Which environment did we prefer? asked our parents. Hard to answer such a cosmic question.

The Hoekzemas knew enough about our circumstances to realize that without intervention, our Christmases might be a little meager. So they always intervened. Each Christmas they sent our family a huge package filled with the most extraordinary things. That package—surrounded, to be sure, with our numerous smaller gifts to one another—was the centerpiece of our family party on Christmas Eve. Those Christmas presents of my youth that I can still name came from the Hoekzema Christmas packages, and several of them I retain to this day: the toy ski jump still works and the locomotive is still unrusty and its cab is still shiny and the bell has not lost its tinkle. One year I received a Tinkertoy set with 106 pieces, every one of which was duly counted and returned to the box whenever we played with them; the set was intact enough to pass on to Carl, ten years my junior.

My Tinkertoy set and Gladys's doll that cried and Marvin's black Lionel train that ran on its own track and Nelvin's red armored tank that shot sparks—the unforgettable toys of childhood arrived in the Christmas packages from the Hoekzemas. In the packages were also things for the baby and handkerchiefs for Mother and cigars for Dad and oranges and fruitcake for us all; and the interstices of the box were jammed with nuts and candy. We held our breath for that Christmas package, expecting to be knocked over when we opened it; and we were.

Someone showering gifts or spreading unsolicited goodwill at Christmas: it's a blessedly recurring part of the human saga and a magnificent old cliché now, bearing echoes of an older Gift of millennia past. Or so the churches keep reminding us, as well they should. Add children or poverty to the story line and you've got a plot that drips with sentimentality. Let it drip. Back then, it seemed cut-and-dried: of course we'd get a package from the Hoekzemas this Christmas; we always did.

Whenever the Hoekzemas rolled up in the big Hudson, they also brought sacks of good things to eat—raisin bread and pastries and fruit—and always cigars for Dad. Those luxury items made a strong impression on us poor country cousins, but perhaps no stronger than the impression made on *them* by my mother's canned meat, canned fruit, apple sauce, and homemade bread. To us those were commonplace offerings, but to them these country things were like manna from heaven. The appreciation they expressed for—of all things!—*bread* was a revelation to us. Jaded children of the land, we casually consumed a dozen loaves of my mother's bread every week, not realizing that it was twice as nutritious and tasty as the "boughten," or "baker's," bread that we always craved and seldom had. "Give us this day our daily bread," we always prayed; but when the Hoekzemas were with us we ate each other's bread and fruit and gave a happier thanks. The taste of raisin bread and oranges with the smell of cigars in the background—even today it can summon images of the holidays that the Hoekzemas brought to our farm.

9

Good-bye to Cream of Wheat and All That

The young in our household swallowed a tablespoonful of cod-liver oil every morning throughout the winter. The oil was a spiritual tonic, obliging us to endure misery without complaint, but I do not recognize any other benefits—except possibly the ambivalent satisfaction I may have received from spooning it into my younger brother Carl when he was a helpless five and I a strong fifteen.

Although you can predict the amount of winter still left in the weather by the groundhog method in February, we didn't do it that way on our farm. We did it by counting the loaves of tallow left in the cellar: like the cod-liver oil, the tallow would last until spring. This way of calculating isn't as obscure and scientific as it sounds, but perhaps a little explanation can make it so. For this purpose I must say something about the garage. That will eventually lead to cream of wheat, and from there to better things. It's all connected. Everything is connected on a family farm.

So, the garage. Besides the outhouse and the barn, the principal outbuilding on our farm was the garage. Other alleged buildings— pig house, corncribs, rabbit warrens, brooder coops—rose and fell as need and neglect determined. The garage had started life as a woodshed and occasional shelter for the surrey, then graduated to a full-time garage when we got a car in 1936 and put the buggy out to pasture, and then, challenged with a new garage in the later forties, it reverted to a woodshed again.

The centerpiece of the garage was a shelf, once a workbench, so burdened with tools and the general wealth of a working farm that we didn't see its surface until the day in the late forties when we emptied the old garage and moved its produce to the new one. "Produce" is the correct concept here, for it is provable that artifacts of iron and steel reproduce in broad daylight on garage workbenches, shelves, and floors, just as surely as mice multiply and rats grow in dark corners of granaries.

A tin box sat on the workbench. Into it went bent nails, dull screws, crippled cotter pins, used staples, worn-out nuts maturing into future washers, and other small, hard, and rusty objects for which a future use was fondly imagined but seldom found. In tin boxes of this ilk are the keys to the real archives of the farm; dig down there and you dig up pieces of the past. Fragments of sociology, pieces of history, smatterings of rural economics lie there, awaiting only excavation and extrapolation. Here is an antique flat wrench with a cracked jaw, circa 1902; and here is an insulator from the first telephone line that came through; and this is a gear from a Sears Roebuck apple parer. With a good forty-penny nail as an archaeological shovel, a bored boy could spend a pleasant hour stirring up the box to see what trash or treasure might surface: a bent washer to attach to a pea shooter, links from a small chain that could dress up a jackknife, a flat nail with a square head that could be traded in school. For the good stuff you dug deep.

One day I stirred up from this storehouse of antiquities a short, cylindrical metal object, three inches long and a half-inch in diameter, slightly tapered and open at both ends. Just a bit of metal rolled into a cylinder, it appeared; but it was too interesting to rebury in the box, so I pocketed it for future reference. (There was a second, identical one in the box, which I left for seed.) Days later I showed it to my mother and asked what it was—asked *her* because at that hour my father was on the back forty cutting firewood. She didn't know its name, but she knew its function. Suspecting that I was onto something important, I went to the garage to investigate the one that I had replanted. Sure enough, in a week it had produced another, giving me now three of them.

"Can I try them out, to see if they work?"

My mother was evasive. "Dad's in the woods; why don't you go and talk to him?"

To the woods then. Such a glorious March Saturday, a day suddenly full of meaning and bright purpose—snow heavily crusted from last night's frost, brilliant sunshine streaming down and shattering into millions of sparkling pieces. Valuables in hand, I followed the lane eastward toward the woods, toward the sun, toward the sharp, beckoning ring of my father's ax, till I arrived at the tramped-down circle of his work among the sugar maple trees.

My father plucked a shining icicle from a branch, nibbled off its end, and handed the rest to me. "Try it," he said. It was sweet, far better than the icicles we regularly sampled from the eaves of the house. All around me were riches I had not encountered before: stumps, logs, and countless cut-off branches were decorated with sweet icicles hanging from the places where the ax had been the day before, where the maple sap had seeped from the wound overnight and frozen. I sampled some icicles, dropped them, and reached for more. Those sights, those sounds, those tastes—they are stamped indelibly into my memory because that was the day when I was first infected with a disease which, though it sometimes goes into remission, has remained chronic to this day.

The symptom of this nameless disease is an irrational springtime impulse to work long and hard hours at making small quantities of maple syrup. There is no cure.

My contagion began in innocence. I gathered my wits to lay out my plan, more than a little fearful that my father would be discouraging or worse. I'd have to be subtle.

"Dad, I want to make maple syrup. Mother said you would show me how." This latter claim about Mother's complicity involved a slight extension of what she had actually said, in accordance with the classic formula for cajoling parents: divide, reinterpret, conquer. Then came Exhibit A: I pulled from my pocket the three spiles (also called spouts or taps).

"Here are the things," I said. "Can we put them up here?"

Did I have the idea that Dad would take my spiles, stick them into a maple tree right there, and milk out a squirt or two of maple syrup while I held the cup? Maybe I had no coherent idea at all. Everything I knew about maple sap and syrup was contained in the sweet icicles I was sucking.

"We'll see once, this afternoon," he said. And I knew I was home free.

Evidently, I would need a few lessons in the production process and my father would have to improvise, for I later learned that he himself had never seen the thing done. I also learned that years earlier he had bought the spiles inadvertently at a farm auction when he had recklessly bid twenty cents on a crate of odds and ends, including spiles, and had simply put them away in the tin box where I had found them, intending to try them out sometime. Every farm harbors a rich collection of unimplemented good ideas.

We had never tasted maple syrup. Nobody we knew made it. My parents thought they remembered that Abe Cavanaugh had once said that his father knew someone who used to make it and had declared that it was easy to do and that the syrup was better than anything you could buy. That was the kind of solid evidence we regularly depended on for decision making. Moreover, those were wartime days of food rationing, and our family, like many others, was preoccupied with ways to stretch the sugar allowance of half a pound per person per week—much less than our palates and much more than our health required. Our sugar stretcher was Karo corn syrup, bought in tin pails, ten pounds at a time; anything free and better than that was sure to be a bargain. The proposition was that maple syrup might be the bargain we awaited.

I didn't marshal all these arguments; they were just in the air somewhere. I lucked out. To my surprise, I got Dad's full support and help—he who was normally selective about which youthful follies he encouraged. No doubt the sugar shortage as well as my entrepreneurial spirit and his own curiosity aided and abetted my case; so we returned to the woods that afternoon fully armed. We took just two spiles, because that seemed the right number to him, believing as he did in moderation in all things. And we took a brace and bit and two one-gallon Karo syrup pails and a few rusty sixteen-penny nails from the tin box. We selected the two biggest maple trees in the woods, drilled holes into them, watched the maple sap ooze out, and then inserted the spiles. I tapped them firmly into place with a stick of wood. We hung the pails below the spiles on nails. (Wrong method, of course, for that wounds the tree and lets the sap leak and go to waste. You should hang the pail from the spile itself; but nobody said so at the time.) As the first sweet drops of sap tinkled softly into the tin pails, we inaugurated the Maple Syrup Business for Missaukee County and, for all we knew at the time, for all of Michigan itself. By late afternoon enough sap had accumulated so that I could lift the pail to my face and drink. I became an addict.

From the front door of the house to the nearest of my two trees in the center of the woods was a distance of about two thousand feet, more than a third of a mile. Each day after school during the spring sap season I took a milk pail and tramped off to the woods to collect the day's yield. Being forest trees, my trees did not have large, branching tops for good sap production, and it was a very good day if the gallon pails were full. Nevertheless, carrying even this modest amount of sap, six or eight quarts, over the snowdrifts along the way to the house was an arduous task for a youngster, and there were days when I nearly despaired. I would wallow or slosh through the drifts to the woods, perhaps walking in yesterday's tracks or sometimes treading lightly on the crust as if walking on eggs, but my returning weight, augmented by fifteen pounds of sap, created new challenges. The situation required snowshoes, of course, but they existed only in books. Indians had snowshoes. I had difficulties. Of course I would stumble sometimes and plunge my tired arm elbow-deep into a pail of cold sap just before upsetting the pail itself, causing the sap to disappear instantly into the snow without a trace. Too well I know that melancholy sight! Better that it occur in the woods, where no one could see the humiliation and tears of frustration, than, as it sometimes did, within a snowball's throw of the house.

Did I like my hobby? I loved it, just as I loved the sweet maple syrup I produced. I studied the woods, picking out the young maple trees, estimating the years before they would be large enough to produce sap, dreaming of a major maple-syrup business when I was a farmer. Tapping maple trees was my turf, and territorial rights were conscientiously regulated within our family. Among my siblings I had exclusive rights to the privilege of tramping through knee-deep snow each day for three-quarters of a mile to haul in the sap. It was understood that this was territory that I had discovered and that it was mine to conquer or surrender. Surrender did not occur to me. I supposed that there was probably a silent sibling watch out on me and the maple syrup business, waiting for me to falter and relinquish the field to others. Therefore I did not falter, no matter how often I fell. With hindsight I would guess that maybe something else, quite the opposite, was going on, namely, a design to keep me going.

Tom Sawyer got the fence painted by inducing his friends to think the job was so privileged they should pay for permission to help. I would have been one of the suckers who paid up and went to work. Getting the sap was a strenuous chore that I addressed with ardor and performed as a special right and privilege, and it is doubtful that anybody in the family ever wanted any other arrangement.

When it arrived from the woods, the sap went into a large pot on the back of the kitchen stove, and there it slowly, very slowly, simmered toward syrup. Each day the quantity was diluted with the fresh sap, and after a week or so we had something that began tasting very sweet. If it wasn't sweet enough, we simply left it on for several more days. We didn't boil it but we should have. Syrup that is made by slow evaporation without boiling usually has a poor flavor, but I didn't know that until years later when I read about Helen and Scott Nearing's experiments in *The Maple Sugar Book*. To our taste the syrup we made was heavenly stuff—a judgment not now up for reconsideration. However, our simmering was not always carried on long enough, and the syrup we canned sometimes developed mold. Not knowing that that was because its sugar content was too low, we concluded that maple syrup simply did not keep well in mason jars and thereafter we consumed it within a month or two of making it. Not hard. We seldom made more than a gallon or two, even in later years when I found another spile and extended my operation to four pails. The Michigan wartime economy assimilated the impact of our syrup business without difficulty.

If there are, within certain tolerances, wrong ways to make maple syrup, there are no known wrong ways to consume it.

For us maple syrup usually supplied a brief and exciting alternative to corn syrup, which we ate with what we called "dipfat." Dipfat was usually tallow—pork fat only in a pinch—heated in a skillet to the point where it sizzled with a certain vigor when you dropped a crumb of bread into it. Every one of us had perfect pitch in telling, by the bread-crumb test, when the fat was ready. We then took half a slice of bread, affixed it properly to a two-tined fork, and dipped it lightly into the sizzling tallow. We put the bread on the linoleum-covered table, handed the fork to a waiting sibling, applied syrup to the hot, betallowed face of the bread, and then devoured it before the tallow clotted.

Cereal followed by dipfat and a beverage was the standard winter breakfast for the younger members of our family. When the beverage wasn't milk it was Postum, the thought of which reminds me of warmed-over, weak, week-old coffee; but in fact we liked it because it was perked like real coffee. After Easter and throughout the summer, a fresh boiled egg replaced the dipfat. On this alternating schedule, year in and year out, none of us ever tired of eggs or dipfat—which was precisely my mother's intention.

On Sunday, because it was a special day, we had relief from oatmeal in the form of cornflakes. Still, oatmeal six days a week gets to be a tiresome story, so periodically there were other alternatives to it, none very interesting. The first was cornmeal mush—to wit, cornmeal cooked into a mush, which we occasionally ate with syrup instead of the usual warm fresh milk and sugar. When we put maple syrup on the mush, we were within striking distance of reinventing Indian pudding, but we did not know anyone had ever been there before. The second alternative to oatmeal was cream of wheat—to wit, wheatmeal cooked into a mush, whose destiny it is forever to sport lumps and eventually to be warmly loathed and detested by all healthy, upright kids. The third item in this declining sequence is cocoa wheat—to wit, wheatmeal cooked into a mush and tainted with cocoa flavoring. The options began to make oatmeal look pretty good again. Neither of the latter two wheatmeal sins against the palates of youth is to be laid wholly at the door of my parents—after all, they got the stuff in boxes from the store. We ate what was set before us because that was the rule; it was the same spirit in which we took cod-liver oil. Dipfat was never so good as when you had earned your way to it through a bowl of lumpy cocoa wheat.

So we consumed rivers of dipfat. For a few months each year we upgraded that delicacy by replacing the corn syrup with our own homegrown nectar of the maple. Although medical science is bent on robbing the human race of certain sweet and greasy delicacies, it happens that our family has long been unusually healthy, and this might be attributed to the one thing that differentiated us from our neighbors: we ate ten times more fat than anybody else. Ah, innocence! *Dipfat* was a household word, and *cholesterol* was a word unheard. (I have no evidence to implicate cod-liver oil in our good health; everybody took that stuff.) We secured suet from the neighbors when they butchered, ground it up with a food grinder, heated it, poured the shiny liquid tallow into bread pans for firming up, and saved the residue; then we stacked the hardened golden loaves in the basement. When the stack was diminished to two or three loaves, we knew spring was on the way.

Each morning my mother cut slabs from a loaf of tallow and put them into the skillet. The residue from the rendering process formed the crowning morning delicacy: cracklings in English, but we knew them by their Dutch name, *kontjes*. (If you translate *kontjes* into Latin and then Greek and finally into English, you get "ambrosia.") We put the sizzling tallow and the syrup on the bread and then spread hot, dripping *kaantjes* on top. The gods may break their fast on that.

Homemade bread, homemade dipfat, homemade *kaantjes*, homemade maple syrup. Only the poor could be so rich.

❧ 10 ☙

Dividing Turf and Multiplying Hobbies

By the time a country boy is old enough to whistle, he is also old enough to feel that he ought to start collecting things. *What* things is less important: colored stones, postmarks, Indian-head pennies, tinfoil, marbles, chains of paper clips. Starting the collection is vital; carrying on is a detail that may fall by the wayside or run amok among sibling rivalries.

My parents collected string. "Storecord" we called it, and it came from the grocery store in bits and pieces, to be frugally tied together and wound into a ball and stuffed into the string can. If one of us started a hobby that required storecord, we were automatically tied into our parents' hobby and we knew the recycled string was there—third shelf in the cupboard, on the left. It was that sort of household.

My first collectible was what we called "match folders," the discarded empties of matchbooks. This hobby required storecord, a sharp eye, and persistence. I proceeded in this manner: Between two nails on the bedroom wall I hung a string, and on it I hung match folders side by side, covers carefully closed. When I had filled one string, I started another and another, encircling the room in double, triple loops of match folders, row on row. There was but one rule: each match folder saved and hung had to be unique; duplicates were worthless. My hobby was always on display, its own visible reward.

But there was also an invisible payoff, the latent magic of the hobby, and that was its power to transform every windblown corner of any public place where debris gathered into an inviting spot, to ensure that street gutters were not messy and sordid but recesses where valuables might lie in plain view, free for the taking. At the friendly edges of parking lots near churches and schools there were treasures among the trash, and though my young eyes were blind to the trash, I could see the match folders. Often they were smudged and had to be cleaned before they were fit for my wall.

The sheer variety of advertisements on match folders astonished me, and as I put each one up on the string I fixed its design in memory so that I could tell at a glance if a new find was of value or a worthless duplicate. Before age ten I was well launched in my career as connoisseur of discarded match folders, fancying myself one of Michigan's authorities on that arcane subject. Maybe I had the notion that I was collecting a finite number of objects, that eventually I might get a specimen of every one: a complete collection of match folders! That they were proliferating in varieties as unending as the casual ingenuities of the advertising industry may not have occurred to me. With hundreds of them on permanent display, I would give an illustrated lecture on the topic at the drop of a hint to anyone who would listen. Occasionally a visitor did.

In September a small package arrived for me in the mail. It came from Momence, Illinois, from Rev. Cornelius Maring, our long-time pastor who just that year had left our West Branch Christian Reformed Church for a new pastorate in Illinois. Long, long ago, he had been the one who helped to soften the hard heart of my grandfather; he had officiated at my parents' wedding and had baptized us five children, and he had a special fondness for our family.

I opened the surprise parcel to find a treasure trove. Match folders! Dozens of them! A magnificent addition to my collection. Each one was unique and, most astonishing of all, every last one was different from any of mine. How could he have avoided duplicating anything in my collection? I concluded that Illinois was an extraordinary place—wherever it was. A letter from Mrs. Maring told us that "the Domine" had picked up the match folders from the streets of Momence and saved them for Ronny.

Did the magic in my hobby have the transforming power to make interesting even the grimy gutters of distant cities? Rev. Maring was a pastor of the old school, a man of God and reserved, never without his dignity and never without a tie. He lives in cherished memory, this good and pious man stooping to gather scraps from the street to please a little farm kid in Michigan. The image was not lost on us at the time, either; but I was equally struck by the bright array of new colors. I installed a brand-new piece of recycled storecord for the match folders and hung them up in glory.

Hobbies and many other things were governed by several regulatory principles at our home, some of them a little quirky. Heading the list was the Principle of Seniority. *Seniority* was a word we never heard, but we took in the concept with our mother's milk. What we absorbed was the idea that there existed a scale of entitlement corresponding exactly to our relative ages, older to younger. Four of us had arrived on the scene at approximately two-year intervals—Marvin, Gladys, I, and Nelvin—and therefore that is exactly the way we were lined up before the duties and privileges of life. Carl came after an eight-year interval and therefore was either a far fifth in line or first again, depending upon circumstances. Favors went to the eldest, as did responsibilities. Seniority prescribed the eternal order of things. That was that.

By the seniority code our bedtimes were appointed—on a carefully graduated scale; by it we arranged ourselves in the car (the smallest tucked in the unprivileged positions between the largest, out of sight and out of seeing); by it we arranged ourselves on a church pew and received our calibrated monthly allowances. The seniority code indicated when and in what order we were entitled to develop certain hobbies, to raise pets, to select radio programs, to go along to town with Dad, and to choose the domain for our various juvenile projects. We had access to the funnies in the *Cadillac Evening News* in accordance with our seniority, and it was not unusual for the Sunday cake to be cut into sizes proportional to our ages. Had not all such orders been ordained by God himself, who had brought us to the family in precisely this sequence?

A code that stresses seniority may just be amplified common sense, but my parents saw much more than that in it. They saw propriety, order, structure. They saw also a good management tool (how else decide just how the youngsters would line up their boots at the door?), an antibickering device, and a silencer for the eternal clamor: "How come he can do that and I can't?" ("He's older than you are.") "I wanna go too." ("Next time.") And they saw also a moral teacher, for the code induced habits of patience and acceptance, virtues both. Patience: if he could hold out that long, Nelvin could plant watermelons next year as I was doing this year. Resignation: with patience and fortitude I could eventually escape the shackles of being only ten years old, but I could never escape being third in line; I might as well accept that.

The seniority code was complex: there were unwritten subsections, judicial interpretations, executive orders, and a body of parental common law that fleshed things out. But it was comprehensive, and sometimes serenely wacky. Couldn't the littler ones just once in a while ride to church at the privileged window seat so they could see the passing show? Ah, but the code frowned sternly upon so whimsical an approach to life. My parents were not about to disturb the universe.

How easy for children to internalize such a code! They learn with alacrity to lord it over one another, especially if they are merely enforcing the natural hierarchy of things. We worked at bringing one another up in accordance with some vague idea that we had to earn our place in the sun not only by virtue but by endurance. When Carl finally joined us, eight years behind Nelvin, we siblings were so practiced at bringing up children that we took on the task of rearing him with enthusiasm, ganging up on him, giving him the moral advantage of having more strictures thrust upon him than any of us had had—a blessing he somehow survived. Extravagant affection may have helped, too.

By no means did the seniority code always work to the advantage of the older sibling. A first claimant did not automatically control the territory forever; he had to cultivate the turf and also be prepared to move on to other fields. Marvin started trapping skunks and muskrats for their pelts, for which there was a fair market; but when he went on to trapping foxes, which required more equipment and far better skills, he relinquished muskrats to Nelvin and skunks to me. We were all satisfied with this arrangement—even the skunks, I believe, for their composure was very little disturbed by the way in which legal access to them was transferred to me within our family councils.

However, for two years I became a reader of skunk literature and an avid student of skunk lore. I bought six shiny steel leg-hold traps at the hardware store and hung them up to rust—as Marvin had taught me—so that they could be more easily camouflaged when I set them in the doorways of dens. Together, Marvin and I surveyed the stone piles and stump heaps of the neighborhood, searching for skunk dens, sniffing droppings, following tracks, locating lairs, planning strategy. But when the season opened on October 15 and I set my traps and caught a skunk, I had to face the music alone. Fortunately, I was not often successful as a skunk trapper—just twice, in fact. It is a sport with which one is easily satiated, and that may help to explain why Marvin assigned the skunks to me and went on to foxes. Indeed, no skunk pelt was ever worth the trouble it cost the youthful trapper—to say nothing of what it cost the skunk—but it took me a season or two to appreciate that. The skunks among us were fairly rare and perfectly harmless unless molested. So why did we trap them? Because we had bought into the trapping mystique, and because we had the magazines that told us how to do it.

On projects that the younger ones had to wait in line for, it was often possible to profit by observation and be ready to move into the niche when an older sibling had outgrown a passion or simply defaulted. That's what had happened with the match folders: Marvin had started a collection but seemed to lack commitment. Later, Marvin raised rabbits and after that chickens, and I saw that chickens weren't much entertainment and that rabbits were, and made my plans accordingly. I saw too, or thought I did, why he was giving up on rabbits: they kept digging out of their pens and running at large. When my turn for rabbits came, I was ready with my devastatingly clever solution: build better pens. Simple as putting up longer strings for match folders.

One summer day I proceeded to fit action to philosophy. With my own money I bought a roll of chicken wire, and then I set off to the woods with a hatchet and returned dragging the essential materials. I picked a spot in the orchard off the beaten track and spent a day and a half nailing things up, far from prying eyes. But Marvin tracked me down. He stood there, chewing on an apple and contemplating what I thought of as my handiwork, with that sort of brotherly look that did not make my spirits soar.

"What in the deuce is *that* thing?"

"It's a rabbit pen," I told him flatly.

"*That?*"

"It's a good one, too."

"Yeah!"

There went the feather from my cap. Big brothers are good at that.

I was in no mood for receiving help, but his hoot and snicker were not really an offer of help, either. Was I supposed to know that he had already exhausted the entire range of sound rabbit-pen designs available within our skills and material resources? At any rate, that first pen of mine turned out to be somewhat beyond the pale: framed with long green poles, it differed from all previous models in being so clumsy and heavy as to be nearly immobile. During the ensuing weeks, as the green poles cured and stiffened, the contraption became even more formidable: a rigid, boxlike monster, it could not conform to the contours of the ground, and consequently, when put to use it promptly leaked rabbits on every side and corner. It might have served as a pen for pigs, but as a rabbit pen it was a firm technological step backward. The rabbits were jubilant, and they blithely broke all previous escape records on the farm.

It was at about that time that Nelvin took himself out of the running for the privilege of raising rabbits. He got interested in something stable, less likely to cut loose and run—raspberries, I think it was. Gladys, two years older than I, was probably automatically excluded from many such projects just because she was a girl. It was essentially a boys' world that we siblings created, and she had to thread her way through it as well as she could, enduring some arbitrary exclusions. Did she want to raise rabbits or ducks or watermelons, or shoot sparrows or hang a wren house or make a bow and arrow or have her own cat or rock collection? Or trap skunks? She had to be a tomboy to survive and a girl to prevail. That cannot have been easy, and I don't know that her brothers saw it as their job to make it any easier. As for Carl, with all the advantages of eight years of hindsight, he could survey the whole field of entrepreneurial triumphs and flops and pick the best of them. Meanwhile, he had the privilege of petting my rabbits—when we could catch one.

Evidently, with our hobbies and projects we were playing at farming, testing it for size and feeling. We were only vaguely oriented toward the market, and even now it is hard to recall, for example, just what did happen to all the rabbits born among us. We didn't eat many, believing that the wild rabbits we hunted were tastier. We sold some rabbits as pets and gave some away; I traded some to a friend in school; predators got some; some ran away; disease got many of them; one beautiful doe froze to death; we saw the cat get a few young ones and we suspected dogs may have too, and no doubt the foxes took their nighttime share. The profit margin on the rabbit enterprises was always pretty slim. It was like farming.

As with any farmer, there came a time when I needed money and had a crop surplus, so I decided to take three large rabbits to a market in Cadillac. They were black-and-white females, friendly pets, always willing to be held, and each of them had given me fine litters of young. Still, it was a practical decision, and I thought, If I'm offered a good price, I'll sell. I took them to Cadillac in a cardboard box, which I carried two blocks from where Dad had parked the car. They are sold and bought by weight, I was told, and someone directed me to take the box to the man near the scale. That would be awkward: how could I put my rabbits on the scale and expect them to stay there for weighing while we discussed the price? But I was at a meat market, not a pet shop. Without ceremony or even a glance my way, the scale man picked up a heavy tool and lifted my rabbits one by one from the box, and with three swift strokes, taking only a second apiece, he transformed my pets into carcasses that he calmly deposited in a neat, quivering stack on the scale. Their pink noses ran red. Then he took the scale reading and told me that I would be paid. The thing had been done so routinely, and in less than half a minute! I was utterly speechless. Was that how I had imagined taking leave of my pets? Not at all. Not at all. Without words, I took the money and hurried away, feeling that I had never been poorer in my life.

As we grew older our hobbies and projects became more ambitious. It fell naturally to Marvin to initiate the big ideas, to talk up ambitious plans, to scout the outer limits of parental indulgence. He also surveyed the literature: magazines and reams of pamphlets that we collected from the Agricultural Experiment Station in East Lansing and the U.S. Department of Agriculture. In practice that meant he was often running interference for me, knocking holes in the resistance but not always able to score himself. In our seniority system, being top dog had its down side.

"I think Dad's really getting interested in squabs," Marvin said to me one day.

"Think so?" I said.

"Nah, I really don't, I guess."

For some years, Marvin read copiously and talked endlessly about raising squabs, but when it came down to the wire what he bought was chicken fence. Although I don't know just why he turned to chickens, I suspect parental pressure. (Indeed, what exactly *are* squabs again? It was hard to remember, and we had never seen one.) Nevertheless, all his squab talk certainly helped clear the way for me when I started talking geese, which are just as exotic. However, my career as a gooseherd was preceded by a brief and intense fling with honeybees.

Marvin had inserted honeybees into the family discourse, laying a philosophical basis that I could later build on. His theme, soundly based on the literature from the USDA, was that bees were immensely beneficial to a farm: to be good farmers we needed a few hives of honeybees. Dad had a lethal weapon against such reasonable arguments: he ignored them. True, he listened carefully, was genuinely interested in an abstract sort of way, said "maybe so, but we aren't trying it just yet," and only then did he forget about it. He had not been brought up to base his actions on the scientific literature; he based his farming practice on, well, the farming practice.

We of the younger set had to learn to be resourceful in persuading reluctant parents to go along with some of our far-out schemes. A straight-out proposal (such as I had lucked out with in the maple syrup case), though it might involve good theory, was usually bad politics. Here lies one of life's gentle ironies: Whereas youth has a keen sense of the arts of cajoling, conning, and convincing parents, many former kids have forgotten its sly techniques by the time they are parents, and they find themselves cornered by the very strategies *they* once employed to such good effect. (I write as a parent.) Adulthood forgets, but youth understands that cajoling parents is a strategic game. Reputed as I was to have been uncommonly successful at that game in my prime, I now dredge from memory and summarize for posterity those few and simple maxims that the young invariably grasp better than their adult adversaries. Here are the trade secrets from a kid emeritus:

First: Talk up your project. Do it in general terms and only intermittently and over a sustained period of time, but *not* to the point of setting out plans definite enough to provide an opening for a parental veto. *Second:* Enlarge your base of support. It's important that others besides you get involved in the project, for that gives your parents an imprecise target at best. *Third:* Manipulate the vagueness. Let only your demeanor and your offhand remarks casually indicate that you are consolidating plans for some indefinite time in the future. *Fourth:* Watch the timing. Success in difficult cases usually comes because there was never a good moment for parents to say no; it was always too early and they didn't want to be peremptory and negative, *or* it was too late and your plans had somehow gotten too far advanced.

Armed with those insights (unarticulated as they were), I spent more than a year on the work-up to my honeybees. I started with a subscription to a bee journal, from which I read aloud enlightening excerpts at suitable occasions. Beekeeping had been prized even among the ancients, we learned: the Romans had written about the arts and pleasures of beekeeping thousands of years ago. But only in modern times had it been realized that the worker bees are all females, that the hive is a complete matriarchal society without a king, and that among honeybees all males are bums. Bees talk to one another by dancing, I read, giving directions to the nectar fields by elaborate spins and rolls, and by tap dances, pirouettes, and back flips. My campaign theme—far more potent than the pale argument that bees are useful—was that bees are incredibly interesting and we'd really like them. Anybody could hum a lot of variations on that tune.

Came the time when I had to make a move, for I was fourteen and convinced that for me and the bees it was this year or never. I knew exactly what I needed and by now so did everybody else in the house: two hive kits from Dadant and Sons, a mail-order bee-supply company; miscellaneous equipment, such as frames, wax foundation, gloves, smoker, hive tool (all long since picked out and explained to anyone who would listen); and two five-pound packages of bees to be sent express from Georgia. The fact that the plan had some exotic features—bees by mail, for example—stimulated interest and worked to my advantage. But as I tried to feed everyone's curiosity about bees, exploit the vagueness of my plans, and watch for the timely moment, I was worried about Marvin's squab precedent: to my mind being diverted from squabs to chickens was the moral equivalent of being diverted from honeybees to bumblebees.

Perhaps I need not have worried, and perhaps my strategies paid off—you never really know. "All right, you can try it once," said Dad with his usual enthusiasm. So I tried it once.

The hive kits arrived, and I spent a few weeks after school putting them together and painting them white. The frames came, forty-four of them, and I assembled them with hammer and tacks; and then the wax foundation for the bee combs arrived, and I inserted it carefully into the frames. I bought ten pounds of sugar to be dissolved in water and fed to the bees after they were in their new hives, and for that purpose I took a syrup pail and pounded some small holes in its lid. In everything I went by the book. Now it was the last week of March: the maple syrup season was winding up; the buds were swelling; I was ready for bees. My new pets would live on sugar syrup and pussy-willow pollen for the first week, awaiting the first blossoms from the red maples.

I met my thirty thousand bees at the express depot in McBain, where they had arrived in two boxes, each screened on four sides and about a foot square. They had been promptly banished to the farthest corner of the waiting room, where they emitted a steady hum. Another customer was regarding them from about twenty feet away, indicating that he intended to keep his distance. Equipped with a pail of sugar syrup in one hand and a paintbrush in the other, I set about painting sweet syrup on the screens of their boxes, following exactly the instructions from Georgia, which recommended dinner upon arrival. The bees were ecstatic at this welcome, and said so by instantly switching keys from a minor hum to a high-pitched hymn of gratitude. I was conscious that the entire depot staff had paused to watch the action as I went at my task with trumped-up professional ease. Actually, the depot staff consisted entirely of Mr. Watson, who had a peg leg and didn't get very close lest he have to run from a sudden attack. I gathered that he had been amazed to see the buzzing bees arrive in his shop and that he would not regret seeing them go.

From the first the bees were a great hit, fascinating the family, casual visitors, neighbors, relatives, and all who stopped by and could be recruited for a brief lecture by me on the ingenious ways of honeybees. I read everything about bees that I could get my hands on, studied the subject more assiduously, I'm afraid, than my school textbooks, and still retain a good portion of it. We lived in bee paradise. Meadows unnumbered were loaded with red clover, white clover, and alfalfa; other clovers thrived in hundreds of waste places; flowering weeds and wildflowers festooned the fencerows and roadsides. On a hot July day you could see the bees by the thousands as they buzzed and wallowed in the bliss of the wild yellow clover. In the autumn I left most of the honey in the hives to ensure a strong colony in the spring, and I sheltered the bees for the winter in a safe hollow in the orchard. Perhaps within a year or two I would start recouping my investment from the surplus honey.

Beekeeping is like rabbit raising, is like farming: the best-laid plans . . . gang aft a-gley. In mid-March, sudden hard rains melted the snow and drastically enlarged the pond before the ground had thawed to absorb the rising water. In an unprecedented event, the swollen pond behind the barn washed over the lane, poured into the orchard and then into the very hollow where my bees had quietly wintered. In the dark of the night the little hollow filled with swirling water and my hives were instantly overwhelmed. In the light of the morning I gazed out in horror upon a sea of disaster. The two hives, covers off, lapped by waves and ice floes, listed against a brush pile where they had come to rest, and all about them thousands and thousands of dead bees littered the water and collected in deep, dark layers along the shoreline. For me, a spectacle so utterly sad as to lie beyond tears.

Had I acted immediately, I might have ordered more bees from Georgia in time to begin the process again, but I was too despondent to make a swift move. I had been saving my money for geese, and I had other dreams to dream. A hard choice. How such teenage decisions are made is mysterious to me, and the process leaves no traces in my memory. I know only that youth does not normally look back and that what I did was to look forward to geese. I fished the two hives to the shore, salvaged a few chunks of combed honey, dried out the hives, and put them into storage.

Nearly thirty years later I dug the hives out and lugged them to New Hampshire, where they have now waited a decade for me to put them to use. And I may still do that. Or I might get some geese again instead. Match folders? Nah.

❧ 11 ❧

McBain, the Smallest City

Like Lake Wobegon, McBain is a little city that time forgot—
and, indeed, time even forgot just when it originated. It's true that
McBain celebrated a centennial with balloons and parades in
1977, but I'm not drawing any historical conclusions from that.

In the 1880s a few lumber mills, houses, and then a store appeared where Riverside and Richland townships met, at a station
on the new Toledo, Ann Arbor and Northern Railroad. The
settlement was called Owens when a post office opened at the railroad station on August 27, 1888, but by September of the next
year the station was renamed McBain. Very quickly it became a
noisy little three-saloon lumber junction, and it was incorporated
as the village of McBain in 1893. More and more Dutch was being
heard at the general store.

By 1907, with the lumber business winding down and farming
gearing up, it was just another little backwoods town that had sold
its woods. That was something of an identity crisis, and the creative response to it was to reincorporate McBain as a city. The
smallest city in the country—that was then the boast of its two
hundred residents. Over the years it has been reasserted, and although the population has since doubled, I don't know if the claim
has been challenged. If the vintage of the village is a little vague,
there's no knocking its pluck and enterprise. Now they say it's the
biggest small city of its size anywhere. We always called it a town.

Our town's Main Street was, and is, a block long and half a block
wide, and from the time I first knew it, things were arranged there
according to an order laid up among the stars. Members of the
McBain family had once owned most of the land under the town,
and accordingly, in McBain, when you walked up to the counter of
the general store, at the corner of Main Street and the main road,

you read your grocery list to Mr. Jim McBain himself. The store occupied the first floor of a blunt rectangular structure typical of the cheerful architectural inanity of the late nineteenth century: a homely three-story façade on a homelier two-story rectangular building. For decades this style was repeated up and down our Main Street, echoing ten thousand other little main streets all across America.

I glance at an old photo of Main Street and I see the truth in bold print: to the craftsmen of that generation it simply wasn't allowable that a store should look like a house—or like a mill or a barn or a church, perhaps the only other structures with definite, known forms. A McBain store was made to *look* like a store, a flat bland face that would face the flat bland faces across the street.

It is said that our town also once had an opera house, but it is not said whether it had any opera. Again a faded photo of Main Street suggests that the opera building may have had a mansard roof, which may also be why it was called an opera house, under the theory that a highfalutin style merits a highfalutin name. That is speculation, not history; attested history is meager in McBain. Anyway, they put a bank in the opera house eventually, neutralizing the exotic. All that was long ago.

McBain, the cultural and commercial center of our world, five miles from our farm, had one each of most things we needed: school, general store, drugstore, bank, newspaper, barbershop, doctor, depot, blacksmith shop, and so on, ending with a bar—called by us a beer garden and conjuring up scenes of debauchery such as probably never transpired in McBain since the last drunk lumberjack died in the prehistoric town of Owens. They told us McBain was officially a city, but we weren't fooled. Cadillac, nearly twenty miles to the west and two thousand strong and with a couple of traffic lights and brick streets and factories and a Woolworth store: that was a real city.

Jim McBain's general store was a solid institution, bearing modest success without pretensions and without illusions. When I came to know it, it was just the sort of place one would now imagine such a place to be: from the piles of Rockford socks and the sweet-smelling stacks of blue bib overalls to the cast-iron stove with trim of chrome and the bottomless barrel of dried salt herring.

In the thirties my parents, like many others, were not always able to pay for everything we needed, so Jim McBain did quite a bit of credit business, waiting hopefully for the farmers to sell the beans or butcher the hogs to put their hands on a little cash. When the bill was paid, which my parents were extremely careful to do before it ever got discouragingly large, Jim McBain would tuck a little sack of candy, gratis, into the grocery bag. If the candy was peppermints, it went straight into the square box in the cupboard, to be dispensed only on Sundays before church, two apiece for each service; but if it was another kind of candy, we sampled it when the groceries were unpacked. I took it that somehow peppermints and only peppermints were appropriate for church, like sermons and knickers and neckties, and had been invented for just that purpose.

The business we did at McBain's store was invariably called "trading," as in "Why don't you folks trade by Jim McBain?" as put by my mother. (The *by* here was a nearly universal Dutchism, deriving from *bij*, meaning "at" or "with"; and the question is blunt because that was my mother's way.) *Trade* was a lingering usage, but not inaccurate. For years we traded eggs and sometimes fresh pork for groceries, and for a few years in the forties we traded lots of strawberries, too. In fact, during the brief intense strawberry season we got ahead of the grocery bill and then McBain owed us money, a pleasant turnabout from the depression years just a decade earlier.

At various times there came and went one or another smaller grocery store down the street from McBain's, but it was not until I was in high school that there was any serious competition. Eventually, another store put in some newfangled features—freezer locker, self-service, cash register, tape instead of storecord for binding packages—and Jim McBain retired, the last of a famous breed, sole proprietor of the town's sole general store. It escaped my attention that an era was passing.

"It might be only whooping cough again," Dr. Masselink said cheerfully. In fact, that *was* good news, since scarlet fever had been suspected.

He was a country doctor of the old school. For more than half a century Dr. Masselink's practice radiated outward for untold miles from McBain through a heavily settled rural area. No one physician could really minister to such a huge clientele. What eased the pressure on his time, if not on his mind, was that many families, ours included, did not call or visit the doctor casually. Serious sprains or even broken fingers never received a doctor's attention—pain was designed to be borne—but the threat of a serious illness did.

As a man he was imposing and portly and kindly, wore a dark suit and vest, carried a black bag, and sometimes gave candy to children. He lived in the largest house in town, as befitted his status. It is not possible to imagine him in overalls or, say, with a hoe in his hand. Day or night he made house calls and he personified the dignity and formidable authority of the world of medicine; his very presence spoke volumes about sickness and health and gloom and reassurance and mystery. No doubt he had some scientific or diagnostic talent, but we wouldn't have known: he was the doctor and that was that.

Dr. Masselink put down his black leather bag on the cold linoleum floor of the kitchen, and we children gathered round as he snapped it open. In went his hand and out came a stethoscope, tongue depressor, green liquid, thermometer, jar of pink pills, whatever. The hubbub always subsided as he went about his mysterious business, never hurried, under the prying eyes of three or four of the more or less healthy children. As I understood it then, the stethoscope was not so much a diagnostic tool as the first phase of treatment, perhaps a kind of external aspirin. Today, I've little doubt that many of the colored pills and bitter liquids that Dr. Masselink left in his wake were placebos, but it's also true that his attention and counsel and his dark suit and the stethoscope and the black bag and the pills and the bitter red fluids almost always left the patient feeling better, whether the working was biological or psychological or merely mysterious.

There *were* serious and dangerous illnesses that stalked the community, preying on whole families at a time—scarlet fever, polio, diphtheria—in addition to the regular epidemics of measles, mumps, pinkeye, whooping cough, strep throat, impetigo, chicken pox, and various forms of flu that swept through the neighborhoods, winter after winter. We lived in what was known as the "goiter belt" of Michigan: lack of iodine in our soil and water resulted in innumerable thyroid problems, especially among middle-aged women. Appendicitis was very common; appendectomies, I think, even more so. Tonsils were removed by the hundreds. Dr. Masselink had a fifty-five-year tenure in McBain, and shortly after he had helped deliver his last baby, at age eighty-three, he toted up his career production: more than 4,000 babies delivered. That too was almost exclusively an at-home service—if he could get there, which he sometimes didn't. In our family two of the five of us were jointly delivered by the responsible parties, my mother and father.

"She needs lots of doctoring." That's what my mother always said of one of the neighbors. I didn't get the irony at first, didn't realize that Dr. Masselink had to deal with a full quota of neurotics—like this neighbor whose good humor if not her health itself depended upon her constantly being reassured that she was indeed ill. Her "doctoring" took the form of regular office calls, a dollar apiece, and bottles and bottles of harmless pills. She outlived both Dr. Masselink and his successor, as well as nearly all her once-healthy neighbors and relatives. When I last inquired, I learned that she was free of complaints and approaching age ninety in full stride. Obviously, Dr. Masselink had prescribed the right stuff.

As he neared retirement, there were inroads on Dr. Masselink's reputation. Had he been too busy keeping us all going all those years to keep up with new knowledge? Probably. Moreover, he had an increasingly fastidious clientele, less inclined to repose medical confidence in the wisdom of age. It may be just as well that we didn't really know whether he was a genius, as we sometimes thought, or a hack, as we occasionally feared when the fever didn't break and the cough persisted, or, as is more likely, just a very good and able man who never took a vacation and devoted his life to others.

At the other end of the social spectrum from Dr. Masselink was Glen Daley.

Everybody knew Glen, the village idiot, though we wouldn't have used so harsh a term. He was "simple," we were taught to say. He was pathetic, of course, but as youngsters we were a little unclear about the distinction between the pathetic and the amusing. Inevitably, Glen was the butt of our youthful jokes and sometimes the victim, for the young are not kind to deficient adults. True to type, Glen showed up at every social function in McBain, and if food was available he got plenty of handouts. Cheerful, harmless, incompetent, supremely homely Glen—nobody would have charged him for anything.

Glen had one remarkable talent, which he was justly famous for. He could put his nose into his mouth.

People usually didn't believe it until they saw it; then they usually didn't forget it. Kids would tell friends about it—"He can swallow his nose!"—savor their disbelief, and then go and prove it to them. We'd spot Glen somewhere in the gathering and edge over and hang around until one of us dared to make the move. That one would shuffle over and offer him a bottle of pop as a friendly gesture.

"Kin ya swallow your nose, Glen?"

Glen wouldn't say much; he'd just reach up and grab his bottom lip with his fingertips, sometimes using both hands, and then effortlessly stretch it up and over his nose. He'd stand there, lower lip implausibly parked just under his eyes, and gaze about him with evident satisfaction, indeed, with a kind of pleased Popeye grin—though it's awfully hard to tell if a man with his nose in his mouth is really grinning. We'd gape and nudge one another nervously, for it was impressive to the point of being a little frightening. Later, we'd try it at home in front of the mirror and realize that it really was quite a stunt. You had to give it to Glen Daley. I like to think that his one talent may somehow have made his bleak life just a little brighter.

"All the churches are just the same, you know; that's why I don't believe some of 'em. Religion's okay sometimes, though. My grandmother was religious. Judas Priest, was she good at it!" Mr. Teft was preaching a sermon from the soda fountain, as was his wont. As usual it was not easy to catch the drift.

For school kids heading downtown at the noon hour, Teft's Drug Store was a natural stopping place: it had the town's only soda fountain and its best candy-bar display, and the proprietor, Floyd Teft, though a marked man in the community, was rather more interesting and accessible than most professional adults. Moreover, there were dark and vague rumors about Teft, no doubt the darker because of his manic ability to be vulgar, sentimental, high-minded, profane, or pious—or all of those at once—as the occasion warranted. His barely believable gossip and his deadpan seriousness shocked and fascinated young people, as they were meant to. So Teft's Drug Store was an attractive place, and often a busy one.

Did Mr. Masselink write prescriptions to be filled by Mr. Teft?

Hard to believe. As a druggist he supplied families with the salves, iodine, unguents, rubbing oils, hydrogen peroxide, cloves, cough syrup, and Epsom salts that were the staples of medicine cabinets. We assumed that those items were overpriced, whether we had any evidence of that or not.

"When you're young you can remember stuff easy; so that's when you ought to do it. Getting a good education is what you should do, because that's something they can't take away from you." Mr. Teft was giving me a learned sermon on learning when we were interrupted by a customer, who then lingered to chat. I couldn't help overhearing the tales they exchanged, complete with lots of dicey four-letter words. That accomplished, Mr. Teft returned to me and the merits of education without seeming to miss a beat. He was a versatile man.

Indeed, he was the sort about whom it was altogether too easy to imagine sinister things. There was his mincing gait and his greasy seductive charm, and his winking insinuations that he knew more about so-and-so than anybody else did, including the relevant spouse. And those gifts of character and reputation were embellishments on his standing distinction: he was reputed to be an extremely adroit shortchange artist. He had a knack for provoking a serious conversation about, say, how teachers were underpaid, which served as a timely distraction from the fact that he had not returned your thirty-one cents in change. Simple enough. But there were more colorful stories about how one might be "gypped" by Teft: ten-dollar bills split into two halves and both palmed off on the unwary, fake coins, miscounting, changing the price as you purchased the item, clever distractions. Thus, if he was silently suspected of many unnamed venial sins, he was openly credited with petty thievery. He not only thrived on gossip himself, but he triggered it as well. The public paid him the grudging respect of exaggerating his presumed infractions. "He can gyp you without you even knowing it," we assured one another. Arraigned before irrefutable evidence of that caliber, I imagine he might have smirked and pleaded guilty.

However, I'm afraid that Floyd Teft finally wasn't any great shakes as a bad man. We sorely needed a good example of badness, though, preferably one visible enough to serve as an example of what we shouldn't become, and Mr. Teft was the strongest candidate we had, so we had to make do with him, harmless small-town faker that he probably was.

Maybe Ben Minier of the McBain *Chronicle* wasn't a bad man either, but his business came to a bad end. He burned down his printing shop, presumably to collect insurance; but he collected instead only lasting notoriety and a new home in the county jail. That was the end of the weekly McBain *Chronicle*, a newspaper, so-called, of which he was owner, reporter, editor, typesetter, and publisher. A subscription to the paper was officially two dollars a year, but actually it was free. That was an effective strategy, for it made many of us feel lucky that we got it.

Ben Minier was not much to talk to, but he was something to look at. A huge man with a large mane of gray bushy hair, he had a face that was knotted and gnarled like an old pine stump, pockmarked, with a bulbous nose and warts and wens of prodigious size. He looked like a man with a past. Seeing him, I thought of pirates: give him bandanna and cutlass and he was the stuff of fiction.

Unlike its publisher, the *Chronicle* itself wasn't much to look at: local ads, announcements, tidbits about who had visitors from Cadillac, a column of "personals," and lots of filler copy: last year's weather in the Great Plains, something about Eskimos, an item about Calvin Coolidge, and a lesson on growing peanuts. At times the paper did fairly well by the school, with regular little articles from each classroom. No doubt the paper had other contents and merits, easily forgotten.

They were an odd couple, Ben and the *Chronicle*, and in retrospect they prompt solemn thoughts. I think it was hard to fill the pages of the paper, and I can guess why. Here was old Ben's problem, and it wasn't really his fault: the social culture of that locale was composed of numerous overlapping but rather closed sub-groups—churches, clubs, lodges, farm bureaus, circles, societies, and even city, township, and county offices. In each case the relevant activities were known by grapevine and hearsay to those *within* and thought to be of no interest to those *without*. So the principal units of the community seldom generated anything called "news," and consequently all kinds of activity never got into the public record.

The fact is that the prevailing concept of "news" itself was at fault, and the fault was simply its sheer, unmitigated inanity.

News was understood to be the fact that the mayor and his wife traveled to Lake City last week, not what the mayor proposed to do with the city budget. When local news as defined by that arid tradition ran to thin soup, as it always did, Minier thickened the broth by simply leaving some of last week's boilerplate in the press, re-printing from it, and changing the date, some headlines, and some swatches of Linotype. You could read those bits about peanuts, the Eskimos, and Coolidge every week for a month. The McBain *Chronicle* got to be like the old radio soaps: you could miss several weeks' production without really missing much of anything.

Still, historians will not disparage even minor local publications like McBain's *Chronicle*, which, after all, yield up their own little fragments for the larger mosaic. Indeed, such chronicles may serve society best by the way they serve history. It's a pleasant irony that local history can scarcely be written without the resources of the town newspaper, which was scarcely worth reading at the time. Though the *Chronicle* was a frail thing, its demise may have been more of a loss to history than to the community; for most of its archives went up in smoke, too.

It takes but a little exaggeration, a little poetic imagination, to see a fateful symmetry in the paper's final career, when all the news seemed to peter out. Since the *Chronicle* was getting pretty re-petitious, with more and more of last week's boilerplate remaining locked up in this week's edition, perhaps, back then, one might have extrapolated to a time when the new week's paper would completely duplicate the previous week's, word for word. What then? Then the paper would simply wind up? Perhaps in some weird or cockeyed way, grizzled old Ben Minier saw something like that coming. Suppose it came: one week he just didn't find anything at all that was new and worth reporting. Nothing about the doings of Jim McBain or Dr. Masselink or Floyd Teft or Glen Daley or the rest of them that the folks didn't already know. No new type needed. Ben Minier's pen was dry. So, in my fantasy, instead of going with last week's news and just changing dates, he divined that his task was now done, his life's work complete. As far as he could tell, the news had ended. So he just rang down the curtain and sent his *Chronicle* billowing to the skies.

Things like that can happen in the country's smallest city, and when they do there is no paper to report the news.

12

Life with Livestock

Livestock. The word may summon images of cattle and sheep gamboling on scenic hillsides, but a farmer's field of imagery is usually homelier than that. *Livestock* means "chores."

Morning and night, day in, day out, week in, week out, farmers and their sons did chores. *Chores* is not a generic term but a specific reference to the humdrum routines of livestock care that all farmers performed twice daily at set times, year in, year out. Feeding and watering the chickens; milking, feeding, and bedding the cows; gathering eggs; cleaning the stable; carrying the milk to the house, cranking up the separator, carrying the skim milk back to the barn; tending the calves, the pigs, the horses, the cats, the dog. Repetitious and boring, repetitious and boring, repetitious and boring.

But the tasks were also routinized to the point where they were part of the natural order. There was not much dignity in disliking chores, and no sense, either, so we didn't bother. Our chores were not heavy, for we never milked more than eight cows, and during the mid-forties my father usually had a choice of three boys to help, and a fourth coming up. No point in sending a labor force of that size to the barn twice a day; so one or more of us was left in the house to help with the dishes, a policy that made doing chores somewhat more attractive to a self-respecting country boy.

Like most farm boys we were vaguely fond of the animals, and, in their fashion, the animals vaguely reciprocated. It's a winter morning in the stable. The cows greet us as we enter by first heaving a heavy sigh and then heaving themselves slowly to their feet, glancing glumly, dumbly our way, not saying much. Invariably the horses blow their noses in gratitude as we stuff their mangers with hay, expelling blasts of air that make their nostrils wobble and rattle. The dog yawns and stretches, yawns again, and then returns to his warm circle of straw. The cats circle our legs negotiating for milk foam, ready to trip us as we step across the gutter. Although the society in a cozy stable on a cold morning is not very subtle or articulate, it has its own form of undirected cheer, and there is something sensually satisfying about coming in from the cold to sit down between a couple of warm ruminating cows. The calm mood will be bitterly broken if I get a gutter-dampened cow tail swatted smartly across my face, one of the major occupational hazards of farm chores. But the kerosene lantern puts everything in the best light, its dull yellow glow creating a cheerful circle that belies the normal daytime dinginess of the place.

Historically, farmers are reputed to be a reticent lot; and of course they keep reticent, stoical company. Yet winter stable sounds are comfortable and harmonious, a rustic symphony: horses snorting like snare drums, cats stringing out their meowing, calves bawling and trumpeting for breakfast, cattle stanchions rattling like tambourines. And there is a just-discernible rhythmic background: the steady crunch, crunch of alfalfa hay being methodically ground up into cuds for the cows' late-morning snack. Like many farm boys I found a deep and elemental satisfaction in all this even before I was a regular milker.

There were various steps toward becoming a regular on the chores staff. The first was learning to feed the calves, which many a farm boy started at a very early age, perhaps five or six. A bit later he starts to gather eggs and throw down hay from the mow, and eventually—it is the big and masculine step—he learns to milk. At first, milking is much harder than it appears and exceedingly tiring; but soon forearm muscles develop in response to the exercise and it becomes as easy as it looks. Since a twelve-year-old boy is usually too slight to handle manure or to take on some of the other, more strenuous and onerous tasks, it is not hard to get the idea early on that farming is mostly fun. I expected to become a farmer from the first time I was allowed to follow a furrow or feed a calf.

Calf feeding was primarily a wintertime enterprise on our farm, and to explain why that was so I must relate the standing theory about livestock breeding. The gist was that cows should be bred so as to calve in November; that helped to sustain milk production throughout the dark winter, and then, as they started to slack off production in May, turning them into the fresh spring pasture brought on a new burst of production. Thereafter, as the pasture grasses slacked off growth in the dry months of August and September, the cow too was drying off in preparation for the new calf in November. Nothing much wrong with that theory. Attuned as it was to nature's order, it has probably been practiced for thousands of years. But it is disappearing from today's dairy farm, where cows are often not pastured but confined and formula-fed the same diet the year round. If today's farmer tries to concentrate the freshening times of his herd, he is likely to aim at springtime, aware that milk prices, which reflect increased human consumption of ice cream, may be higher in the summer. The guiding idea now is not the rhythm of nature but the estimate of the market.

However, what our system meant to me was that we usually had calves to feed during the winter. At the age when a boy is too young to help with the chores but old enough to "help," I pursued calf feeding with a special ardor. The morning routine: Dad got up and lighted the kerosene lamp, lighted the stove, wakened me, and went to the barn. I rose in the dark, felt my way down the cold stairs, took my roll of clothes from the stairway where it was kept, and dressed by the kitchen stove, which was just beginning to throw a little heat into the uninsulated and drafty house. I followed Dad's tracks through the snowdrifts to the barn, leaping from hole to hole, and made my way to the stable, which seemed warmer than the house I had just left, and probably was. Near the outer reaches of pale lantern light I would see my father parked between two contented cows. "Did you feed the calves yet?" was invariably my greeting; and "Did you feed the calves yet?" was invariably his mocking reply. I knew then that he hadn't.

Half a dozen winters swirl and merge here into a composite recollection, and of course in their time my brothers participated in very similar ceremonies. Dad poured a few quarts of warm, fresh milk into the pail and I headed for the calf pen, where the first overeager calf always began by plunging its nose straight to the bottom, then surfacing with a snort. The calf gulped the milk and, following an instinct to butt the udder to stimulate milk flow, butted the bucket with great gusto, while I cranked up all my courage and held on for dear life. Keeping control of that bucket, not dropping it or spilling the milk, until the calf had worked its way down to the bottom corners, and then getting the bucket away from the calf—for a youngster of about six that was a big step toward becoming a farmer.

But drinking from a pail is not instinctive to a newborn calf; it's learned behavior, and teaching the technique is a fearful pleasure for a young boy. It's done like this: First, following my father's example, I dip my hand into the warm milk and then quickly force a pair of fingers into the calf's mouth between its toothless gums. I'm about eight years old now, and this nearly drains all my courage right at the outset. But I repeat the finger treatment until the calf catches the taste of milk and responds with instinctive sucking. First success! With fingers still in place, I now exert a mighty effort to pull and push its mouth down into the milk, recruiting all my strength and probably some of my father's. Not yet a day old, the calf is already much stronger than I am, and it snorts and blows and balks and slurps and generally misbehaves while it also begins to experiment with its orifices—mouth, eyes, ears, nose—to find the one best suited for ingesting milk. "Hang on!" calls my father, and I hang on as if the farm depends on it. Eventually the combination of fingers, sucking, and milk comes together for the calf, and after a few stormy and successful sessions I can withdraw my fingers slowly and the calf sips milk without the teat surrogate between its gums. A stirring moment for boy and calf! Another husky little critter is on its way. Usually it meant that the calf was on its way to an early career as veal cutlets, for at about eight weeks most of our calves went to the weekly stock market. Each year we kept and raised one or two heifers as herd replacements.

Our cows had slipped out of the pasture on the far side and sneaked around into the cornfield. When we rounded them up, the Calvinist cow—the one with the guilty conscience—tried for a short-cut back to the pasture by leaping the fence. She should have remembered that the fence was barbed wire, a reminder that came when she caught a sharp wire barb on her left hind teat and ripped it wide open, a gash three inches long and half an inch deep. How do you milk a cow in that condition? And how do you avoid mastitis if you don't milk that injured quarter? Keeping the animals to-gether and healthy was a constant challenge for every farmer. We didn't call the veterinarian often, but we used a lot of stuff called Man and Beast Salve.

Sometimes the challenge was truly formidable. After calving, one of our cows developed an alarming condition known officially as a prolapsed uterus—though the farmers' phrase for it was that she had "cast her withers." Such an extravagantly gory scene! Here was a young cow lying in her stall, chewing her cud, and behind her in the gutter lay about a bushel of her intestines, all attached. She had spent the night quietly expelling them, as if they were an-other calf, turning herself inside out. This situation required more than salve. We got the veterinarian, and he and my father together started to ease the whole slimy pile, by the handful and armful, back into place through the torn opening. ("Like putting spaghetti through a funnel," said Dad.) The cow's contribution was to work valiantly against their efforts by tightening her sphincters to expel the package as fast as they fed it in. They finally prevailed—the veterinarian had faced this situation before—and then sewed her up with thick black rawhide cord.

Alas, the cow had other ideas: the next morning she was inside out again, once more the whole bag of guts in the gutter. Again the veterinarian came and helped slide it all laboriously back into place and apply more stitches, more salve to the sutures. For the next two days we put a round-the-clock watch on her, tapping her gently with a stick whenever she started straining. That worked. Afterward, she seemed to become a normal cow, but it turned out that her condition was far beyond salving. She could not conceive again, and thus had no future as a milk cow. We had to assign her a new career as canned beef.

I felt a certain ambivalence about the whole business, as I think Nelvin did. He and I had had a few earlier encounters with that cow, and though they were unconnected to her subsequent prob-lems, they helped to etch her story into our minds. As a young heifer she had spent a summer, maybe two, tethered in the yard as the designated lawn mower. Two young juvenile delinquents looking for excitement as matadors, Nelvin and I figured out that we could safely pester the heifer without real danger to ourselves. Here was a new and exciting sport, so we experimented with various provocations, sticks and stones being preferred. When she went for us, we knew exactly how far she could get before the tether brought her up short. So when we wanted a thrill, one of us put out a sharp eye for parents and the other proceeded to the pleasant task of teasing the young heifer. Either we got good at this game or she did, for it became pretty easy to stir up her wrath. She would see us coming and lower her head and paw the sod at the end of her chain. How exciting! And how ironic a format for developing the virtues of courage! We did this in precisely the same mood—careless malice—in which we would stir up a bumblebees' nest: prod the nest with a stick until we could hear the bees sizzle and come boiling out to attack, then take off at high speed. Every time we got away with it without a sting, we were the more inclined to do it again. Danger has its seductions, as the cult of bullfighting plainly shows.

However, once our sport with the heifer was discovered by our parents, it was all over in a hurry. So we forgot about it.

We did. Not the heifer. Unbeknownst to us she nursed a healthy grudge, as well she might: she had sustained a wound that time did not salve. Several years later when the heifer was among the cows, Nelvin happened to be in the barnyard one evening as the cattle came home from pasture. Suddenly the young cow saw the young matador and saw also the long-awaited opportunity to settle an old score. She cornered Nelvin between the stable wall and the barnyard gate and then she lowered her horny head and made straight for him. In a panic, he began to scramble up the gate just as she closed in on him. The gate was made of poles and fortunately it was flexible. The exact sequence, too swift for any intervention, was a little unclear, but Dad's oft-repeated summary is probably accurate enough: "He started to climb the gate and she helped him through it." Nelvin was conveyed through or over the gate and tumbled to the safe side with only minor bruises on his body, but both of us sustained major lacerations on our consciences. Your sins will find you out, said the message. And we were duly awed.

Still, it was all a bit baffling. That was precisely the young cow who the very next year developed the ghastly problem with her reproductive system. Was there any lesson in *that?* Was it just that we were not supposed to forget any of this? Is it purged now that I have told?

Farm animals come to be viewed comparatively and often in moral perspective: cows are bland and mysterious, horses stoical, calves fun, chickens willful, dogs warm, cats aloof, sheep dim-witted and lovable. Pigs are often disgusting. In fact, pigs are greedy, dirty, smelly when closely penned, noisy at mealtime, and sometimes savage beasts. A calf will eventually drink, munch hay, and chew cud with something like serenity, making no comment at all on the passing show. A pig habitually grunts and snorts in menacing guttural tones, does a lot of pointless squealing before being fed, and invariably says its grace before meals by sticking its filthy paws into the soup. In fact, a pig that doesn't stand in its own trough while eating lacks the enterprise normal to the species, for that is the best way to fend off the gluttonous sibling competition. It is true that a fat sow in spacious summer quarters mothering a sadistic gang of piglets presents a scene of undoubted rustic charm; but a typical pig in its typical narrow quarters can be a thoroughly unpleasant slob.

I will admit that these are retrospective judgments; at the time I didn't blame our swine for being such pigs. I suppose that a pig has a perfect right to wallow in its basic values: gluttony, ill manners, hostility, and mud. And a pig is certainly the best contrivance yet designed for manufacturing tasty bacon from wormy apples, swill, weeds, and garbage. One year in the late thirties my father could find no market for the potatoes he had stored all winter in the basement. He cooked up hundreds of pounds of them in the copper wash boiler and then successfully processed mashed potatoes into ham, sausage, and pork chops. You can't pull off salvage operations like that without pigs on the premises.

There was the year we threw dozens of bushels of surplus apples into the pigpen. Fastidious as always, the pigs first trampled the apples into the grit and the grime and then happily slurped up the apple sauce and squealed for more. The next year we thought to save ourselves some work: before the apples ripened we put the pigs into the orchard to keep the grass down and to harvest the green apples as they fell. As intended, the pigs ate the green apples and, as unintended, they turned next to the bark of the trees, tearing it off in long, chewy strips. It is an exquisitely droll sight to behold a fat sow parked with her rump in the wallow while she chomps contentedly on a two-foot-long plug of fresh bark from a Duchess apple tree. My father was not amused. He sought to wean them from this vile habit by putting black axle grease on the tree trunks. No problem: the pigs just ate the axle grease. Not for nothing did *pigheadedness* get into the rural American lexicon as a term for a peculiarly virulent strain of stubbornness. Eventually we won this orchard battle: first we turned the pigs out of the orchard lest they eat it to the ground, then we clinched the argument by eating them. Fabulous bacon!

People have affirmed that if we eat the flesh of animals we should sometimes participate in killing and dressing them, and the implication is that this would give moral validity to our eating habits or perhaps even change them. Much ink is shed in semiphilosophical circles on such questions, regarding the moral and aesthetic implications of lifestyles. (Might it also be argued that if we enjoy beefsteak we should be willing to fork manure for a spell?) There was a strong strain of puritanism in our Reformed religion, but the idea that to secure the right to enjoy something pleasant we ought to do something decidedly unpleasant directly connected with it was not part of either butchering or religion, as I remember them. And it didn't occur to the farmers that to be willing to kill what they were willing to eat was a moral achievement. For them it probably wasn't. It was merely necessary, a thing they saw with a clear, cold eye.

Whatever the moral requirements for enjoying bacon, I do not recommend that anyone participate in the kind of hog butchering that fascinated and repelled me when I was young. Uncle Henry or Ben Baas always came to assist my father with the job, and were paid for their help with fresh meat. Requirements for butchering: skill, strength, a certain callousness, cool weather, enormous quantities of boiling water. Also, at least one hog. Sometimes the water was heated in a barrel over an open outdoor fire, augmented with still more water heated inside in the copper wash boiler. The entire carcass had to be dunked repeatedly into a barrel two-thirds full of scalding water. This loosened the bristles so they could be scraped off (like scaling a fish), and it washed the carcass at the same time. It was a two-man job.

For youngsters, slaying the beast was the focus of the drama. First the animal was cornered and hog-tied, rope around the ankles. Usually it was a lazy and fat old sow, serene and ornery by turns, lugging a hundred pounds of lard, her flabby flanks rippling with bacon as she walked. She would then be driven to the place of execution, snorting defiance and squealing all the way, for hogs are suspicious critters and one in a butcher's custody has something to squeal about. But we hadn't heard anything yet. The butchers would deftly flip the hog onto her back and hold her there, at which she would emit piercing, nearly deafening squeals, high-pitched and full of terror and fury. Sharp hooves claw the air in desperation. I do not recall that my father ever handled the knife at that point. It would have been his way to defer to someone else, generously assuming that they had more skill at it; it may also be that he just wished not to do it. Doubtless he would have preferred a soundless, eyes-averted method, like putting the sow in a sack with a rock and dropping her into the water hole, as he did with surplus kittens.

In a typical case my father would hold the front feet, balancing the fighting, squealing animal on her back, and the assistant would thrust a very sharp knife deep into the hog's throat, swiftly making an eight-inch incision. It was important that this be done quickly, correctly, and completely. The hog was immediately released and would struggle drunkenly to her feet, blood pouring in a wide, thick stream from a mortal wound. Presently the squeal would die away into a raucous gurgle, and the stream of blood would soon thin to rhythmic spurts, driven by a failing heartbeat. Then the hog's legs would stiffen; she would try to take a step, stagger, and collapse into a red sea of her own blood.

Pop-eyed and stop-eared, we children would watch this blood sport from a safe distance, perched high on the granary steps. It was raw theater, such as we could not turn away from. Calamity is riveting, whether for children or adults, and blood in such quantities is shocking—for us an unusually compelling demonstration that animal death is part of farm life.

As for the hogs, experiments by our neighbors in later years showed that the ceremonies might have been simplified, if simplification was wanted (which I doubt), by putting a .22-caliber bullet into the hog's brain as a first step. My father had reservations about that method.

"Awfully small target," he said.

Most farm animals were of mixed strains—horses, cats, and pigs being of no known breed at all. Our cows were mainly Holstein, but there was enough Guernsey and Jersey in their veins to make calving time more interesting than if they had been of pure lines. Not only was there little purebred stock in the community; there was very little serious attention to genetics at all. How easy for a farmer to lapse into the thought, A bull is a bull; whether it came from a long line of scrub cattle is of secondary importance, and nothing can be done about it in any case. Thus generations of poor stock were perpetuated, and our animals were inevitably part of that.

On our farm there was one exception to the rule, and it early caught the attention of the aspiring farmer within me. Each year we ordered day-old Leghorn chicks from a southern Michigan hatchery, which mailed them to us in boxes, a hundred fluffy yellow peeping chicks to the box. The chicks' cost was calibrated to their alleged pedigree: those whose ancestors had laid an average of 325 eggs a year cost more than those from a 312-egg-per-year strain, and so on. My father paid careful attention to those figures, never purchasing from either the best or the poorest lines. That means, at least, that he passed up the cheapest option, believing that, from the point of view of the science of farming, the cheapest was not the best buy: the chicks might look the same, but they wouldn't be the same. Now *there*, I believed, was a satisfying line of thought! Perhaps if more options about seed lines and bloodlines had been that clear-cut, my father might have approximated the progressive farmer I so ardently wished he would be. But if not he, then I. So I brooded, so I vowed.

I could work off my frustration with my father's generally casual approach to modern farming by trying to carry out my ideas in my own hobby enterprises. After raising scrub rabbits for a year, my reading led me to believe that I needed some purebred Flemish Giant rabbits. Eventually, I located and bought three of them for breeding stock. And indeed they were bigger and healthier than the scrubs. On the other hand, they were uniformly light brown and not nearly so attractive as the colorful scrubs, and they had less in the way of rabbit personality, too. But yes, they were definitely superior rabbits—if you are raising rabbits for meat. But there's the rub. My somber experience had been that raising rabbits for meat somehow missed the point. Later, turned temporary goose herd, I saved my money for a pair of Toulouse geese, which I concluded were best adapted to our conditions, and I had a pair sent to me by express mail from Iowa. I presume it was a good line, and they thrived for years, but nobody else had any geese for comparison. In the same vein, I devoured a lot of advertising about honeybee strains before I selected mine from Georgia. Perhaps I thought that the farther I went for stock the better it would be.

Although none of my youthful bloodline adventures amounted to very much, they certified to me that a modern approach to farming that followed and went beyond my father's strategies with Leghorn chickens was possible and desirable. Later, I got a chance to experiment successfully along the same line of thought with seed potatoes.

Was I perhaps really thinking of agribusiness? Unwittingly, we dream subversive dreams.

13

War News

Children of the radio era had a special pathway into the fertile and secret places of the imagination. That era began abruptly for us—I was in the second grade—when we came home from school one day to find two men scrambling about on the roof of our house. My father said there was a storm coming, so they were wiring the two chimneys together. *Wiring chimneys together?*

Having enjoyed his little joke, Dad pointed out the thin wire that ran between the chimneys and down over the edge of the roof, dropped along the wall, took a sudden turn, and sneaked into the house under the window sash. Inside, we saw that it was attached to an ornate box two feet long and a foot high—a brand-new Philco radio from the McBain Hardware Store.

Within the radio was a very heavy battery that was the focus of an energy-conservation lesson learned so well that very day that I can still report that batteries for the radio cost $6.60 in those 1940 dollars. Electricity was still far in the future and the battery radio was undoubtedly a luxury. It worked like magic: the aerial between the chimneys was mystically connected to Detroit and East Lansing and Chicago, and very soon we all became radio addicts. Good-bye Victrola! Hello Amos and Andy!

With one eye on the cost of batteries and another on the discipline of children, my parents laid out rules: there would be family programs and there would also be an individual program for each of us. Thus we all gathered round on Thursday night for "The Aldrich Family," our favorite, and on other nights for others, such as "Quiz Kids," "Dr. I.Q.," "Truth or Consequences," and what I think may have been Dad's favorites, "Lum 'n' Abner" and "Amos and Andy." "Fibber McGee and Molly" might have been on this list, but it fell on Sunday night and was deemed too frivolous a closing for a day largely devoted to churchgoing, Corn Flakes for breakfast, Sunday School, and the reading of somewhat selective literature. Among the news reporters and commentators, Gabriel Heatter was easily the most memorable, although we children didn't so much listen to the news as overhear it, which was perhaps not a bad way to learn.

As for our individual choices, siblings might listen in on another's program, and usually did, but that was understood to be through the good offices of the one whose program it was. The program's proprietor got to turn on the radio, determine the volume, and assign the seats. Gladys carried the sharing further than any of us and basically turned her Saturday morning "Children's Bible Hour" into a family program. We three boys had our favorite daily serials. For a long time "Captain Midnight and the Secret Squadron" was my territory, "Tom Mix" was Marvin's find, and Nelvin's was "Jack Armstrong, All-American Boy." Sometimes all three of us joined in on Saturday night's "Gangbusters."

Thus we took part in the world's derring-do. The heroes of those overblown landscapes stirred our idealism and, in my case at least, considerably influenced reading habits and flights of fancy. Leaning close to the Philco, volume turned low to spare the battery, we took what we heard and constructed what we saw in the television of our minds. Offered breathless voices, banging doors, and revving airplane engines, we could fill the skies with epic dramas. From a plot sketch and echoing hoofbeats entire cavalcades emerged to march across the vistas of the mind's eye, vanquish the alien foe, and fade into the golden sunset. Perhaps radio youth developed an intuitive sense of how much guts and gore to include in the most strenuous battle scenes, an internal violence-monitor, and we had acquired early practice by hearing Old Testament stories read to us. Thus our imagination was stimulated and fed by radio but not bombarded with an excess of violent images.

Not long after Marvin introduced me to Tom Mix, I also caught wind of the Lone Ranger and Tonto. With that, the door was open to the entire home-on-the-range gang and to what I mistook for the western literary tribes: Red Ryder on the newspaper funnies page, Zane Grey in the school library, and the X-Bar-X Ranch boys on the shelves of western juvenilia. I could smell saddle leather and purple sage through the covers of any western dime novel. One feeds on what is available, including junk food, and my reading diet put an idea into my head. Before settling into farming, I would go immediately from high school to Texas or Wyoming and become a cowboy, spreading honor and justice in a broad swath. Reading fiction can do that to your mind, as Don Quixote learned. Anyway, my own western loyalty seemed confirmed when, for a Corn Kix box top and fifteen cents, earned by pumping water for the cattle, the Lone Ranger himself sent me an adjustable gold-plated ring with a secret compartment underneath its U.S. Air Force insignia. Patriotism permeated everything in those days: even the Lone Ranger was part of the consensus on the war effort—though it is hard now to think of him as a proper part of the military-industrial complex.

One evening Marvin and I learned on the regular broadcast that the Lone Ranger's great white horse, Silver, had sired a son, a beautiful jet black colt with a perfect white star right in the center of his forehead. That is what they said, and they were in a position to know. If I suspected that they were fooling us, their game plan put my doubts on hold: the faithful were invited to suggest a name for the colt, with a cool one thousand dollars going to the first person to send in the name eventually chosen. No fooling there.

I talked to Marvin and he agreed that we should pool our wits and come up with the best of all possible colt names. We would split the money fifty-fifty, which I thought was pretty generous of him. I promptly suggested Star as the name, and Marvin promptly scowled. "Nah—everybody will send that in." How would they think of that? I wondered. We considered our own farm horses of the day, Tom and Barney by name, but concluded that the Lone Ranger wouldn't appreciate those names—perhaps their sound lacked the requisite hint of somthing wild or western. Wrangler sounded about right to me, tough and masculine, vague and poetic, but that was what they called one of the sidekicks of Tom Mix, so that way was closed too. Silver was a terrific name; so what about Gold for the colt? ("Come on Silver! Come on, Gold!") I sensed that Marvin was losing enthusiasm for the whole project; indeed, it was his role to observe that Gold was no name for a black colt. At last we came up with a doozy of a name, Diamond Star, which sounded so stunning to me, so richly evocative, that I easily overlooked the fact that it was, well, in a word, stupid; in two words, very stupid. So we sent that name in, whereupon they immediately named the colt Victor, and that was that. We should have tried Wrangler after all. Or Shooting Star.

Undoubtedly the radio brought into our home an imaginary world. It also brought home to us a very real world, which was just as fantastic.

The background shadow of our days, something vague and menacing called Hard Times or Depression, yielded its place when I was nine years old to something more vast and vague and menacing. It was called the war, to be combated with something called the War Effort. When the Japanese attacked Pearl Harbor, in December of 1941, my teacher Mrs. De Hart took time out the next morning, Monday the eighth, to discuss world affairs with her third- and fourth-grade classes. It seemed an occasion most solemn and illuminating, although I do not remember much that she said. Something big and terrible had happened, something confusing for a child, and it was hard to grasp the mystery of what was going on. The teacher's classroom discussion seemed to clear the air, filling us all with an immediate surge of hopeful gloom. The whole country was at war, we had been attacked, though just now the battles were far away and we were completely safe. But we would all have to help. Then she taught us the words of Irving Berlin's "God Bless America": "When the storm clouds gather / Far across the sea, / Let us all be grateful / For a land that's free. / Let us all be grateful / For a land so fair, / As we raise our voices / In a solemn prayer: / God Bless America . . ."

The words were etched into our tender years and traced themselves around a thousand pictures. In the land of the free we lived well beyond paved roads, beyond the end of the power line, but not beyond the reach of distant battles, for friends, cousins, and neighbors were in uniform far across the sea. High patriotism set the tone for an endless stream of images and actions that entered the fabric of our country life and drew its patterns in relief: rationing, defense stamps, war bonds, scrap drives, "Uncle Sam Needs You," paper drives, Japs and Nazis, home on furlough, price ceilings, Colin Kelly, gathering milkweed pods for life jackets, Edward R. Murrow, "Remember Pearl Harbor," Gabriel Heatter, recycled tires, the service flag in church, zinc-coated pennies, the fate of the Aachen cathedral, victory gardens, General Patton, gold-star mothers, D day, WACS and WAVES, Tokyo Rose, "Praise the Lord and Pass the Ammunition." The war effort affected everything, merged with everything, became everything.

Old iron collects and multiplies in the footprints of farmers, and the war machine snatched it up and beat the plowshares into swords and the pruning hooks into spears.

All the farms in our neighborhood had riches to contribute to the national harvest: first from the dump behind the house, then from the piles beyond the barn and beside the stone pile, where lay many a broken hunk of cast iron and various abandoned implements of rusty steel. They had accumulated and moldered through the years, and now they would be reborn as guns and tanks. Behold the venerable wagon wheel that had leaned against the maple tree since Armistice Day, had leaned there, in fact, so long that the tree had embraced it and seemed bent on digesting it whole—rim, spokes, and hub. Chop it loose now at last, liberate the wheel and drag it to the scrap pile for a nobler destiny. So it was on every country place, for scrap metal is indigenous to farmland; it thrives like the thistle and the green tumbleweed. When the war came it required but a few years for decades of this heavy metal growth to be swept from the farmyards, altering the appearance of the American countryside. A good riddance for a good cause. The war effort ennobled us.

It also made us wary. The countryside lives by hearsay, some of it occasionally reliable. Scrap trucks came to the door unannounced; today they were looking for aluminum donations to go to Detroit for airplane wings. We were willing to give our scrap aluminum to the war effort, but was this *that?* Or a private effort to turn an easy buck on the sentiment of the day? We had been coached: several of us children wandered aimlessly about the premises with the aluminum man, managed not to find anything more than a pot cover, and then bade him farewell. In fact, we had a little cache of flattened aluminum kettles and worn-out separator parts that we had salvaged from our dump for the war effort, but when complete strangers came unannounced to our door we just couldn't find any of it.

After the heavy metals came lighter stuff—small steel, aluminum, rubber, tin, paper. Our school put on scrap drives, and different grades competed with one another. We took packages of newspapers and old rusty pails full of bits of scrap iron to school on the bus, and we threw the iron on the pile west of the school. Week by week the pile mounted higher, and as it rose so did our pride in our country and in our school. We would keep those caissons rolling along, whatever caissons were. (I had no idea.) You could get admitted to a basketball game with fifteen pounds of scrap iron or twenty-five pounds of paper. In 1943 our school set out to collect enough scrap to pay for a jeep, which is how I found out what a jeep was. (I had no idea.) They said it was a war machine so tough and nimble that it could climb right up that row of steps in front of the school. Holy mackerel! Back we went for more scrap, more jeeps to fight more Japs.

Defined at the time and held in memory by sharp sentiments and clean emotions, it was, we now say, an old-fashioned war, without troubling ambiguity. President Roosevelt himself had four sons on the front lines, said our radio, and the battles of the Old West, the Old Testament, and the World War sometimes seemed to blend into one another. The world was young then, and the struggle, like every proper struggle in far-off times, seemed chaste and moral, right against wrong.

We whose early years were punctuated with scrap drives have sustained a mark on our souls, leaving us forever unreconciled to the wholesale discard of reusable materials that became the hallmark of the modern economy. We pricked up our ears when recycling edged timidly into the public consciousness in the early seventies. Recycling was a *new idea?* Only the word was new, of course. It had long been a way of life, merely common sense; repressed by avarice and gone dormant for a quarter century, it is now reborn as a virtue. But for rural Americans, the war had enforced what stewardship or poverty had already loudly asserted: everything usable is to be used, what is broken is to be fixed, even a bent nail is not to be discarded.

Rationing, which is but the other side of the recycling coin, was the preeminent fact of life, and we came to assume that much of what we wanted was scarce or unavailable. Gas for the car could be had only in small quantities, tires and tubes not at all. Near the war's end, Dad laced up a long tear in a tire's sidewall with baling wire and buckskin to keep the tube from oozing out. It was a neat job but it didn't last, so he inserted a lumpy slab of rubber from a discarded tire. That worked better, but you could feel the thump of that lump in the tire like a bump in the road. Yet it was as easy for rural people as for anyone to accept restrictions, for the countryside was still feeling the Depression, was used to austerity. And some of the rationed food items—meat, eggs, butter, and the like— affected farm families like ours not at all since we produced those things. Late in the war rumors were rife that whereas butter was scarce among all the Allied nations, the Russians were using it for axle grease. I couldn't figure out whether the Russians were being credited with evil or ingenuity.

The memorable challenge for us was sugar rationing, since our lifestyle, generally austere as it was, was also heavily accented with sweets. Put bluntly, we found our sugar allotment restrictive because we all had corrupt palates. Sugar rationing was probably good for our health, but it did nothing to improve our tastes, for after the war we all went back to our sins with gusto. A heaping teaspoonful of sugar went into every cup of Dad's coffee, a standard we all earnestly aspired to for our own beverages—cocoa, Postum, and Kool-Aid. No mother in our community could ever make enough cookies, cakes, pies, puddings, and candy to satisfy her family, and we were no exception. The bribe and reward system in our household was usually structured around sweets: there was sugar in the bottom of the tablespoonful of cod-liver oil; when we were very young we got a lump of brown sugar if we submitted to a haircut without tears. When sugar was too scarce during wartime for all the cloying concoctions we loved, there was corn syrup and sometimes honey. Since we felt deprived if a month slipped by without cake, we eventually worked out a successful system for having our Sunday cake and eating our sugar, too.

It worked like this. As a family of seven we were allowed three and a half pounds of sugar a week. A pound or so of it was reserved for general cooking and baking purposes, and on Saturday night the remainder was carefully apportioned into seven identical open glass jars, each with one of our names on it, which were placed together on a tray. At every meal the tray of sugar jars was parked in the center of the table. Everyone had his or her own jar. It was always available; we used what we thought we needed. Rules were few: if we wanted to eat our week's allotment on Monday morning's cereal, we had that chance. The goal of the enterprise was to preserve freedom of choice for everyone while sequestering as much sugar as possible. There were a good many things on our table besides cereals that we sought to improve with sugar: rice, buttermilk pop, cold pork fat on bread, sage tea, tomato soup, spaghetti, whipped cream, bread soup, plain macaroni, Postum, Kool-Aid.

Only our frail achievements in self-restraint stood between us and our addiction. While the prospect of cake on Sunday was a strong inducement to juvenile self-denial, there was another force at work as well, for that tray of seven named sugar jars spoke volumes in praise and reproach. By midweek the sugar levels in the jars were no longer equal, and we could read whatever we wished out of the evidence. Who seemed to be saving the most? (Certainly not Dad, who merely tolerated the whole scheme, usually borrowing some from Carl, who, as a mere toddler, was not yet a heavy consumer.) On Saturday the remaining sugar from the seven jars was poured together, sometimes ceremonially so that the heavier savers among the sibling rivals were suitably recognized, and Mother calculated whether there was enough for a cake for Sunday or perhaps for a small batch of cookies. It has to be said that the frosting on those cakes was very, very thin: you could see the cake through it.

Always there were drives to sell war bonds and stamps. We bought war stamps for ten or twenty-five cents apiece and pasted them into the book; and when the book was full we had invested $18.75 in the war effort, had loaned that much to our country. For a child it was a savings discipline of years' duration. She exchanged the full book at the bank or post office for a twenty-five-dollar Series E War Bond, made out in her own name and redeemable in ten years. She overheard her parents tell the neighbors of her achievement, and she swelled with a patriot's pride. Before war's end I had two of them.

When you are eleven years old, two war bonds are a patriot's achievement and a large savings account. It scarcely matters that the ten years to maturity are nearly a lifetime away, for you are prepared for the future. But when you are twenty-one and a decade of inflation has taken its toll, the bonds so ardently eked out half a lifetime ago seem to trickle away like rivers in the sand. By the time I redeemed mine, all the ardor had gone out of the project and a good bit of the purchasing power had gone out of the bonds. Economically, cashing a war bond in the early fifties was a vapid exchange for someone facing the expenses of college. Two days at my summer job and I could earn the equivalent of one of those bonds. Had all my early zeal come to this? A few dollars for a few books?

If there is merit in having children earn and save money, it has more to do with character and causes than with economics. I suppose I understood that at the time but forgot it as the war passed into history and the investment, not the experience or the memory, was the tangible symbol left. The essential deposit may not have been monetary: we had invested a part of ourselves in the war effort, in something noble that utterly transcended our modest lives. And the memory is the dividend.

D day, 1944: one of the days, like October 14, 1066, around which history pivots. We had had plans for June 6, but they did not concern the war; we had planned a large gathering of relatives at Uncle Pete's, a family reunion. Dad usually turned on the radio in the morning for a weather report, but this morning the weather in France was vastly more important than ours, and every station was exulting that D day had finally dawned. Family plans were put on hold and the contingency plan was put into operation: all across America that night churches would be filled with people praying for the success of the Allied invasion of Europe, and we would be among them.

Small things can get stuck in an eleven-year-old's mind. After breakfast I laced up my high-tops and Dad and I went out to work on a little stretch of unbroken land south of the woods. He carried his double-bitted axe, I a hatchet, and we talked about "the invasion" as we went; but by the time we got to the woods we were talking about the land we were clearing. Today we would pick up the brush and burn it, tomorrow he would plow the land, and the next day we would plant potatoes there—for that particular patch of earth, the first field crop since the foundation of the world. Near a brush pile on the western edge of the plot I spotted an unusual shrub—odd that we had not seen it before today. Chest high and prickly, it bore at its very top one exquisite bloom, which proved to be a wild rose. Somehow that beautiful flower seemed to remind me of something, but I could not grasp exactly what it was. Nothing of the sort had ever been seen around here before, Dad said. Today was D day. I picked the red rose at noon, Dad helping me with his jackknife, and carried it home. Mother was cooking dinner and listening to the war news on the radio. I presented the rose. She dried her hands on her apron to accept it, then she smelled it and smiled and thanked me. She loved the rose.

The wild rose and D day became forever linked in my mind. Such an implausible combination, such an unbreakable connection: the momentous and the incidental. The fate of nations was in the balance, and I had plucked a tender wildflower from a virgin field. And the two became as one. Whatever it was that the D day rose aroused in me remains as obscure as ever, although I still can hardly think of one without the other. Perhaps there *is* some hidden significance in the bond, and I have often hoped that I could find it or be successful in inventing it. It may come to me one of these years.

With the war's end the dawning of a new day in agriculture was proclaimed, and the air that farm boys breathed was made heavy with dewy optimism—all of it leading to uninspiring conversations at our home.

"Dad, maybe we could get a jeep."

"Why not a tank, while we're at it?"

"No, really, I mean it! It says here that thousands of war surplus jeeps will be sold cheap to farmers to use as tractors. There's a place you can write to. We should do it."

"Well, not just yet."

"Why not?"

"I guess jeeps don't run on hay, do they."

"It says gas rationing will be over next year."

"Then they're going to *give* gas away?"

"Come on, Dad! We need a jeep. Be cheaper than a tractor."

"We'll wait and see."

Farm magazines that came to our house fed the visions of modernity: heaps of new products would soon be available now that we had won the war. Farming would be fun again. Atomic power would make electricity cheap enough for everyone, even us. DDT, which had saved thousands of soldiers' lives from the ravages of typhus and malaria, would now save the farms of Americans from pests and diseases. Who wouldn't want to be a farmer now that real farming was about to begin? I soaked up the heady atmospherics and fell to dark brooding. Even a cheap jeep seemed out of our reach, and a new tractor or car was totally unrealistic. Here we were on the threshold of the modern wonder world toward which all history had been yearning, and our family still rode around in a very tired 1932 Chevrolet with well over a hundred thousand country miles on it. In the gush of postwar boosterism I dreamed of presenting the family with a brand-new 1946 Buick.

It would work like this, according to a full-page advertisement in the *Farm Journal*. I had to supply the best entry in the contest to state, "in twenty-five words or less," why Robin Hood flour was superior to all others. Although this brand of flour was unheard of in McBain (I checked), and although I had never baked anything more elegant than a mud pie (I admit), I was not to be easily deterred. I simply composed my short and vivid testimony about "delicious cakes and pastries" (as I cleverly put it), mailed it in quietly, and awaited results.

If there was a dash of earnest insincerity in my twenty-five-word

Robin Hood sermon, there was none in my ambition for the car. In the pictures, that 1946 Buick, grotesque and gorgeous in uncertain proportions, made all prewar cars look like toys. It was a doozy. True, it had no white star, and it was called DeLux and not Victor, and it had a most implausible grille, like a bright chromium face with a very serious overbite. I studied Buick advertisements wherever I found them. How reassuring the refrain "When better cars are built, Buick will build them." And it is still reassuring to think that there was a time when advertising had even that vague hint of modesty. The claim turned out to be not only modest but true: the following year Buick put chromium braces on the overbite, corrected it year after year, and by 1949 the car had nearly swallowed its dentures and reduced its grille to a big toothy grin. Maybe the later cars were better, but the memorable one was that '46 model, approved by Robin Hood flour.

Perhaps I suspected that the merry men at the Robin Hood firm might not be very modest, for I considered and rejected as my entry "When better flour is ground, Robin Hood will grind it," and then went back to the clever pastries pitch for my testimonial. In fact, I looked up *pastries* in the dictionary, a fancy word that made your mouth water if you said it often and that I had seen somewhere in the company of cookies and doughnuts. It seemed a more suggestive word than *bread* and *biscuit* and more sensual than *bun*, so I worked it in twice, for I was intent on that Buick.

They gave the Buick to someone else. They also ignored me for the other prizes: washing machines, trips to Florida, refrigerators, radios. Not for years did I tell the family how fervently I had striven to fulfill my postwar dream for us all. So we didn't get a new car after the war; we got a couple of new tires and tubes for the old one, and it rolled along for a few more years. We didn't get a tractor. We didn't get a jeep. And we didn't get a new radio, for we were still beyond the power line. There were lots of things we didn't get. And we didn't get over dreaming, either.

14

Matters of Taste, Matters of Fact

Across the dinner table my son catches my eye before venturing cautiously into irony: "Ah, delicious! Vegetables in the good Dutch tradition, eh Mom?" Flipping me a wink for self-protection, he wants to nail down my sympathy in advance, just in case there is a reaction. We both know the phone rang just as the beans got hot, which is why they are overcooked now, and he has heard so many parental tales about how we were raised on overcooked food that he can already predict my comment. I provide it on cue: "My mother wouldn't have served beans like these—too raw." He laps up the reassurance that in the good old days things were pretty bad.

At least they were different. It was not a fancy cookery that the Dutch peasants brought to Michigan and passed on to their children. It was a meat and potatoes and bread culture, and while the bread was always available and always good (twice a week our house smelled like a bakery), the rest of the basic fare was another story. Meat was boiled till it was soft and then fried until it was crisp. Vegetables were just boiled until they were soft. That's about it.

Consequently, the best home cooking involved dishes just outside the boiled-meat-and-vegetables staples: baked beans, scalloped potatoes, chicken soup, goulash, casseroles, pot roasts— things done slowly in an oven or on the back of a kitchen range, dishes that needed no timing and got better as they simmered. With the ingredients of a casserole a woman might venture to experiment, but seldom with the basic diet of meat and vegetables.

But "the good Dutch tradition" certainly simplified things. We could tell if something was sufficiently cooked by the way we could flatten it with a fork or by the way it just fell apart. What did not meet these basic conditions was simply not yet fit to serve, for food on the plate was never to be tackled with a knife, not even meat. A broiled steak (which we never had) or any fresh cut of meat quickly sautéed in a skillet (which we never had, either) would have been dismissed out of hand as tough and chewy.

The boil-it-fry-it rule for our meats was not quite so perverse as it sounds. Much of our beef and pork had been canned by my mother earlier, and that process, three hours in a boiling bath, had thoroughly cooked the meat and also preserved all the juices. Preparing it for serving then involved simply opening the mason jar and putting chunks of meat and fat into an iron skillet for frying. There is probably no better way to treat canned meat. With fresh chicken the boil-fry sequence made good sense too, for our chickens were all fat old hens, retiring from a life of egg laying, tough perhaps to begin with but tasty and almost tender after being subjected to this process. Something similar goes for wild rabbit, of which we consumed a great deal. When I add to this list such noble exceptions as salt pork, bacon, ham, dried beef, and slow-cooked pot roasts, I realize that our meat cookery, parochial as it was, was not all that bad. Besides, we always had splendid gravy.

It was in the vegetable department that the real culinary crimes were committed and went unnoticed and unpunished for generations. Potatoes, even new potatoes, were supposed to be mealy: soft, flaky, dry. Eating potato skins, even of new potatoes, was unheard of. We would as soon have eaten apple cores or banana peels. We never baked potatoes; we only boiled them and fried them. Salad consisted exclusively of chopped lettuce doused in vinegar and sugar. A true garden salad of mixed fresh crisp vegetables with a plausible dressing was never served on our farm as long as I lived there, and I doubt that grocery stores even carried a genuine salad dressing. It is likely that a true salad would have been spurned as "raw." In the same lofty spirit we children usually met asparagus, peas, and broccoli with cold defiance, partly because they had been cooked to a dull gray and partly because we were just perverse. In sadness I remember the fate of fresh garden beans, typically treated as if the aim, which was often achieved, was to rid them of their offensive natural color, vitamins, and appearance. A favorite trick was to chop the beans to bits before overcooking, the better, perhaps, to expel the taste and texture.

The casual abuse of green beans was partially redeemed by the splendid things my mother did with ripe beans. She would dispatch one of the children to the barn with a small pail, to the area known as the "threshing floor"—the earth floor of the hay barn, deeply covered with the accumulated chaff of half a century. Countless times over the years newly harvested beans had been stored in the barn, where they were subsequently threshed. The process had spilled some beans to the floor, where they mingled with the chaff and awaited the day when they might be salvaged. To do that we simply pawed aside the surface chaff and started picking up the beans, one by one. It was not tedious; it was fun. There were several kinds of beans lurking in the chaff; red kidney, which I didn't especially like since they were large and meaty; yellow eye, a white bean with a bright yellowish eye surrounding a black pupil; and the smaller white pea bean. In half an hour we could scrounge a quart of beans. It was easy to blow out the chaff, and it was fun to bring the booty in. Mother washed the beans and set them to soak overnight, and the next morning they were puffy and wrinkled, breaking out at the seams. She treated them to brown sugar and molasses and slices of pork and smoked bacon and chunks of onion and perhaps mustard and other seasoning, and then they spent the full day asimmer in the back of the oven, radiating a sweet aroma throughout the entire house. Now that's beans!

So, it was a mixed bag. And there were reasons why most food was overcooked. One was that it had always been done that way, and housewives had little time to make fussy changes in longstanding habits. Besides, so much of our food was canned, and therefore by definition heavily cooked, that the standard for taste and texture tended to be set by canned food. And there was the banal fact that most adults had dentures, often ill-fitting to boot, and they simply relied on their cooking to do what their molars couldn't. Moral: False teeth in one generation may lead to false palates in the next.

And there were notable exceptions. Nobody ruined sweet corn by overcooking it, and there is not much temptation to overcook apple sauce, either. About those delicacies we knew and practiced almost everything there is to know, and indeed, apple sauce, which we consumed in enormous quantities, we treated not as a fruit but as a vegetable. Good thing, too; for it covered a multitude of dietary sins. In general, we were not encouraged to develop independent tastes. "Just eat what's set before you" was the prevailing maxim. Sometimes that was easy, for kitchen talent among Dutch housewives ran heavily toward desserts. They all managed kitchens that never had to purchase and never could exhaust the rich supplies of cream and butter and eggs, and they whipped these things up with lots of sugar and poured them lavishly into and over cakes and pastries, and they vastly enjoyed eating what they made. A matter of taste. Who could be so graceless as to spoil the simple pleasures of life by thinking of slimness as an ideal?

Even so, when I reflect on the exhausting schedule of the typical farm housewife of that period, it seems remarkable that most of them managed to become plump and stay there, when they might have been worn to a frazzle.

Monday was wash day.

Now and then a family was rumored to wash clothes regularly on a Tuesday or Wednesday, but such tales were hard to credit. Why would anyone step so far out of line? Still, one summer a family moved to a farm just half a mile to the south of us, and they proceeded to do their washing on Saturday afternoon! Neighbors simply shook their heads: such perversions of the natural order could not endure. Within a year the new folks had conformed, but within another year they had moved away again. Many had spotted them as unstable types right from the beginning. The normal woman's workweek began very early on Monday morning, amid a common neighborhood understanding that the clothes were to be on the line early, where they could be seen by other housewives. To hang clothes out at 10:00 A.M., when others were taking in their first batch, was about as explicit a way to advertise slackness as you could find.

Our routine was straightforward. Before breakfast Dad fired up the spare range in the "summer kitchen" (our name for the utility room) and put on it a copper boiler full of water. Until I was twelve we pumped and carried all the water into the house; thereafter it was piped but still hand-pumped. The water heated during the morning chores and breakfast, and then my father ladled it into the tubs and put on more water. Then my mother took over.

There were three possible modes for washing clothes: the Tub, the Washer, the Washing Machine—ancient, medieval, and modern, a natural sequence. We used them all.

In the beginning was the Tub. Housewives simply dumped the clothes into the tub with the hot water and the shredded brown Fels Naptha soap, and pounded them down and beat them up with a clothes stomper. Then they let the children take a turn. Some clothes had soaked overnight and some needed to be rubbed on the washboard, but this general method had served womankind for countless generations, vying during much of that time with the prehistoric alternative of beating the clothes on rocks at the river's edge. In our community ancient times lasted right through the Depression.

Then there was the Washer. Sometime around 1942, with a new baby in the offing, our family graduated from the ancient tub-stomper-washboard method to the washer, a large half-moon-shaped tub fitted with a mechanical device to which we applied a tedious back-and-forth motion that stirred and swished the clothes through the warm suds. It involved less drudgery than stomping the clothes in washtubs, and it could be conveniently operated by renewable local energy, namely, child power, which we had in abundance. It was conventional Monday morning wisdom that the washer didn't really get things as clean as the old-fashioned tub and stomping procedure. And I am sure that in days of yore and for similar reasons the tub and stomper had been slow to prevail over the known virtues of rocks on the riverbank.

After the Washer came the Washing Machine. Shortly after the war, when appliances became available again, we got a Maytag washing machine, powered by a smoky and noisy gasoline engine that much preferred not to start. On those cold Monday mornings when Dad had to spend a half hour to get it going, he developed some doubts about the advantages of progress. Perhaps it was because rural history had been compressed by the war that our family experienced all three major phases of clothes-washing history within less than a decade during the forties. My mother welcomed these changes, but I think the pace of life worried my father a little.

Tuesday was baking and ironing day. Ironing was another of the farm ceremonies in which common sense and the lure of rituals of cleanliness fought each other to a standstill. Ironing clothes in the days before wrinkle-free fabrics, steam irons, starchless collars, and relaxed Sunday dressing codes—how vastly complicated and laborious it was! After the washing my mother prepared a batch of liquid starch into which she dipped aprons, shirt collars, and cuffs and pleats of blouses, and hung the garments up to dry. Dresses, linen dish towels, blouses, shirts, handkerchiefs, and other garments (which had been thoroughly dried on the line on Monday) were then sprinkled with water, rolled up tightly, and packed into a basket to get them to the right degree of dampness for effective ironing. Later, my mother or Gladys would unroll them and iron everything, giving special treatment to the starched clothes. They heated the flatiron on the wood-fired kitchen range, and tested it for cleanliness with a damp cloth and for temperature by the sound of the sizzle from a wet finger—too hot and it would not only fry a finger but also cook a white shirt collar brown.

All this toil and moil seemed to be accepted as matter-of-fact routine, necessary and inescapable; but surely it was energized by strong ritualistic impulses as well. True, it made some sense to starch aprons, for they stayed clean longer that way, and of course the satisfactions of producing nicely ironed clothes are not to be denied. At about age ten or twelve each of us in turn went on an ironing binge, starting with handkerchiefs, but I doubt that those brief spasms of helpfulness lightened my mother's labors by very much.

Wednesday was mending day. Darning cotton socks (Rockford socks for boys, brown lisle stockings for girls) headed the list, and patching denim overalls ran a close second. It's unlikely that any housewife was *ever* caught up on her mending, and most women made a lot of clothes for the family as well. During the war, chicken feed was sold in a cotton sack that was designed to be recycled as pillowcases, skirts and blouses, pajamas, curtains, and underwear; and some brands of chicken feed came with appropriately varied prints for that purpose. Those possibilities elicited from many women a certain pride in their skill and frugality, but they also gave them more work. Every household needed a daughter to help with the housework, and my sister did her share, though she often preferred being a tomboy outside with her brothers.

Occasionally, a housewife without a teenage daughter took in some extra help in the house, and one doesn't have to wonder why. I look at the summer of 1942: my mother had four children under fourteen; she had no indoor plumbing, no electricity, no refrigeration; and she was pregnant, hemming diapers in her spare time. To keep washing, cooking, ironing, sewing, cleaning, and mothering from becoming overwhelming, she sometimes had help on Wednesday or Thursday afternoon from my cousin Gertrude, and that gave her a midweek break to attend meetings of the church Ladies Aid Society or the neighborhood Home Extension group.

On Wednesday nights we might have company. Not that this meant idleness: the women would darn socks while they talked, and the men would catch up on their smoking.

One night when we had company, Marvin was put in charge of seeing the younger boys to bed—making sure the lantern was lit and turned low in the hallway, and so on. We said good night, went upstairs, and when I noticed that something was amiss, I marched down again and stood in the center of the kitchen, where I could be heard throughout the house. I shouted aloud to no one in particular:

"Hey, where's the pot?"

An explosion of laughter came from the living room full of adults, and Marvin popped up from somewhere to try to repair the social damage I had wrought. He spoke softly:

"Mother, we need the chamber."

More adult laughter. That word *chamber* sounded ridiculous to me on his lips, and perhaps it did to adults as well: it was a mother's euphemism, not a boy's. But any youngster knows that when adults want to snicker and guffaw, there is no reasoning with them. For our part, though we never called a spade a spade but rather a shovel, we always called a chamber pot a pot.

The pot was for reserve, not for regular use, for there was always the great outdoors and within it the little outhouse. There is something memorable about standing with bare feet on the cold stone doorstep in the dead of night in the dead of winter answering a call of nature. If you move quickly, hard-packed snow is not quite so cold on bare feet as is fresh-fallen snow, but it's less interesting, too. We did not tend to linger over these pleasures. However, years later I came to associate memories of these nighttime moments with a line from Shakespeare's *Julius Caesar*: "For this relief, much thanks, tis bitter cold."

Thursday was catch-up day, and the day for such extras as pie baking, making soup, gardening, and making butter. For years mine was the task of churning the butter, a pleasant honor gladly accepted. Experience had taught us that slightly soured cream not only churned to butter more effectively (instead of whipping) but also produced a more flavorful butter than fresh cream. We poured about a gallon of thick cooled cream into the churn, a squarish metal device with a small hand crank and a wooden paddle that worked the cream. During the churning, which might take twenty minutes or so, it was important not to interrupt the action until the cream coagulated, which it did very abruptly. It was easy to identify this moment by the sound of the paddle in the cream. Then I'd stop, put in half a cup of cold water, and crank for another minute. And that's it: large curds of shiny yellow butter were now bobbing about in a sea of genuine buttermilk. We poured off the buttermilk—to be used as a beverage or in place of soured milk in a recipe—and my mother worked over the butter to expel the last of the milk and also worked in a bit of salt. Thus we arrived at the proper moment to reach for a loaf of homemade bread and a jar of wild-strawberry jam.

We made our own butter because we couldn't afford not to. Today I own that venerable churn, still serviceable and scented with memories of the ton of butter I must have made in it, and I have a dream that someday it will make butter for me again. What I lack is a gallon of unhomogenized cream—and what I fear is that if I could find it I couldn't afford it.

Friday was for making bread again and cleaning and for monthly and seasonal tasks. Monthly: washing some windows, waxing a floor, cutting a child's hair. Seasonal: heavy canning in summer;

quilt making, butchering, and meat processing in winter; house-cleaning in spring and fall, a room a week. We'd empty a room *completely*. Everything went outside, where we children beat the furniture with a broom; curtains got washed and starched and strung out on curtain stretchers; floors got mopped, walls sponged or completely repapered, rugs pounded. Most Dutch housewives followed all these rituals—at least once a year for each room, twice for the living room—or felt guilty if they didn't. Undoubtedly they were serving obscure ceremonial purposes and cleanliness at the same time.

Also on Thursday or Friday we might get a visit from the Watkins man or the McCannon man—pharmacist, herbalist, pur-veyor of minor kitchen wares, household nostrums, spices, teas, and every imaginable sort of small boxed, packaged, capsulized, or bottled consumable. They were interesting hucksters, and I think my mother was intrigued by their products and welcomed their vis-its. Certainly children did. From yellow sugar-coated cold tablets to vanilla extract to salves and saccharin and snake oil and ginger and garlic and tooth powder, they could produce piles of weird and wonderful stuff from those big black briefcases and from the bot-tomless trunks of their cars. With the displays came a nonstop dis-course, which, if my mother had time for it, ranged throughout all the domestic arts and sciences and to the state of the world be-yond. A visit from the Watkins man was like an hour-long TV commercial in a world without TV. Everybody knew these products and knew these merchants by name, and the consensus in the neighborhood was that they were all right. However, they never left us any salad dressing.

Maybe my mother didn't want a whole bottle of cough syrup or lime extract—just enough to refill her own bottle—and she wasn't afraid to say so. She could be wonderfully matter-of-fact when she was confidently astride her own turf. Without any effort at all she drove a firm, clear bargain, Mother did, and Dad couldn't bear to watch; he went out to the field. The Watkins man was obliging: he simply poured the right amount from his jug into her bottle, disdaining a funnel and not spilling a drop.

During the war these amiable traveling merchants had to peddle what they could get. Imitation pepper, for instance. Mother took one sniff and told it like it was. "T'aint real pepper," she said, looking the man in the eye. She wasn't being censorious, just matter-of-fact. He buried it deep in his briefcase and changed the subject. As the war went on she got to sniffing lots of things, lots of imitations as it turned out, and she boldly called them as she smelled them. In her own kitchen she trusted her own nose. Poor innocent chaps, they got so that they'd twitch when Mother reached for something and raised it to her face. They had just been bragging about their stuff, insisting it was the real thing. "Real *what?*" she'd say, detecting imitation vanilla at arm's length but putting it to her nose anyway, locking the man in on the way up, eyeball-to-eyeball. He'd always blink first. Then she'd offer him a cup of coffee. Real coffee, rationed coffee, scarce and expensive, and served with real cream and real bread and butter and wild-strawberry jam. I don't wonder they kept coming back.

Saturday was an even fuller day for the housewife than the other days. She had to get ready for Sunday, which was to some extent a day of respite from housework—cooking and dishes excepted. Maybe my mother and sister intended to bake a cake Saturday afternoon, but before that they would blacken the stove, wash the kitchen floor, clean the lamp chimneys, scrub the privy with disinfectant, dust the living room, and get somebody to polish the shoes. On Saturday night we children took turns taking baths, the setting being a washtub in front of the stove. When we were young, several siblings might use the same tubful, since it would be a shame to waste warm soapy water. Later we figured out a way to curtain off a corner of the kitchen for basin baths. But we were more fortunate than most: in summertime we had a pond to bathe in.

Last of all, on Saturday night Mother peeled potatoes for Sunday. She had served baked beans for supper, never better, and tomorrow we would have meat and vegetables "in the good Dutch tradition." Should I be censorious if the vegetables were over-cooked? Probably not; but as a matter of fact they were.

Not to worry, though: dessert might be huckleberry pie.

15

In Pursuit of Huckleberry Pie

Although Robert Frost harvested blueberries in New England and gathered poetry along with his crop, some of his lines invariably point me back to the prosaic huckleberries of Michigan. Picking wild berries was the sweetest and best of our vagrant summer plea-sures, the fruit sometimes abundant beyond belief. If we had to drive some distance to get them, so much better the berries, so much stronger the mystique. From experience I can testify that we may take Frost's word for it, in "Blueberries," that

> It's a nice way to live,
> Just taking what Nature is willing to give,
> Not forcing her hand with harrow and plow.

Berry picking was a regular part of our family routine and we did not take it lightly, accepting it rather in the rare, high spirits of picnic-in-the-offing, almost a festival, aware that gathering from these unharrowed, unplowed fields was a serious part of our domes-tic economy. It's a nice way to live. Three or four times a summer, berry picking was our excuse for a full-scale family outing, a respite from the routines of haying and hoeing, and satisfying as diversion even if the berry crop was a bust. Huckleberries in July and blackberries in August were what we sought, and there were years when my mother canned more than a hundred quarts of them.

These berries grew profusely in the extreme eastern and northern edges of the county, exotic areas known to us simply as the "Plains"—large cutover timber tracts of an earlier generation, the soil too poor ever to have been farmed, now partially growing up to scrub oak, jack pine, and wild berries. The Plains were treated as public reservations, although we were a little vague about questions of ownership.

On the appointed day, as determined by the neighborhood grapevine report on the berry crop, or by the calendar, or simply by our success at badgering our parents, we prepared for the excursion by tying a ten-gallon cream can onto the rear bumper of the '32 Chevy, fastening it securely with recycled baling wire at the bottom and binder twine at the top. The can would hold the berries, for there would be no room inside the car. We equipped ourselves with a recycled Karo syrup pail apiece, and, in case we would be gone through midday, my mother and sister prepared a stack of sandwiches. A green gallon jug made of light metal and heavy crockery always went along filled with Kool-Aid. The Kool-Aid was too weak, because it was cheaper to make it that way; too sweet, because our young palates were already spoiled; too warm, because this was before ice cubes arrived in our neck of the woods. We loved it, though parents didn't drink such stuff.

The blackberry Plains was an hour's drive to the north; the huckleberry Plains, an hour to the east. (*Plains*, like *oats*, was often treated as a singular.) En route to the Plains we stopped at a grocery store to buy bologna to put into our sandwiches; we also bought chewing gum to shore up our willpower. Gum was rare at home and forbidden in school and was therefore one of the minor attractions of the occasion. The family rule about berry picking was concise: pick first, eat last. The gum made compliance easy, since you can't chew gum and eat berries at the same time. Fathers did not chew gum; they chewed Red Man tobacco. Mothers went without, needing no props to sustain their willpower. Kids went straight for Black Jack gum.

We knew several homemade substitutes for gum, but since they were always available they could not very well serve the high purposes of berry picking. Paraffin wax was one of our common substitutes; white, crumbly, quite tasteless, and prone to becoming brittle on the bedpost at night, it's a poor boy's gum. A better substitute is a handful of wheat kernels, which, with a bit of practice and conviction, you can work up into a passable excuse for gum. Rye will serve too, but only with difficulty, as it lacks the gumminess of wheat. Oats won't do at all, since it has husks. Another alleged substitute, spruce gum, which oozes from the bark of spruce trees and crystallizes in lumps, was unknown to us at the time—we must have read the wrong books—but the chances are less than zero that we would have liked it. It tastes like paraffin wax soaked in turpentine, surely an acquired taste, though not, as yet, acquired by anybody that I have met outside of books. The books we read also recommended the inner bark of slippery elm as a home-grown gum, and in pursuit of that alleged delicacy I have gnawed an embarrassingly large amount of bark, but never found any with a decent bite. Compared with those alternatives the mere mention of Black Jack chewing gum, our all-time favorite, could activate the glands.

Having secured the bologna and the Black Jack, we headed toward the Plains, eventually turning off the gravel road into a twisting, sandy lane, a pair of ruts that had started life long ago as a lumbering road and was now kept open by hunters and gatherers and others similarly unauthorized. We seldom saw other cars in these remote plains, miles from the nearest farm. We parked the Chevy under a tree, preferably the same one we had parked under last year, inhaled the pungent air, distributed Black Jack and syrup pails, sampled the Kool-Aid, and then scattered to the four winds in pursuit of adventure and berries. Intriguing territory, with infallible power to stir the adrenaline. Endless acres of possibilities. Nature unforced. We could go where we wanted to go, yield to any straying impulse, follow any path, any animal trail, any distance. If ever there was in our hearing a call of the wild, it came from here.

We were especially keen on the huckleberry Plains because the landscape and flora were utterly different from anything in our neighborhood. Here was soil too sandy, too dry to support a decent sod. How odd! Young jack pine and small white oak and huge white pine stumps of Michigan's golden timber age flanked intermittent clearings where shadbush, bracken, and sweet fern formed a framework for millions of low huckleberry bushes. None of these things were to be seen near our farm. Anthills and deer trails and fox dens and hornet nests and bird songs were interestingly different from what we knew at home. The Plains revealed itself again as an invaluable public resource, recreationally and emotionally; it was the closest we could come to genuine wilderness. Wasteland, perhaps, thousands of acres of it, from the viewpoint of harrow and plow; but beyond price from the vantage point of the spirit. Here was Nature giving lavishly, and no one here was forcing her hand. The rich ambience of the Plains in high summertime, its eerie silences and wildness, its beloved scents of sweet fern and of hot sun on dry pine needles, still mingles in memory with the taste of warm blue huckleberries, and with the sense that life in the countryside could be very engaging and very good.

If the regions near the parking place had been picked over, we would wander far afield, except my mother, who would usually stay nearer the car with Carl, when he was still young. This was one of the rare times when there wasn't a volunteer baby-sitter among us older siblings, for the tug of the Plains was stronger than the charms of playing big brother or big sister to a toddler. We had learned that the fun soon goes out of trying to keep a huckleberry-crazed two-year-old from stuffing his face with a cheerful blend of green berries and leaves. Returning with full pails we often found that Mother, besides baby-tending, had filled and emptied her pail already, having found excellent picking nearby. Even without the support of Black Jack or Red Man, she was a first-rate berry picker, astonishing her offspring, who too easily imagined that women's talents were restricted to indoor sports. She told one of her secrets: "My mother taught me to pick with both hands, like this. Watch." We watched. Impossible—too many fingers, leaves, bushes to keep track of. "Just work at it; it'll come." It came. But not right away, not that year. And she was right: it's a nice way to pick.

After the first pailful it was easy to believe that the best berries were farther off, still undiscovered—eastward where the trees thinned or beyond the cutoff trail, beyond the fire line, past the tall pines and the big swale and a bit farther, then left or maybe right, to some remote and sun-soaked sidehill. Surely there was such a place where the bushes were thicker, the berries bigger and sweeter than anywhere else. Tracing them to their secret clearing, gathering up a pailful, and finding the way back to the car armed with the fruit and its full complement of bragging rights—is any adventure of woodland or field so fair as that?

Inevitably there were times when we went to the Plains and found almost nothing. Once, searching for huckleberries, we were wandering about in circles of frustration among the barren bushes, appalled at the thought of going home to the hoeing fields, when we found some tall bushes loaded down with deep purple berries. This was strange fruit but not forbidden, so far as we knew. We tasted them cautiously, and when we were not struck down in our tracks, we tried more. They were tart and juicy, rather intriguing. Yes, we would have some more. But there were bushels of them free for the taking, a gift outright; why go home empty-handed? On the other hand, what would we do with them? We bent the bushes and filled our pails with the strange berries, staining our hands in their juices a deep, dark purple. We brought the berries home, cooked some up into a sauce, and pronounced the results okay. We then urged Mother to try the definitive experiment, which was a pie.

By this time we were calling the new fruit by a Dutch slang name which, though it probably was not our family's invention, may never have been committed to writing until now. The berries were *smeer-pootjes.* (If this name were translated, which I don't recommend, it would come across as something like "little hand-stainers.") Well, smeer-pootjes pie passed our critical palate test very well: maybe not quite up to the scale of huckleberry pie, a very lofty standard, but not bad at all in a lean year. Once we had tasted and named the berries and accepted them into our repertoire, we had no further scientific interest in the bush, though we kept an eye out for the smeer-pootjes thereafter, especially when the huckleberries made a poor showing.

It was probably decades later that we identified the plant as shadbush, or juneberry, a many-specied genus (*Amelanchier*) of the rose family. Careful observation since then has assured me that the chief difference between the New England shadbush and the Michigan varieties is evident only in July: in New England the berries normally shrivel into hard and seedy little beads, tasteless and barely capable even of staining your hand, suitable at best for bird food; but in Michigan, if the rains come in season, they often turn into juicy and tasty smeer-pootjes, suitable for ersatz huckleberry pie.

Once my father and I were far from the car, picking blackberries side by side with pails nearly full, when we came upon a berry patch so copious and lush with ripe fruit that it brought tears to our eyes. Here were gifts far beyond what our pails could possibly hold. "I have an idea," said Dad. "The car's quite a ways off—you want to wait here while I go as quickly as I can to empty the pails? Then you can guide me back here by calling." *I* stay *here?* I didn't dare to say yes to this plan, and I didn't want to say no. So I did the daring thing and said yes. Off he went with our full pails, telling me emphatically to stay right there. We kept contact with shouts until he faded, faded out of hearing. I sat down to wait. Endless acres of silence spread out in every direction. And all the silence looked the same. I was very aware now that I was all alone amid the blackberries and that the berries were all alone amid the vast, mysterious Plains.

In which direction was the car? Hadn't Dad seemed to circle a bit? Did he really know where the car was? There was probably not another person within shouting distance of me. Just to check this out, I tried it. Right; no answer. What if Dad didn't find the car, just kept on walking? Did he ever get lost? Daniel Boone said that he had never been lost, but he admitted that he had been bewildered once for three days. I was bewildered already; lost might be next. In the midst of the Plains, where only God and the birds and the blackberries could see me, I sat and pondered. Did birds ever get lost? How did they find south when they had to go? Which way is north? Could I find the car if I had to? How would I know how long I had to wait before I had to do something? The blackberries around me seemed to shrink.

The Plains was a light and airy region: many clearings, few large trees, scarcely a forest, not intimidating. Still, I had no idea at all where I was or where *anything* was. How extraordinary, baffling, disorienting. On the flat and open terrain of our farm community we could always at least tell directions, for we were seldom out of sight of roads and fields that ran north/south and east/west. Now a sense of direction and place, when I wanted to lean on it, simply wasn't there at all. Could I even point north? As hard as a youngster could, I tried to stave off the silence by thinking about how I could tell directions, how we find our way in strange environments. I had plenty of time to think, for it took about two hours to get through the next twenty minutes.

But I mark that remote spot in time as the point when I first began to think that there are two kinds of people, those who have an inner compass and those who do not.

To have an inner compass is to have, for example, a ready answer to the question, Which way *seems* north? Those lacking an inner compass have no intuitive answer; they can only contrive one. Put another way, those with the compass have a mental quirk by which the back of their mind is always busy noting directions, making corrections, generating constant low-level interest and information about north-south-east-west. They may not always be right about directions, but something always seems right. In contrast, those without an inner compass can move for days, even through unfamiliar places, entirely heedless of directions; normally they simply don't care about them. People with an inner compass do care; for them the difference between north and east has a vividness like the difference between left and right. They want to have what *is* north also *seem* north; so they work at it. It's a thing you might find yourself thinking about in remote places like the Plains.

None of this is based on scientific observation—just observation. It's evident that those with an inner compass have a certain advantage and bear a certain burden. The advantage is that the compass is often uncannily right and a powerful ally in finding the way, whether one is mixed-up downtown or wandering through the blackberries in the Plains. The burden is more mysterious. The inner compass may sometimes point the wrong way, or even get stuck off course. (I knew a man who moved to Iowa and there found his directions mixed. He couldn't fix it. Day after day the sun rose in the south, set in the north. For nine months his world was always distressingly ninety degrees askew. Then he returned to Michigan and had to relearn to trust his intuitions, which were in tune again.) To those without an inner compass, that could not happen and, in fact, it usually strikes them as a preciously loony problem; they simply consult the objective facts about directions and make the mental correction. Those burdened or gifted with the little compass inside cannot always correct it, for it lurks in a place beyond the reach of their will. They are the victims of their talent.

Neither is that based on science—just observation. Further observation: in general, the rural folk of Michigan have a livelier inner compass than those of New England. If that is true, the explanation may not be far to seek. More of Michigan's rural folk live on straight roads and in houses built square with the world; directionality is a blatant part of their environment, of their daily expe-

rience, of their consciousness of place and position. Much of the
Midwest is like that; not much of New England is. On our eighty
acres, rectangular and four-cornered as it was, every row crop was
laid down in lines that ran either east/west or north/south, and we
learned to think and communicate automatically in terms of the
directions of the earth. For those destined to have one, the inner
compass was being fine-tuned every day of the week.

To psychology and sociology I leave it to discover, if they can,
how much of this is true; and to philosophy to help resolve the
quandary, if it can, of what facets of the inner compass belong to
nature and what to nurture. I am aware that readers of these observations may find them provocative if they have an inner compass—and somewhat peculiar if they do not.

Very faintly my father's distant voice drifted from the vastness
into the directionless patch of Plains where I kept vigil with my
blackberries and my thoughts. I bellowed response and waited. Silence. Exultation and despair. Then another call, then another,
and then I guided him in; and then the blackberries, which had
shrunk to insignificance, swelled out again to luscious fullness. We
quickly filled our pails once more, and then we tossed away our
Black Jack and Red Man and filled our stomachs. Those blackberries loom in memory as being thick as a man's thumb and almost as
sweet as jelly, the standard against which I forever measure blackberries. When we were ready to go, Dad, pointing, said, "We'll
head off that way, just a little to the right of the sun, and when we
get to the third clearing we'll bend more south." We did that, and
the route led directly to the car. Sometimes a sense of direction is
very elementary, relying on obvious data like the direction of the
sunlight, the remembered landmarks, the lay of the land. An inner
compass needs the support of outer cues.

From that day I began to pick up on the fact that fostering one's
own compass involves drawing habitually on all kinds of data, slant
of the light and shape of the terrain among them, and on cultivating in familiar territory and inadvertently at first a lively roster of

mental habits, mental mappings. In time it became a point of pride among us—my father, brothers, friends—to work our way through strange forests without becoming disoriented, a skill that can become a sixth sense in foresters and hunters, or even in wandering berry pickers. That ability stood us in good stead in later years when we hunted rabbits and deer in the Plains, or ranged farther into other untracked tracts of wildness. Those of us who grew to adulthood on a mental landscape that nurtured an inner compass have probably lost the ability to shake it off: everywhere it shadows our steps, unforced, like a gift of nature, whispering directions, quietly pointing.

We were in no hurry to leave the rich-giving Plains. We had filled our containers, filled our stomachs, nearly filled our souls. When we got home we were comfortably behind schedule, a reminder that the day had been unusual. By the time the chickens were fed and the eggs gathered and supper prepared and consumed and the cows milked and the milk separated and the calves and pigs fed and the dishes done and the table cleared and the toddler packed off to bed, it was dusk. But fresh berries do not keep, certainly not in a hot, closed cream can, so they had to go into the canning jars tonight for processing tomorrow. If the fruit was blackberries, they would go almost directly into the mason jars with only the most cursory sorting needed. But huckleberries required more attention, since young, unskilled, two-handed pickers, incited by the drama of the Plains, also collect refuse with the berries. Under the eyes of our parents, we had to learn to sort the good fruit from the chaff.

Imperceptibly, those excursions off the home grounds became parables for us, inadvertent and unrecorded as such but not without effect—tokens of the larger adventure of life. The Plains, which seemed so vast and giving, so unbounded, so alive with the scent of mystery, yielded a sweet and simple berry harvest and something far beyond that. Whole landscapes of possibilities were prefigured there. Gifts unforced. There, if anywhere, were intimations that somewhere we might gather where we had not sown;

there were hints of uncharted territories of the future where we could no longer take our bearings from serene and cozy farmscapes, but would have to extract them hopefully from the scattered data in a larger, wilder world, from the source and direction of light, and from an inner compass, probably nurtured unconsciously but yet mysteriously aligned, one might hope, with the encompassing moral order.

But right now we had to get the farm chores done. That accomplished, we assembled around the kitchen table, dishpan heaping full of huckleberries as centerpiece, each of us equipped with a flat tray, its bottom covered one tier deep with berries. The kerosene lamp above the table, the kitchen's only light, was suspended by an adjustable chain; so we pulled down the lamp until it brooded low over the berries, until its round glass globe had combed all the superfluous light down off the kitchen walls and gathered it on the table directly in front of us all. Seated in the pale glow of that family circle, heads bent over the berries, arranged in our best Norman Rockwell pose, we might have appeared to be praying. But no; that we had done already. We were moving the berries from one vessel to another, from cream can to dishpan to sorting tray to mason jars, performing the last of the simple ceremonies of the harvest, carefully picking over the entire batch, tray by tray, getting the last fragments of the Plains out of our berries. Getting the Plains—though only temporarily—out of our system, too. Tomorrow would be hoeing and haying again. But we were also closing in on the next day's huckleberry pie. It's a nice way to live.

❧ 16 ❧

What We Know of the Sparrow and the Crow

One summer day I interrupted a large garter snake at its dinner in the strawberry patch, ingesting a live baby bird, head first; the snake was about halfway through its meal, and the birdling appeared to be much too large to go the rest of the way. I didn't linger to find out. So appalled was I at "Nature red in tooth and claw" that I dropped my box of berries and quit the field in a hurry. I waited three days and then returned, carrying a big stick. But the nest was empty, the berries were spoiled, and the snake was nowhere to be seen.

Not only for scenes like that, but for reasons more obscure, we took snakes to be our natural enemies on the farm. Normally we killed them on sight, cheerfully abetting a deep, possibly instinctive human aversion to things that crawl and creep. We knew about rattlesnakes, but they were so rare that if we ever saw one we didn't recognize it. We knew very well that there were serpents in the Bible and that none of them were any good, beginning with the first one in Eden, "more subtle than any beast of the field." There was probably a certain amount of minor sport in running down a snake to destroy it, but for the most part it was less sport that we were practicing than sheer habit. We killed snakes, I'm afraid, mainly because it was our policy to kill snakes, just as it was their policy to swallow birds. Today I understand that garter snakes prefer to dine on slugs, eating them whole, often head first, and I tend to view them kindly on that account alone, for I now regard slugs as natural enemies. I presume there were no slugs in the Garden of Eden and that the snake got an unfortunately bad press.

On the farms after Eden there is a firm imperative to keep predators at bay. This requires hardening your heart, and it's an attitude that has consequences. The unceasing war on insects and weeds and potato bugs extends to mice and rats and snakes and intermittently to sparrows and crows and gophers, and perhaps also to rabbits and hawks and foxes and weasels, with an occasional woodchuck and skunk and badger and porcupine thrown in. Sometimes even a pet cat that has turned to prey on pet rabbits. Subsistence farming is harsh and single-minded: what the farmer does not sow or reap, and cannot eat or feed or use or sell, is in danger of being thought a weed, to be casually uprooted, for whatever is not part of the produce may be suspected of preying upon it. In so utilitarian an environment the margins for impartial contemplation, or for aesthetics, are usually very, very narrow indeed. Matters of life and death on a farm are a mixture of necessity, ecology, sport, habit, cold indifference, and sentimentality. There is room for wantonness in such an atmosphere.

Take hawks, for example, the aesthetic opposite of snakes. Rather than low and insinuating, they are lofty, aerial predators with grace and elegance to spare, and are almost universally admired by birders. "Persecuted and misunderstood, but important in the ecosystem," says my bird book. Not important to *our* image of the ecosystem. To us they were just predators of cunning and deceit, and we loathed them, for we knew that they would attack young chicks. We had seen it. Had we known that they would also happily dine on snakes, that might have modified our attitudes; and, indeed, the idea that the lowly slug could go up the food chain, via garter snakes, to soar with hawks and eagles is peculiarly satisfying now but was unavailable to us then. Our one experience with the chicks put a decade-long blot on the reputation of the entire family Accipitridae.

It was high noon and several of us were in the yard near the brooder coop when a hawk, probably a buteo, glided in over the orchard treetops, dropped upon our brood of young chicks, pounced, and then began beating its wings furiously to get aloft with its prey. First we just stared in amazement; then my mother shouted and waved her arms and ran toward the hawk as it struggled to rise above the apple trees. Fifty feet in the air the predator released its prey. The chick fell like a stone. We rushed to the spot to stare at the clump of bloody feathers; then I reached down to pick up the chick in my fingertips by one of its fragile wings. The limp body was headless! Farm families never forget these things and enduring attitudes are formed by them. Although such hawk attacks are un- likely, young chicks don't think so, for their instincts command them to cower and hide whenever a large bird or the shadow of one passes over. For the next decade each time we saw the chicks flee to cover, we were confirmed in thinking that hawks are farmers' enemies.

Like snakes and hawks, English sparrows fell into the category of automatic prey for us, for they preyed upon what was ours. Our attitude toward them was not quite so unreasoning as toward snakes: if we had a vague and unrecognized need for helpless victims, we also had some vague ecological reasons for killing sparrows that did not differ essentially from our reasons for swatting flies. Sparrows were a nuisance in the barn and they fattened on grain from our granary. We despised them. In our moral ecology sparrows were only a cut above rodents, more akin to rats than to wrens. Just as there were good insects and bad insects—bees and potato bugs, say—so there were good birds and bad birds. Sparrows and hawks were bad always, crows sometimes; robins were good, wrens were good, swallows and bobolinks were very good. Nesting barn swal- lows that had the courage to pester the cats by dive-bombing them as they came out the stable door were absolutely tops! Conven- tional wisdom settled these judgments without any dispute. As for sparrows, their malignity was confirmed, if confirmation was neces- sary, by the fact that they didn't sing. Didn't even try. They would jabber, they were noisy like chickens, but it wasn't the sound of music. We thought it pretty obvious that they had a parasitic and slum mentality: messy housekeepers, their nests mere tufts of hay stuffed under rafters, their droppings everywhere in the barn.

So they were fair game, and we gave no quarter. We'd poke out the sparrow nest with a stick and hope that when it fell there would be some young ones. Then we'd call over the cats and hand them each a tasty hors d'oeuvre of fresh, warm prefledgling sparrow. Thus we early learned recycling and showed concern for the happiness of cats. Alternatively, we would take the hairy birdlings in hand, back off, and pitch them hard against the barn. "Splat!" they would go—a quick and painless death. On the ground the cats danced in circles of ecstasy, meowing excelsior and staring up at the barn wall, whence the juicy morsels of heavenly manna fell. In summer this wantonness was routine minor sport for us, a picnic for the cats; however, we would not have engaged in it, would not have been permitted to, but for the fact that it was intended to help maintain an ecological balance on the farm. Whether demolishing their housing projects, which gave us real satisfaction, affected the population of the predator sparrows I do not know, but it is likely to have had more of an effect than another squalid thing we did, namely, to use sparrows as targets for practicing with a BB gun. You can stun a sparrow with BBs, a possibility that made it fun. That's the way it was. Wincing came later.

Crows as predators were far worthier adversaries, and our quarrels with them were more sporting. Crows were clever and interesting, but it was well understood that they could be a big problem in a newly planted cornfield. When young corn plants are up an inch or two, crows love to yank out the new shoots and eat the swollen, moist kernel at the bottom; that's a crow's idea of Indian pudding, and they were surely enjoying it long before the paleface got to these shores. A band of crows invading a young cornfield can do enough damage that major replanting may be necessary, and the farmer's first level of retaliation was to tell exaggerated stories about the malign capabilities of crows. In spring and summer, swapping crow stories was a standard part of rural discourse. Unlike most predators, crows had a reputation to live up to.

It was threshing day and we were in the southeast oats field. Two neighbors, Cleo and Bill, were leaning on their pitchforks, waiting for the next wagon to appear from the barn. We were "threshing out of the field" and I had just taken a jug of water out to those who had been assigned to the field. As I came up the question being agitated had to do with smart birds.

"Now you take a crow," said Cleo, and he sent a spray of tobacco juice careening into a shock of oats and then took a long pull on the water can. "You take a crow—that sucker kin tell if you've got a shotgun or just a pitchfork in your hand. I dunno how they do it but they do it, sure as shootin'."

Bill didn't know how to top that. He took a cool drink while Cleo warmed up to his subject.

"Say that blinkin' crow is sittin' on a fence post, watchin' ya. Open field. You think you can walk into range of that crow with a shotgun? Now say you're carrying this here fork—heck, he'll eat corn right in front of ya. I seen it more'n once."

Bill allowed that this was so—a crow knew a pitchfork from a shotgun—but Cleo wasn't done yet.

"Course it depends how you walk," he said. "You *can* fool 'em. Tell ya how. Say there's a crow in that there tree over there; you take and walk straight at that tree with the crow sittin' in it, and that sonofagun will take off, specially if you've got a gun. But now you take and go 'kitter'n' like, and make to walk *past* that tree—don't walk straight at it—and that crow'll set right there and let you walk by 'cause he thinks you don't see him! They know when you're going for 'em."

"Oh, they're smart all right," said Bill. "I didn't see a crow this whole spring until I got my corn planted. Then they come floppin' in like turkeys."

"Well, I guess they was over to my place before that," said Cleo. "My corn was up first, proley. Anyway, they don't always wait for it to come up, ya know; you plant it on the square and they'll go right to it and dig it up. I don't plant corn on the square anymore. No sirree! They're smart bastards, crows."

This last was the most interesting item on the crow's résumé: the allegation that it would follow the rows of newly planted corn and dig it up even before it had sprouted.

We always planted our corn with a small hand planter, and to plant it on the square we had to mark out a grid on the prepared field. We did this with a marking pole, a long pipe to which strands of twine were attached at three-foot intervals. At the ends of the twine trailed several feet of chain, which made the marks in the soil. A man and two boys then marched abreast back and forth across the field, carrying the pole that dragged the chains that made the marks. Having finished the field one way, we did the same thing again the other way, perpendicular to the original rows, and when it was completed the field was a grid, entirely reduced to three-foot squares, a microcosm of the whole state of Michigan as the surveyors had plotted it. At each three-foot intersection we planted a hill of corn with a hand planter. The growing corn could then be cultivated "both ways," east/west this week and north/south next week. Without such a system of cross-cultivation, the corn, which was usually planted on newly broken sod, would become so infested with quack grass that its growth would be stunted. Although the job of marking the field was tedious, the planting itself was pleasant enough—light work punctuated with the brisk and steady clickety-click, clickety-click cadence of the planter.

While we marked and planted the cornfields, the crows bounced from trees to fence posts, cawing and cussing, feigning indifference, watching our every move. We knew that they had caucused and figured out what we were doing: if we had been planting potatoes, they would have gone off to spy on the neighbors. Cleo was not alone in believing that crows could find and follow the chain marks in the field; Bill insisted that a crow could spot the grid pattern from the air and flop down at the intersecting lines, dig there and come up with the corn, proceed to the next intersecting lines, and poke a beak in again. When it lost the mark, it would take to the air and get reoriented. Opinions differed as to whether only some crows were smart enough to do this or whether all were. And did the parents teach the young? Or was this criminal talent instinctive? Cleo also had a corollary to his various theories about crow genius. "Heck! They probably don't even need the chain mark," he said. "They can smell the corn."

Whatever their talent, one planting season we set out to foil their plans by doctoring their dinner. We took a tubful of seed corn and stirred into it a sticky black substance advertised in the *Michigan Farmer* as something even the crow with all its wiles would loathe. It was supposed to make them gag and choke, and it had a vile odor that seemed fully up to the task of sickening a crow; but in fact its principal effect was on the operation of the mechanical corn planters. The black sticky goop gummed up the mechanism so that the planters choked and malfunctioned. Our problems with the planters were more frustrating than the problems with the crows had ever been. Another round for the birds.

With so resourceful an antagonist it is not surprising that we took the direct approach: we hunted the crows with guns. The normal seasons for game hunting were fall and winter, but it's a long dry spell for the dedicated hunter from one winter to the next autumn, so it was natural to fabricate a reason to be out with a gun in the spring. The sportsman needed something wild to outwit in the woods, and crows provided the perfect excuse. It was our policy to try to have at least one dead crow to hang up in the cornfield as, well, a scarecrow.

The most dramatic type of crow hunting took place just before the young crows were ready to leave home. We'd find a nest and disturb the fledglings with a long pole until they squawked and set off a general alarm; then we'd enjoy the tumult and the racket that ensued, an old-fashioned crow riot. Crow relatives and neighbors from miles and miles around would pick up the signal, repeat the rumors about young crows being molested, and flock in to add to the commotion. Circling around the treetops, perching and shouting, swooping, dive-bombing, keeping just out of shotgun range, they would snarl and complain and call for reinforcements in a wondrous cacophony of crow nattering that sent our adrenaline levels soaring. The louder the din the farther the signal went out across the countryside—"crow riot in section 15"—and the more young, hot-blooded crows swooped in to join the jamboree.

It was usually a first-class rumpus, more fun for us than stalking crows; and since we couldn't always find a ripe nest, we taught ourselves to imitate the call of young crows so we could sometimes set off the riot by taking the initiative ourselves. We would be concealed beneath the trees making plaintive crowlike squawks, and they would swirl overhead, snarling at the alleged owl (as we supposed they might be imagining) who was savaging some crow babies. Or maybe they thought a giant snake had slithered up the tree to the nest and was swallowing young crows, whole and head first. Actually, we were just getting even for the little matter of the corn. (Once we caught two fledgling crows alive and took them home and put them in a rabbit pen, hoping to domesticate them. We offered them gifts of corn, such as their parents had stolen, which they scornfully refused. It's not easy to turn predators into pets; to our great regret the young crows soon died, perhaps of starvation.) Whatever the outcome, the crow riots we started were good fun for us, and I believe the crows, in their own way, enjoyed them too. It gave them a good party to crash, and it always ended the same way—with a big bang. At the first gunshot, the crows realized that they had been had and that the party was suddenly over. Instantly they went silent, circled once, and then sailed away without a word.

So crows were sporting predators, the best kind; and this redeemed some of the base relations between us and other predators.

Most of the time most of the crows had little to fear from us—as did our corn from them. We had no effect whatever upon the crow population; and only rarely did they seriously affect our corn crop. In fact, there was a kind of chivalrous relationship between the working farmer and the bandit crows. Raids by each upon the other were taken for granted; sly attacks were part of the game. But they were never under cover of darkness; everything was in the open and the adversaries saw each other every day. After the corn was well started, we could ignore crows for the rest of the year, and they ignored us. The annual feud we had with them and they with us was battled out in May and June like any seasonal sport, and when the playoffs—that is, the crow riots we had started—were over and the score settled and the corn knee-high, both sides returned to business as usual. It had really been only a game after all. The cawing that was a taunt in May was merely a greeting in August.

It is true that life on a farm nourishes certain warm affections, as for young animals and other tender growing things; but it also breeds a certain callousness, as toward anything, bird or animal, that even remotely preys on the farmer's interest. Like all farm kids, we were almost daily participants in cycles of life and death—planned and impulsive, painful and casual—and were intimately familiar with much that was tender and some that was brutal but a great deal more that was just supposed to be matter-of-fact.

Many things got assigned to the matter-of-fact category not so much because they were morally neutral but because they were morally complex, too complex for us to sort out and assess. Unless there was an explicit lesson to be enforced, there was no space in the economy of our life to make an event out of the life or death of sparrows, cats, and crows. That had to wait a couple of generations. The underlying idea was that all animals were replaceable—not a very sentimental feeling. But sentiment is the luxury of leisure or of recollections in tranquillity. Poetry would have to wait; we were the working class.

❧ 17 ❧

And Don't Lick the Hoarfrost
off the Pump Handle

We drew our water with a pump in the yard. Perhaps children who grow up where there are half a dozen factory-made beverages in the refrigerator have a different idea of the sources of life than those who were refreshed on a hot summer day only from a pump in the farmyard. Small wonder if a certain amount of literary slush has collected around human experience with wells, springs, pump handles, windmills, fountains, and old oaken buckets. It's damp territory there, oozy with ancient sentiment.

Our pump was worked by hand, not by the wind. Owing to the Depression and then war shortages, people of that era didn't acquire windmills; they had them or they didn't. We didn't. Such a shame, I thought. Water pumping could be absolutely effortless and free as the flowing air, I daydreamed, as God must surely have intended, else why invent the wind and send it across the land? Most neighbors had windmills and we could hear them, their ungreased squeaks and their melancholy sighing as they swung round to catch the shifting breeze. But we did a lot of hand pumping, regretting all the while the wasting of the wind.

The pump was on the slight incline between the house and the barn. We had gravity flow through a makeshift piping system to a stock tank in the barn, but we carried the water to the house. When I was quite young it worked this way: one week I carried water twice daily to keep the crock full in the kitchen, and Nelvin carried wood to keep the woodboxes full; the next week we switched. Seven was the age when we started with these regular chores, so we carried small quantities of water; there was a pencil mark for us on the pail at about the five-quart level. We could barely work the pump handle, barely lug the water. That's why it was fun. At first. When I was about twelve we installed a then-modern force-pump system, which had a valve arrangement whereby the pump drew the water from the well and drove it through underground pipes uphill to a newly installed storage tank in the house. The overflow from the house tank then ran by gravity through pipes to the barn. Still, all the water for the family and for cows, horses, and chickens had to be lifted by the pump handle, and this force pump was also harder to operate than the earlier one. All the more reason to get a windmill, I thought.

Some farmers pumped water with a "pump jack" powered by a gasoline engine. We younger pumpers urgently recommended this device to Dad at regular intervals. It would have required a capital outlay of the kind he was not prepared to make, not only because it was not in his nature to make capital outlays but because he had no capital. He had what he needed for pumping: strong arms and three sons. When I was nine and Carl came along, the household's water demands increased considerably; but by the time *he* reached the pumping age, the advent of electricity had deprived the farm of the fun of pumping.

Sooner or later every young water pumper has an experience like this. Pumping on a bitter, bitter cold day, I paused to adjust the spout of the pipe that carried the water to the barn. Since it was hard to manipulate, I removed my mittens to handle the dripping spout and absentmindedly returned my wet hands to the ice-cold pump handle. Zap! Too late I remembered that I had been warned about that. My hands were instantly glued to the frigid iron, each held fast by a layer of quick-frozen wet skin. Instinctively, I jerked off one hand, and that was another mistake for it tore off thin swatches of frozen skin and left them plastered to the pump handle! Too pained and scared now to jerk my other hand off, I just held on, cold as it was, and let my body heat slowly warm the handle enough to thaw the skin loose. I was freed, but with two sore hands. For water pumpers that kind of possibility comes with the territory, but no one would recommend doing it twice.

My school friends told tales far more graphic: whole slabs of skin frozen and stripped off, sheets of flesh torn loose, careless children who put a wet hand on frozen iron and lost fingers! Could have been a whole hand, frozen solid, ripped right off! You can never be too careful. We loved the stories and shrank from them. Claude said that his little sister once put her tongue on a pump handle and it stuck right there—held her so she couldn't even holler, held her for hours. "What'd she do?" we demanded. "Froze the end of her tongue clean off," came the report. "That's why she stutters."

I didn't always believe Claude, but it was impossible not to draw morals from the stories. On the other hand, there was the familiar and innocent pump handle, face-high to a child; and some December mornings it was covered with the most exquisite and delicate hoarfrost, like a big stick of ice cream. What would it taste like? There are demons lurking within us. We walk near the edge of a high cliff and the demon says, "Jump, do it! *Do* it!" The demon starts to push us and our guardian angel drags us back, just in time. I have felt them warring inside me, up and down my spine, fighting for control of my legs. Sometimes they will do battle for your tongue.

All night long Jack Hoarfrost works on the roofs and trees and lilac bushes, to make the world white enough to meet the dazzling sunrise. He does the posts by the barn and the old dump rake, and turns the woven-wire fence into elegant latticework too utterly lovely to look at. Then he sprays the grass with whipped cream and, just as the sun appears, sprinkles everything with sugar crystals. He does the pump too, every inch of its surface, even the handle, way down to the very end. Sweet world of magic! A small voice whispers into a small ear, "Taste? Just one lick?"

Working a pump handle takes no skill or maturity, merely persistence. But the job sheds its charm very swiftly, even on a bright winter morning. Before the hoarfrost has melted, the pumper is bored. Working the handle endlessly up and down may be the very symbol of the worst of repetitive rural mindlessness. But it did not work out that way in our case; and our experience was the opposite of mindless.

Since pumping a lot of water was necessary, my father contracted the job out. To us. It was not normal policy to pay us children for farm work, but there were a few exceptions. Picking string beans was the principal paying job on the farm, and pumping water was another. In the latter case, the reasons were pretty practical: the job was tedious and had to be done regularly; children were entirely capable of doing it; it would have cost a lot of attention and nagging and bickering to fashion and administer a system that would have gotten the job done fairly and reliably. As good liberals, my parents simply threw money at the problem, and the water got pumped without any difficulty at all.

When I came on the pumping scene, in about 1940, the pay was—and remained throughout the wartime inflation—a penny for every 333 strokes, three cents a thousand. (My parents did not carry their liberalism to excess.) There was not much competition for this employment, but, eventually by my own choice, I did a large portion of it. Before I was twelve I discovered a significant and banal truth: very small amounts of money accumulated on a regular basis over long stretches of time eventually add up to rather startling sums. Three cents a day for a thousand strokes, the minimum daily requirement, produced nearly a dollar a month. That was spending money, to be used essentially as I chose, and it prodigiously supplemented the meager fifteen-cents-per-month allowance that I began getting a few years later. In fact, it made me a swaggering capitalist among my siblings, and I was soon positioned to get serious about increasing my stock of worldly goods. I turned to Marvin, four and half years my senior, as my adviser on investment policy. His name was on mailing lists, and he had exotic catalogs from far-off places, two of which are especially memorable.

One of the catalogs was from Johnson W. Smith and Company, and it displayed and exaggerated every imaginable trinket, joker, gimcrack, gimcrack, gadget, smoke bomb, doodad, bauble, toy, and game, every bag of tricks that could appeal to a boy, plus another range of items, such as jackknives, flashlights, model airplanes, kites, and balsa wood gliders. It was a marriage of hobby shop and joke store, laid out page after beautiful page. What a privilege for Nelvin and me just to *look* at such a catalog, a privilege Marvin duly rationed, of course, pending our good behavior. My first purchase was a large-barreled Eversharp pencil with five different colors of lead, each available at the press of a button.

The other catalog was from the Book Supply Company, and it turned out to be the source from which I early formed the habit, never adequately controlled, of book buying. We leafed through the fiction section, and I was awed: hard to believe there *were* so many books as they offered for sale. The catalog went far beyond anything offered in our very scant school libraries, and we had never seen the inside of a public library. What to do about all these sudden new possibilities? Well, I could do no better, Marvin told me, than to buy *The Mysterious Island,* by Jules Verne, the best book of its kind ever written, he said flatly. For sixty cents, I invested. He showed me how to prepare the order and how to buy and enclose three-cent postage stamps for payment. Now there was nothing to do but wait. And pump more water.

The first book I had ever bought, some years earlier, was a paperback with a yellowish cover called *I Want to Know Book.* I got it for ten cents at Ben Bower's grocery store. It was an assembly of minor scientific facts, and a typical short section was called "Do You Want to Know What Shooting Stars Are?" Well, I certainly did. What it said was that they are *not* pieces of star that shoot off into space; they are just random big hunks of cold rock riding around way up there, and once in a while one just tumbles to earth, catching fire on the way. Well! So that was science! I looked at our rock piles behind the barn. Burn? You might as well say you could burn water. I looked up into the bright blue sky and tried to think of those big rocks waiting around up there—just floating, floating. Must be *way* up there, I guessed. After much thought, I reported this crazy theory to Dad, and he put down his barley fork and looked at me and shook his head. "It probably just goes to show that you can't believe everything you read," he said. As usual, he was right: I certainly couldn't believe that book's story. I could try all morning and it wouldn't do any good. And what was the use of believing it, anyway?

When *The Mysterious Island* came in the mail, I knew I had something I could believe. Captain Cyrus Harding and his stalwart companions, balloon wrecked by a typhoon and marooned on what they named Lincoln Island, reconstituted for their own use and in a few years all the technological trappings of nineteenth-century civilization, gunpowder and telephone included, using only raw materials, their bare hands, their prodigious ingenuity, the salvage from their wrecked balloon—and the unaccountable aid in times of crisis of an unseen guardian presence that inhabited their island and made it mysterious. Nothing so implausible here as floating rocks overhead. What a book! What a buy! The twenty thousand strokes of the pump handle that it cost me—done in less than three weeks, at perhaps forty minutes a day—were nothing when weighed against the hours and hours of pleasure that wonderful book brought me.

Thus stimulated, I never once considered turning back from the spendthrift path I was on, and well before I entered junior high school I owned a fair library of cheap novels. My siblings were building their own libraries too: Marvin was going in for esoteric stuff like Kephart's *Camping and Woodcraft;* Gladys was buying volumes of the adventures of Elsie Dinsmore, the sappiest girl who ever walked, in my opinion, but I read the stuff anyway; and Nelvin was collecting the adventures of the Sugar Creek Gang.

Four novels by Jules Verne were the favorites of my lot and are among the ones I still retain. One is *Twenty Thousand Leagues under the Sea*, which also cost me sixty cents, or exactly twenty thousand strokes of the pump handle. All my purchases of that time were stamped with my name, the letters imprinted with a little hand-held "printing press" that I got from Johnson W. Smith and Company for thirty cents. That's only ten thousand strokes, and a very good buy.

My son has always had access to libraries of books that he has de-voured by the shelf-full, including the best books there are for his age, books that I believe are very good indeed. When he reached the age at which I had acquired it, I put *Twenty Thousand Leagues under the Sea* into his hands. He read it with some effort and pro-nounced it a lousy book, which he finished reading only out of courtesy. Warming to his subject, he said it rivaled even the all-time worst novel, Johann Wyss's *Swiss Family Robinson*. Although not minded to break a lance for the Robinson family, I did tell him that Jules Verne had written two obscure sequels to that famous book, namely, *Castaways of the Flag* and *Their Island Home*, which were among my favorite early purchases, books wherein the Robin-sons' adventures were, I suggested, somewhat less fatuous. He said he'd take my word for it but, thanks, not my books.

So we didn't have the windmill I thought the farm needed. We had the pump handle instead, and working it probably helped to give us the discipline to appreciate the books that it produced along with the water. The books I pumped up happened to be nineteenth-century classics, translated from their original German (Wyss) and French (Verne) and widely circulated in this country a hundred years ago. Unwittingly, I was drawing from traditional streams. Realizing that now, and aware of my son's reaction, I have resisted the impulse to reread them.

And my son has not read Verne's *Mysterious Island.* Nor has he pumped up rivers of water for horses and cows year after year, nor has he seen the tempting crystals of hoarfrost on a familiar pump handle on a frigid winter morning. Part of his experience he has caught and kept in vessels very different from mine, and he has not had the advantages of certain deprivations. It's my fancy, or literary conceit, that there are mythic streams of human consciousness that you can best tap into if you know the special feel of blisters earned from a farm pump handle. Be that right or wrong, it is a fact that our literary culture, from the Bible to Robert Frost and T. S. Eliot, is alive with springs of water as symbols of life and spirit.

So, we continue drawing from old wells. We keep the experience of certain privileged books, like sounds of sighing windmills turning, safely stored in memory. We linger to savor the luminous hoarfrost that wraps the brittle morning farm with meaning, like memory of mist frozen, and keep watching the night sky for blazing rocks, aware, reluctantly, that there are more rocks up there than balloons. We still rely on unseen angels to keep us from the edge. It's a mysterious island, this earth, this life.

18

Boys' Best Friends

His name was Tag. Built and colored something like a very small golden retriever, he had an ancestry far richer than that. Tag was not really a cow dog, for my father had youngsters to send after cows and, anyway, our cows knew enough to come at our call. Not much of a hunting dog, either. Tag was just a lowly farm dog, a friendly family mutt, carrying out the high destiny of dogs: bridging the gap between the human and animal worlds, affirming the kinship of all living things.

Tag had a smart dog's flair for squeezing heroics out of fairly slim materials. On one occasion he taught us that there were certain advantages to the design of our swimsuits, which were worn-out and cut-off denim overalls complete with bib and suspenders. The suspenders were the saving grace. The canonical family version of this episode is that I was splashing about in the pond, slipped off a log, and was promptly in the water far over my gills—a child of six or seven with no known talents for water sports. Seeing a careless child in trouble, Tag dashed into the water, grabbed the left suspender of my swimsuit, and began yanking me shoreward. That more or less pulled me to the surface again and we struggled there together, dog and child, until more help arrived in the form of a father's strong right arm.

Such a tale drips with sentimentality, of course, and as a family we made the most of it. Tag the kid retriever had turned in a performance that we retold and embellished for relatives and neighbors for the rest of the summer, and though scruples forbade us to claim flat out that Tag alone had saved my life—too simple—we were unanimous that that had been his intention. Clearly he was the kind of animal that took pity on dumb humans, especially children, and from this little drama derived the family legend that Tag kept a particular eye out for my welfare. That notion seemed confirmed by the subsequent cherry incident, which suggested that Tag wished to save me not only from my follies but also from my iniquities.

The day after our annual cherry-picking trip to Manton, a large dishpan heaped full of red cherries sat on the workbench in the summer kitchen. I couldn't go in or out without passing the cherries. They were for canning and hence forbidden—that much was supposed to be understood. But some things it is inconvenient to understand. To my young eyes at that moment nothing was more irresistibly appetizing than that enormous heap of cherries. The dishpan loomed big as a tub, and I supposed that it contained millions of cherries—whatever a million was. Nobody would miss a few. I made several ostentatiously casual passes by the red mountain of cherries, assessed the available routes, then snatched a large handful and disappeared out the door as calmly as is compatible with a full gallop.

I should have remembered: my parents had eyes in the backs of their heads. An irate mother was instantly in hot pursuit. "Ronny, stop!" Nothing doing. I jumped off the porch, made a sharp right turn past the rain barrel, and headed for the tall grass behind the house, hoping to lose my pursuer in the underbrush. Came another command to stop, which I was afraid to heed and afraid to disobey. Nothing to do but get out of earshot as rapidly as possible.

Alerted by the sound of my mother's commands and the tone of her voice, Tag instantly knew that she was treating me as an adversary; and he knew which side he was on. He plunged into the scene with a loud yelp, and, just as my mother caught me by the suspenders, Tag caught her by the apron strings and yanked her backward for all he was worth. His vigor and strength, his evident intention to save me from her clutches, plus her own amazement, stopped my mother dead in her tracks. The intervention had thrown her off balance and off guard; she was flabbergasted, then intrigued, then—oh blessed assurance!—she was pleased. I saw her resolve dissolve. I negotiated a quick amnesty, and we both fell to congratulating Tag. Good old Tag!

There were innumerable such tender spots amid the humdrum of those days. They were outnumbered, although not overshadowed, by common events that necessarily involved a good bit of callousness and unfeelingness all around, for farm life in the late thirties, with four growing children, had little room for sentimentality. Perhaps we savored stories of Tag's heroics partly because we had need of them. But none of Tag's gallantry did him any good when he got into trouble and needed a defender himself. Tag was accused by a neighbor of being one of the two dogs that had been seen harassing and killing sheep. The county sheriff came with the accusing neighbor lady and, while children hovered at a distance exchanging rumors about what was going on, adults gathered ominously around Tag.

In later years it was my mother's firm avowal that Tag had been charged and tried on very flimsy evidence. My father's way was to keep his own counsel on such complex matters; neither then nor later did he ever disclose his view of the case. Nevertheless, the outcome far surpassed anything we children had imagined. I don't know if Tag was found guilty or if this was a case of prior restraint or of placating the neighbors; but I know that he was sentenced to death. In fact, I learned that that had been the verdict only after it had been carried out—by my father, in the water hole. Tag was sent the ignominious way of surplus kittens. How else? My father had mastered, and performed without flinching, just one method of putting an end to a farm animal's life. Other ways—poison, carbon monoxide, or a bullet—I do not think he could have brought himself to employ.

Events of this kind we were expected to accept in the way we were to accept the weather, without murmur or complaint. The concession our parents made to our feelings, and to simplification, was to tell us that Tag was gone rather than that he was going. So they were matter-of-fact about letting us fashion our individual resolutions, or none at all; we would gravitate toward the analysis we could handle and savor bittersweet regrets in later years.

Who can say if Tag, a fond pet by day, actually turned killer by night? Even if it were true and I knew it, I wouldn't believe it.

Animals are replaceable—that was our father's stoical philosophy. Soon after we lost Tag a new pup joined our family, a hound, beagle predominating, and he was destined to spend many years as my father's faithful hunting companion. My uncle Henry gave him to us and we immediately assembled a family council at the supper table to decide his name. We settled on Sport, which pleased everybody until we discovered that he had already been named Rover before we got him. That confused us, but it appeared that we would have to bend before the facts. Who had ever heard of a name being changed? I, for one, assumed that such a thing was quite impossible to do; you might as well try to call a dog a cat as change its name. Could *my* name be changed? Clearly not, for who then would I be? Those speculations seemed to be verified, for one of us held out for the name Sport for about a week or so, but it didn't work; it wasn't the real name and it just wouldn't take. Rover he was, Rover he stayed.

Like Tag before him, Rover lived on table scraps, a wholesome diet I have since concluded, but I didn't think so at the time. During hunting season there were other treats: Rover got the parts of the rabbits that we didn't keep—feet, head, whatever he wanted of entrails, and eventually the leftover bones. Our dogs were splendid symbols of farm efficiency: they came free, never saw a veterinarian, and recycled leftovers for a living. A dog cost nothing. Companionship and hunting were a bonus. Everybody was poor, but nobody on a farm was too poor to have a dog.

Still, Rover did not have a completely happy life with us. Because of the allegations against Tag, my father decided to keep Rover tied most of the time, and I think that made him sometimes morose and ill-tempered. How he howled out his bitter complaints when we went to the fields without him! His unhappiness with his chain distressed us children and sometimes we begged to have him freed, and sometimes he was. During the hunting seasons he was free a good deal. I wonder why no one in our community (to my knowledge) kept a dog in its own fenced yard, which would have posed no great difficulty. Keeping the dog in the house was never considered, any more than keeping a goat in the house; by my father's lights a dog was a barn animal. Since Rover was tied at the barn, we did not have his company much of the time and so we tended to think of him primarily as a service dog, whose main service was hunting rabbits. To be sure, this was a wholly honorable and honored life, and I believe my father appreciated Rover completely and without qualms. He was a valued part of the farm economy.

But Rover got old young. I was an early teenager when we began thinking about a hunting disciple and eventual successor for him. The Harringtons were neighbors of ours and one day I was at their barn admiring their litter of beagle pups. Suddenly, they offered to *give* me the one of my choice. Just like that! I was completely astounded. That would be the next best thing to having a baby brother! In fact I *had* a baby brother—Carl was about five then, and wouldn't he enjoy having a puppy to play with! What would my parents say? I raced home to report the offer and to enter a plea for a puppy. Rover was getting old and lazy, I asserted; he needed an apprentice. And the idea that a pup would be great companionship for Carl was an argument I applied for all it was worth. In fact, I proposed that we could even own the pup together, Carl and I, and I would teach him how to take care of it. And so on. My ardor was awash with charity and righteousness, and somehow it prevailed. (Had there been some prearrangement that I was not aware of?) Anyway, the next day I was proudly marching down the driveway with a black-and-tan beagle pup in my arms, to a full-family reception.

A Dog Named Chips was the title of a book by Albert Payson Terhune that I had just read. So I named my dog Chips. We had an agreement that Chips would not be tied, except in extremity. We were to train him to stay home, and somehow we did.

Chips and I began our rabbit-hunting careers together. Before that, Chips had devised his own rabbit-tracking apprenticeship, employing as his agents some of my escaped domestic rabbits. Let's say that I was experimenting with the hypothesis that raising rabbits at large, so to speak, might be easier than trying to keep them enclosed. In fact, it was actually the rabbits themselves who had proposed the idea by initiating the experiment. These erstwhile pets had multiplied that summer in the barnyard and orchard, and they and their offspring took to the fields at high speed whenever the new pup showed more than a passing interest in them. They had been skittish before, but after Chips had been in training for a few weeks they were as agile as jackrabbits and considerably more alert.

Those white rabbits were conspicuous, and at first Chips simply pursued them by sight. His early philosophy was direct and simple: see a rabbit, chase it; rabbit out of sight, rabbit out of mind. Clearly, before he was worthy to trot in Rover's tracks as a hunting hound, he would need to refine his technique. Old Rover used to cast a withering eye on this juvenile fooling around with the white rabbits. In the first place, pursuing domestic rabbits had always been against the rules, so far as *he* knew. You might as well shoot chickens and call it bird hunting. But in any case, what did that crazy young pup think he had a *nose* for? While *we* were amused by Chips's antics, Rover was not impressed with the younger generation.

Well, the young pup simply thought he could run down a rabbit if he could only keep his eyes on it. Trouble was, when he got his eyes on it the rabbit made for one of the crop fields. As the summer progressed, potatoes and corn and beans got bigger and even the rabbits of dullest wit soon learned that they could just hop over a few rows and hunker down, out of sight of that silly pup. So the young dog had to learn some new tricks.

The challenge was to spy the rabbits in the bean field. When Chips lost sight of one fleeing rabbit and didn't have another in view, he leapt high into the air above the beans and jerked his head in a quick semicircle, his big beagle ears flopping while he scanned the field to spot a rabbit. He repeated the searching leaps until he glimpsed his quarry, and then, with yelps of triumph, charged off in the new direction. From the house we'd hear the high-pitched bark—Chips's effort at baying—and glance toward the fields. Sure enough, there was the flop-eared pup racing wildly across the hillside, popping into the air every few seconds as if riding a pogo stick, and rabbits were fleeing to the four corners of the field. By the time Chips had perfected his techniques among the beans and potatoes, the rabbits had learned how to slip off to the corn-field, where the foliage was taller and where Chips was duly compelled to leap ever higher and higher. "Doesn't look like he's got much of a future as a tracking dog," said Dad one day, watching the jumping-jack show. "Guess he's got some kangaroo in his blood."

Chips was in a contest he could not win. It was mid-July and the day was near when he could no longer do the high jumps that would raise his eyes above the growing corn. Hearing Chips's bark from the fields, old Rover would always snap to attention and stare at the weird spectacle: a pop-eyed and flop-eared beagle doing the high hurdles somewhere off in the cornfields and baying for re-inforcements. Rover was not about to answer the call. He glanced up at us, blinked, and turned away in disgust, as if to apologize for the whole race of beagles. Then he lay down and yawned, thus af-firming that for the time being the conduct of young pups appeared beyond rational control. Surely, he thought, this younger genera-tion is going to the—well, I don't know what he thought, but it was no compliment to Chips.

Rover hung back until the time was ripe. Eventually the corn grew far too tall, and all the crops and hay and grass grew too tall. There were still white rabbits around but Chips just couldn't *see* them anymore; he knew they were there but he didn't comprehend how he knew. He'd trot down the lane with his nose in the air, and I could tell that he was thinking rabbity thoughts, but he didn't know why and didn't know what to do about it. That's when Rover gently moved in to offer the young dog a serious lesson in how to keep his nose to the ground, how to find a fresh scent and stick with it, how to circle when he lost it and pick it up again. When autumn came we all went to the woods to try the real thing, and Rover gladly took command. To my delight Chips was quick to learn the new techniques, realizing that his nose was superior to his eyes and to the see-'em-chase-'em philosophy of his puppyhood. I think it began to dawn on him that the hard-nosed and cynical old pro Rover knew a thing or two about life and the pursuit of rabbits after all. And by following his lead, Chips was soon on the path to a career as a superb tracking dog.

❧ 19 ❧

Handwork: The Prose and Poetry of It

Cursed is the ground. . . . thorns also and thistles shall it bring forth. . . .
In the sweat of thy face shalt thou eat bread. . . .
—GENESIS 3 : 17–19

My wishes raced through the house high hay. . . . /
Nothing I cared, in my lamb white days. . . .
—DYLAN THOMAS, "FERN HILL"

To race on bare feet through the stubble of the hayfield was a summertime test of our courage and also of the toughness of the calluses on the soles of our feet. As we grew older the calluses moved to our hands. Tool handles did that for us, those of hoes and pitchforks especially, but also bean planters, potato planters, crate slats. We earned blisters and calluses from beet knives, corn knives, pump handles, shovels, cows' teats, hammer handles. We even got them from handling the horses' reins.

But above all competitors the humble hoe handle, inspired by the awesome virility of quack grass, ranked as the most prosaic and

effective callus producer of our time. We could forget the calluses
on our feet by the time they appeared on our hands, for when we
started hoeing seriously, the barefoot lamb white days of childhood
were fleeing and youth was under way. Summertime now seems to
me to have been inseparable from hoeing, the job never completed. We first sharpened our hoes in early June for the sugar
beets, which had been planted by machine in continuous rows and
had to be blocked and thinned by hand after they were up a few
inches. Blocking: with a hoe we reduced the row of plants to
clumps spaced about a foot apart. Thinning: on hands and knees
we crept along the row and reduced each clump to just one plant.
Six acres of sugar beets could "keep the kids out of mischief" (my
father's favorite euphemism for work) during the first two weeks of
June, and if we completed our own crop in time we found work in
neighbors' fields at fifteen cents an hour. By then it was time to
face the quack grass flourishing in the cornfield.

In our standard crop rotation a field of newly broken sod was usually planted to corn since, better than most row crops, it could
stand up to the competition of quack grass, which had been lying
low in the meadow for several years, quietly extending its roots,
ready to pounce and spread the minute the plow turned over the
sod. Our theology left no doubt: the curse that had spread from
fallen Eden included quack grass; and we had no illusions about
totally defeating it in one year with the cultivator and hoe, artil-
lery far too feeble. Dad's ambition was modest: "We'll just give the
corn a head start; eventually it will put out shade and stunt the
grass." As much as anything, quack-grass control was the inspiration behind our crop-rotation system. Maybe half of it would be
killed the first year in the corn crop, much of the remainder in the
next year's potato crop, and most of the rest in the third year's bean
crop. In the fourth year the field was sown to oats for harvesting,
and simultaneously to clover and broom grass for a hay crop the
following years. Then the process started over again with the quack
grass sneaking back into the hayfield.

Since hoeing was always available and forever necessary, it gave the farmer some choices in assigning work to the younger generation. At any time, he could reach for the hoe and lead his sons to the field or send them there. A farm boy's life was always under siege. Typically a "heavy hoeing-fatigue syndrome" set in before we had finished with the beans, and summer after summer we were inoculated against too severe an outbreak by the renewal of a family pact. The deal was simple: when the beans were hoed we would go cherry picking. That involved a trip of twenty-five miles to the cherry orchards of Manton, a major family outing and one of the principal social events of the summer, a brief reversion to "the lamb white days." Looking back, I suspect benign manipulation. For in fact we went cherry picking precisely when the Montmorency cherries were ripe, and I can't now rediscover the rigid causal link between completed hoeing and cherry picking that we once saw so clearly. There probably was a little confusion there, sown by our parents and nurtured by our ardor. But at least it *seemed* that every dead weed in the bean field brought us nearer to bowls of cherries.

Although hoeing was the most conspicuous and banal of the jobs of summertime, it was neither the best nor the worst of them. Sometimes we amused ourselves with the question of "the best and worst," relieving the tedium of the time in the field by working out a scale of likings and loathings for various farm jobs. From much experience we formed some settled ideas about farm work and its ability to charm or repel us, and I don't know that any research more expert than ours has ever been brought to bear on the subject. Here are a random dozen field jobs properly scaled according to their agreeableness, all handwork tasks, the order going from the detestable to the tolerable. Spreading manure is at the very bottom of the list, and things go up from there: pulling beans, shocking corn, planting potatoes, picking potatoes, hoeing weeds, shocking wheat, husking corn, shocking oats, planting beans or corn, topping sugar beets, piling wood. Those are standard jobs of that era, structured by the rhythm of the seasons. Omitted from the list are daily chores and such other necessities as tapping maple trees, looking for fox dens, watching bobolinks, building stick shacks in the woods, and listening to the patter of rain on the steel roof of the barn.

"Dad, which would you rather do, hoe or husk corn?"

"That all depends, I guess."

We youngsters were absolutists. On the evidence, Dad was a relativist. Whereas we easily assembled prejudices, excuses, and insights into our scale of working disvalues, Dad seemed to have no such simple scale at all. He met each required task not with judgment and passion but with poise and acceptance. How indeed, I wondered, could he *not* passionately *hate* hoeing this stupid quack grass? (Youth has a gift for the keenness of its dislikes!) He didn't really seem to hate it; he just did it. Such equanimity was puzzling and sometimes exasperating, as when he evidently preferred going to the back forty with a hoe to going to the Clam River with a fishing pole. He even admitted that! We hid our faces from the shame of it.

Well, he had a scale all right, and it often coincided with ours, but it also had deeper roots that came more slowly into view. Today I think I can see his remarkable composure in a broader light.

If it was quite clear to me that picking stones was a pretty nasty job—putting kinks in our backs, dust in our eyes, blisters on our fingertips—then it was equally obvious to me that hauling sap from the woods, though much harder work, was really great sport. The difference, not fully evident to me at the time, was that the maple syrup operation was my own enterprise, with all the associated dignity that implied. Hauling stones did nothing for my self-respect; hauling sap did. Exertion was not the issue. Exertions do count in other ways: there are the real pleasures of certain physical efforts, even very exhausting ones. Planting corn or beans with a hand planter demands some effort, but more in the way of skill, rhythm, and constancy. There is a pleasure in the martial cadence of the work—clickety-click, clickety-click, clickety-click—a long, tiring, and satisfying march to the end of a good day.

In time we learned that the satisfaction of hard work is often intimately linked with the products of that work. We could see and admire the neat crates of potatoes, and that itself made potato picking more satisfying; and it's precisely what put a strike against hoeing weeds—we couldn't *see* the difference in the bean field after we were done. Undoubtedly, hard work caters to a latent aesthetic of farm life: a compact woodpile, a bushel of potatoes, a basket of apples, a stack of wheat, a load of hay, a raggedly handsome corn shock. In their comeliness and order, and in the labor they have exacted, those things speak to us of very basic matters—of providership and decorum and of tasks well done—and they may even stimulate the poet or artisan within us. "Every man admires his woodpile," said Thoreau.

Spreading manure is another story entirely. According to a widespread opinion, never successfully challenged, it is an unsavory job of no redeeming social value and no aesthetic value, either. No lyric poets have lifted their voices in praise of spreading manure. It's well known that there is no way to do the job neatly or so that the task is pleasant or so that the results are pleasing or worth contemplating. The standard indictment of spreading manure is that while it's good for the soil, it's bad for the soul and it's bad for the back.

So there is no charm or poetry in the manure pile. Only necessity, fertilizer, and ecology. On our farm we did not have a mechanical manure spreader, so there was a lot of fork work for us, and, looking back, I am awed by the amount of heavy labor involved. All the manure from seven or eight cows, two horses, some calves and pigs, and a few hundred chickens was handled three times by fork before it was mercifully plowed under. Wrestling with manure was mainly a winter pleasure. Very little accumulated during the summer, since the animals were usually outside, thoughtfully spreading their own.

We had two different ways to dispose of our manure. In the first scenario we'd fork it into a wheelbarrow and ease it out the door toward the manure pile, trailing juice all the way. A string of planks formed a runway up the pile, and we'd head full speed for the center of the runway, hoping to get to the top of the pile—failing which, the wheelbarrow might roll back and flatten its driver. Or we might run off the runway with the wheelbarrow, lose control, and get yanked headlong into the soft pile. (Variations on these themes are well known to farmers but not to the agrarian literary traditions.) At any rate, come spring we would dig the manure out of the pile, fork it onto the wagon, carry it to the field and heave it abroad, preferably downwind, and hope for more or less even coverage of the future cornfield.

In the other method we hitched the horses to the dray—a long, heavy sled with wooden runners—parked it in front of the stable door, loaded it up with fresh manure, and then headed over the snow to the field, where we forked the manure off into individual piles spaced about a dozen feet apart. In the spring, when the winter scabs of ice had peeled back to expose the raw face of the landscape, those fields were pimpled with hundreds of little round pustules of manure. Some Saturday when they had thawed and dried a bit, we would tackle the piles and spread them around. It was a boring task, requiring minimal skills and creating magnificent blisters on hands just fresh out of winter mittens. Nelvin and I did a lot of this together each spring; indeed, I reckon that there were at least twenty-seven manure-spreading springs between the time I was ten and eighteen. A lowly by-product of manure spreading was that it made us welcome the hoeing season.

Persons inexperienced in these rural charms have supposed that the odor of the manure would be the worst part of the exercise. In fact, it is but a minor part, which we easily got used to. It's as if your sense of smell gets callused. One exception was the gas-laden chicken manure that had to be removed periodically from under the roosts in the chicken coop. Hoe in hand, we would poke our head way in under the roosts and scrape out the stuff, sometimes filling our pockets or boots and inhaling great drafts of lung-blistering methane, ammonia, and other gases that were cooking in the manure. No one gets used to that; if he does he is dead.

Nothing in these experiences put a dent in my idea that I would be a farmer. After all, it was fairly easy to factor the nasty tasks out of my vision of my farm of the future.

Far off toward the congenial end of the handwork scale lay things like topping sugar beets by hand. "Nice work," my father used to say of topping beets, a compliment he also extended to cutting wood and shocking grain and to a few other things as well. Most farmers of a generation ago, before machines usurped the task, would have agreed with his assessment of beet topping. It had nothing to do with appearances: a sugar beet, even nicely topped, is nothing to admire. A wagonload of them is better but still not prizeworthy. True, for looks, a load of beets beats a wagonload of manure, but not by a whole lot, and it loses to a stack of wheat by a long shot. No, the pleasure is not like that of piling wood, in the profile of the product or in the sentiments attached to it; it's in the physical work itself and in the productivity of it.

Before the beets could be topped and tossed into the wagon, which was the agreeable part, they had to be extracted from the soil. First, Dad or Marvin loosened them with a horse-drawn beet lifter, a contraption somewhat like a very narrow plow. The thing had a long knifelike runner that ran deep under the beets to break their grip on the soil and lift them about six inches. A sugar beet can be as big as your head and can weigh up to five pounds, but when first yanked out by its green locks, slabs of dirt clinging to its face, the thing might weigh ten. We would lift them up by their lush tops, one in each hand, pound them together to knock off the soil, and pile them into long windrows in preparation for topping. Between each pair of windrows the horses drew the wagon, and we hacked off the tops of the beets with a beet knife and tossed them into the wagon box.

A beet knife is a rigid steel machete-like weapon, and from the end of its blade protrudes a curved prong the size of a finger and sharply pointed. The beet topper stabs the beet with the prong to lift it, then grabs and holds the beet in the other hand. With one swift swing he decapitates it, or scalps it, depending upon the preferred imagery of slaughter, letting the juicy tops fall into a neat row, to be forked up later and salvaged as forage for the cattle. Moving smoothly, the harvester flips the beet into the wagon with his left hand while he stabs the next beet with his right. Once we younger beet toppers had mastered these basic moves, and had developed the strength and accuracy to hit the beet exactly, we would settle into a comfortable four-step topping rhythm: Stab beet, grab beet, top it, toss it. Stab beet, grab beet, top it, toss it. It's nice work.

Sugar beets were a cash crop for us but we seldom had more than six acres, even during the war years when the market was strong. Like most crops they demanded a lot of handwork, and it was a blessing that Indian summer often set the context for it. We topped the beets into the wagon, unloaded them into a field pile by hand with a large scoop fork, and forked them again into a hired truck to take them the five miles to McBain, where they were again forked by hand into the boxcar by which they were sent to the refinery in Mount Pleasant, where they were turned into sugar. Although we supplied the raw materials, our sugar was still severely rationed by the war effort.

We were topping beets in the field in front of the woods one bright fall day and were almost enjoying our work.

"Dad, how do they make sugar from sugar beets? I mean, just what do they do to them exactly?"

Dad flipped a four-pound beet into the wagon, looked up, and sent a stream of tobacco juice splattering against the steel tire of the wagon wheel. He slid his engineer's cap to the back of his head and scratched his hair. "Well," he said. Then he turned to the horses. "Geddap," he said, without picking up the lines. Obviously, he was thinking this one over pretty carefully. "Whoa," he said, and the horses stopped at precisely the right place.

"Couldn't we do it?"

"Well, I can't just say," said Dad slowly. Somebody had planted a little seed and, somewhat uncharacteristically, Dad was caught off guard and let it grow. Such a simple and seductive idea: Why not make sugar, or at least something sweet, from our own sugar beets? We raised them by the ton, so why not process a few pounds to ease our sugar shortage? Why didn't we think of that before?

The idea would not go away. Like the strange cat with mange that came to our door that fall, and that we chased away repeatedly on the grounds that we had cats enough, the subversive idea was not to be gotten rid of just because it was outlandish. We finally accepted the cat, fed it, and within a week it died a natural death— just wanted a friendly place to die, we supposed. We accepted the idea, too; it also died.

Did anyone else make sugar from beets? Did we know how to do it? Of course not. But then nobody else made maple syrup, either. Maybe the answer was in a book somewhere, but we had never heard of such a book. We were on our own. We would figure the thing out. "Might as well try it once," said Dad.

We tried it once. We took two large, shapely sugar beets and peeled them and sliced them, then we chopped them and boiled them—and tasted them. Not ready yet, we said bravely. We mashed them and whipped them and cooked them some more. Not yet, we said; but we hadn't expected it to be easy. Then we dried them and fried them. And tried them. Needs more processing, we said. We were growing pessimistic but we were not to be easily defeated. Into the beet mush we tossed, by turns, water, milk, starch, salt, and either vanilla or tapioca. No sugar yet. Must be complicated, we said. We processed the beets in every other way our unrefined culinary imagination could devise, short of baking them into a pie—at which casual suggestion Mother balked. We had to admit it: the results had been getting steadily worse from the raw-beet stage, each step more disastrous than the one before. By now we had a sodden mass of sticky goop of varying unpleasant consistencies and colors and odors and, most memorably, no matter at what stage, of a taste so exquisitely dreadful and sickening that for weeks afterward we all tended to get a spasm in the stomach whenever we looked a sugar beet full in the face. Total failure. We could grow them but we couldn't eat them; and we could no more squeeze sugar out of a beet than blood out of a turnip. We buried the beet goop behind the toilet, next to the cat.

"Whose bright idea was that?" Dad asked at a cheerful family debriefing session after the burial. Nobody owned up. Instead, we firmly resolved to help the war effort thereafter by shipping all beets, every last one, from the farm to the refinery. There, it appeared, they knew something we didn't know, and the rumor in our community was that they weren't telling lest the Germans find out. The Germans?

Dad was usually pleased to conclude an episode with a wisecrack.

"If we could get a recipe for our sugar-beet goop to the Germans," he said, "and get them to eat it, why, we could probably win the war in a month without firing another shot."

In July the grain ripened. Wheat and oats were the principal grains in our region, and we harvested them, together with lesser amounts of barley and rye, with a McCormick binder. Such a binder, horse-drawn, often with a team of three, made a good country spectacle and generated a wonderfully complicated racket. So many things going on at once—cutting and bundling and binding and tying; so many wheels and pulleys aclatter; so many cogs meshing and gears grinding and armatures and pitmans and sprockets squeaking. Like the conductor of a portable band, the driver-operator sat atop this moving heap of clanging, clattering machinery as it waded into the waves of grain. I never actually operated a binder, but I often walked behind one, applauding as the bundles were tied and then kicked out to accumulate in rows across the field, ready to be picked up and assembled into grain shocks.

A *sheaf* of grain and a *bundle* of grain are one and the same, although sheaves are in books and bundles are in fields. Bundles are prosaic, made and tied by machines. *Sheaf* is a much older word, probably Saxon, and an older concept too, redolent of the poetry of the countryside, the rural harvest traditions of story and song, of pipes and dances.

A shock of grain is a collection of bundles arranged to keep the heads of grain off the ground and to give the stalks a chance to dry prior to threshing. Shocking oats was sometimes a pleasant job, primarily because the results were always striking and handsome. After an afternoon's work of shocking grain, the whole landscape took on sharply new and graphic contours: rows of neat and stately structures appeared in what had been just a forest of growing stalks. Farmers of that day did not merely harvest the crops, they created entire country scenes.

Today it's easier to teach the skill of shocking grain than to find the raw material. The instructions are simple: (1) Take two oats bundles, one under each arm, and park them among the stubble, butts down, about twenty inches apart, leaning the heads together; do the same with another pair of bundles, placing them adjacent and parallel to the first two, just touching them; do it a third time. That is the basic six-bundle A-frame. (2) Support the six bundles with one at each end; then add two on each side, and finally one more in the center of each side. (3) Tuck the heads gently in so that they all nuzzle together. That's it. Three minutes, start to finish—the standard Michigan fourteen-bundle shock of oats, ready for inspection and admiration, ready for wind and rain and hot summer sun. For how many centuries, or dozens of centuries, was this design used? Nobody knows. Within a couple of hours a pair of shockers could erect scores of them, like city blocks of new houses, up one hillside and down the other. We treated different grains in different ways. The twenty-one-bundle wheat shock, for example, was an elaboration of the basic oats design, with additional corner supports and a three-bundle thatched roof that actually kept out the rain.

Shocks of grain, row upon row, millions upon millions of them, were once the dominant landmarks on the late-summer farmscapes of America—the expressiveness of the fertile land lavished in eloquent harvest symbols. Since World War II, the combine (which cuts and threshes the unbound grain in one combined operation) has systematically driven the McCormick binder and its neatly tied bundles out of the fields, and all the grain shocks have now moved off to the land of the passenger pigeon and the dodo bird.

Good riddance, say some. Bring on the combines. They are those who have to make their living by the grain they grow and by the sweat of their brow.

Consider wheat. We seldom saw it through the poet's rose-tinted glasses, though we did see that the waves of grain were indeed *amber* waves. But that meant simply that the wheat was ripe, dry, stiff, and scratchy to handle. To avoid mildew in the tight bundles, we could harvest grain only on dry, sunny days, when the stalks were brittle and the beards on the wheat heads were prickly. On such a day the weather was usually hot, but we had to wear long sleeves to protect our arms when we did the shocking, and they didn't fully protect them. Within a few hours our wrists were blistered and our arms were scratched from wrist to armpit, and all afternoon sweat seeped into our scratches, pouring salt into wounds. Frequently, there were thistles in the wheat, and somehow the McCormick binder seemed to know that and maliciously tied the bundles with the thistles on the outside, precisely where we grabbed them.

"Thorns also and thistles," says the Bible, and "in the sweat of thy face. . . ." So we were sometimes grateful for hands covered with calluses from hoes and forks and horses' reins.

Now and again the binder twine on the bundle would break, scattering the stalks. Regathering them, my father would kneel amid the prickly stubble to retie the broken bundle while one of us twisted for him a makeshift thong from a fistful of stalks. We would bend over the grain and sweat would pour into our eyes, blurring our vision to misty vagueness. In the few minutes required to bind the stalks, we may have drifted back into the mists of history, hundreds or maybe thousands of years, back to the time when bundles were sheaves. Only that thin strand of now-broken binder twine (made by a modern machine, used and also broken by the machine) had separated us, modern harvesters, from the identical labors of the most ancient reapers. Rising triumphantly, we would admire what we had wrought; with our own hands we had fashioned a genuine *sheaf* of grain.

20

Working with Horses: Hay and Harrow

Driving a team of horses is a basic, gentle pleasure, especially flattering to a farm boy's self-image. Draft horses are large and mighty creatures, clumsy, usually patient, without much personality, and fairly easy to control if they don't get any surprises. Surprised horses sometimes create memorable experiences. One of the most emphatic lessons my father taught his sons was this: Never get within kicking range of a horse without speaking to it; let the horse know you are there. And none of us ever got kicked by a startled horse. Operating some implements, such as binders and plows, required certain advanced skills and cautions, but handling the team was the easy part. The horses knew what job they were doing, they knew the way to carry the sleigh, and they picked up quickly on the dull fact that they should follow the furrows, the rows, the ruts, walk slowly, turn around at the end, stand, or whatever.

For my brothers and me the first real job with horses—at about age ten—was "driving in front of the loader." This early exercise of horsemanship is vital nourishment to a farm boy's hungry ego. He rides out to the field on the hay wagon with two men, leaning as they do on a pitchfork to steady himself as the horses amble down the lane to the back forty. He is now an intimate part of the working realities of farming and he suddenly realizes—gazing appreciatively at his shadow as it whips over the grass and past the fence posts—what a striking figure he cuts, standing there on the wagon, fork in hand, stalwart as a man among men.

The hay has been cut, wilted for a day, then raked into windrows so that it is bunched sufficiently for the hay loader to pick it up automatically. We hitch the hay loader to the rear of the wagon, and the horses amble slowly down the windrow of hay, one on either side, the wagon straddling the hay, which is picked up by the loader and rolled onto the wagon. The horses have the bit in their teeth and they know exactly what is expected of them. Young and spirited horses will sense that the boy's tug on the reins and the voice at the end of them lack authority, and that sometimes prompts them to ignore the driver; they might simply turn and head for the barn. Veteran horses are more predictable, merely stopping now and then to munch hay and to see if anybody is paying attention.

The loader sweeps up the hay in a long unbroken roll and dumps it gently on the back of the wagon, where two men, movements synchronized, begin to build the load. Up front our boy-man drives the horses. That is to say, he holds the lines (*reins* was a book word, *lines* was a farm word), giving it his full attention; and as the load mounts he climbs aloft on the ladder attached to the wagon's front. The higher the load the higher the honor. At last the driver-hero is nestled against the topmost rung of the ladder, a ton of hay beneath him, hay piled high around him, wisps of hay poking him in the neck. The views from this elevation are exciting: down there are the raspberry bushes, the stone piles, the long fencerows, and there beneath him too are the broad, sweating backs of the horses, still obedient to his every command. Through the lines he can telegraph wordless instructions down to them: a sharp tug ("Whoa!") or a gentle flipping ("Geddup!"); or he can turn the whole vast procession, horses and wagon and loader (sharp "Gee"), to begin a new windrow. A man's world.

The load completed, he relinquishes the lines at last to one of the other men for the triumphant trip back to the barn. Past the apple orchard and into the lane they go, gliding, riding at treetop level on a gentle cushion of twelve feet of packed hay. Would that someone nearby had a camera!

Even before Nelvin and I were old enough to drive the team, we sometimes hitched a ride home to the barn on the hay load. We got permission to climb the tall ladder, scrambled to the top, and settled into the soft and prickly hay beside Marvin, who had been the driver. One day, Ben Baas, a neighbor with whom we exchanged work during haying season, was to drive home the load, and my father was walking. Just as we started out, one of the horses' lines got caught under the front of the wagon tongue. (The tongue is a long tapered pole connected to the front axle so as to command the steering of the wagon; about five inches in diameter, it runs between the horses and is fastened and upheld at the horses' chest.)

The tangled line was a minor detail, but we had to correct it before proceeding, and Ben climbed down the wagon ladder at the front of the load. Instead of going to the ground and walking around, he stepped out on the tongue between the horses to reach for the tangled line. That's the kind of shortcut a farmer might take with his own team, not often with someone else's. These were our horses, not Ben's, and they were startled by this unfamiliar approach and they jumped. When Ben tried to calm them from his precarious position on the tongue, they panicked and broke into a trot. He grabbed the harness hames, and as the horses picked up speed and headed for a hillside, he hung on for his life—literally, for he was standing on the tongue between the runaway horses, and if he had fallen he would have been trampled and run over.

We who were on top of the load had an unexpected ride, very short and swift; for a load of hay is not made for high-speed turns on hillsides, and this one didn't survive it. The hay did not slide off—it flipped off, downhill side, and landed upside down like a pancake. We three boys sailed through the air, crash-landed head-first, and were simultaneously buried under a ton of hay. Nelvin and I were stunned and helplessly pinned down, faces buried in the stubble. I remember being unable to move at all, then eventually hearing Marvin's voice calling me, very faintly and far away, but being unable to answer. In fact, he was only ten feet away; he had pushed himself clear and was digging and calling for us.

Nearby, Ben was getting the ride of a lifetime astride a narrow wagon tongue between a runaway team cutting hillside capers. Eventually he grabbed one line and turned the horses and their empty wagon in sharp circles until they calmed down. By then, my father was on a dead run from the barn back to the field, and Marvin was digging for his little brothers in the pile of hay. He got a grip on my left hand and dragged me out into the sunlight, spitting chaff and panic; and just as he did so he answered Dad's call by shouting that, yes, we were all right. I bellowed after him that we were *not* all right. Marvin commanded me to pipe down and help to find Nelvin. Then he dived back under the hay and came back tugging a leg, this time with Nelvin attached.

We weren't really hurt much, just bruises and scratches aggravated by hysteria. My mother's therapy for the situation, very successful indeed, was threefold: salve for our sores; sage tea, a favorite beverage, for our stomachs; and then to bed on the sofa with the shades drawn. By suppertime we were in good repair again. The next day we were ready to go back to haying.

A plow is a very simple device—basic, precise, and unimaginably ancient. Although farming is not a graceful business, plowing with horses comes close: no gears, no clatter or clutter, only the throaty murmur of the plowshare and the elegant ripples of the furrows across the scenic fields. Some scents of the countryside are sweeter than a new-made furrow, but the smell of the fresh, moist earth represents elemental things. Farmers have ever found an earthy pleasure in turning over the soil with a plow, found a satisfaction in its quiet precision and calm, such as cannot be found in haying or harrowing, in sowing or reaping. I sensed something of that already when I was a five-year-old fanatic, following in the furrows behind my father's plow, hour after hour.

I have read that in some parishes in England, Plough Monday (first Monday after Epiphany) and a service of Blessing the Plough are still observed, in a tradition harking back to medieval Ploughman's guilds. Even secular farmers who have never heard of it would understand that. The senses and the symbols all agree: the first plowman was the first farmer.

Plowing demands considerable strength and skill, and plowing a straight furrow with horses requires quick reflexes, a good eye, and much practice. (What advantage has a straight furrow over a crooked one? Practically speaking, none at all. That is why it is so important.) My father did not teach his sons to plow. He had reasons: there was not a lot of plowing to be done; it was a skill we might not need later in life; he knew we would botch the job with sloppy, crooked furrows, painful to look at; he enjoyed doing the plowing himself. By the time we were strong enough to handle the plow behind the horses, we were already working for the neighbors, plowing crooked furrows with their tractors—an arrangement that satisfied everybody.

Tractor engines have reduced the melodies of farming to a low common denominator, for they sound essentially the same whatever work they are doing, whereas each horse-drawn farm implement makes its own individual country music, its own sensual claims on memory. The cultipacker clatters and clunks and clangs, its heavy iron packers bumping each other as they roll over and compact the soil lately sown to grain. Whereas the harrow is as silent as a plow, the binder is a big bandwagon of noise, of cutting and whirring, of rattling and churning. But the binder's sounds don't carry far; the much gentler rattle of the horse-drawn mowing machine drifts farther across the fields. A half mile away the mower's sound is a steady rhythmic hum, resolving, as it draws near, into a smooth clatter, almost a purr, the prim sound of efficiency. When sounds of mowers come, can fragrances of new-mown hay be far behind?

In a class by itself for the production of sheer unmitigated country racket is the threshing machine. This monster specializes in sensory overload. Once a year it tramped through our neighborhood, noisily devouring stacks of grain, emitting bags of wheat and oats, and spitting straw into large scenic heaps. Threshing day was always a major event: lots of sound and fury, signifying everything, beloved of children. On that day tractors and horses, wagons and neighbors descended on the farm, all in high spirits. When we were very young, Nelvin and I would scramble up to a precarious high beam in the barn far above the threshing floor and perch there to watch the annual pageant below. Gingerly we slid out along the beam to secure bits of dried sparrow dung to drop down on the threshers, scoring a bull's-eye just in time to gaze innocently in another direction.

When we were older we maneuvered to be assigned to drive a tractor and wagon (not a team and wagon, because a team owner seldom assigned horses to a stranger; tractors were not so fastidious) to haul the loads of grain from the field to the waiting threshing machine. When we were still older, someone younger drove the tractor and we handled a pitchfork with the rest of the crew. For a brief period in the late forties, horses and tractors often worked side by side bringing in grain from the fields on threshing day, but the general commotion associated with threshing was not congenial to horses, and that itself often provoked new installments of the ongoing horse-versus-tractor debate. We had a young cousin who actually preferred driving horses to driving a tractor—a disgrace to his generation.

A cultivator is a simple one-horse implement with plowlike handles and half a dozen shovels to stir the soil and uproot the weeds between the rows of crops. With it you can cultivate corn long after it is too tall to run through with a tractor cultivator; you can also use it when the fields are too wet to bear a tractor's weight. (Score that for the horse; and add that horses never get stuck.) Moreover, a boy can operate a cultivator as soon as he has strength to steer the thing and hold it upright. Perhaps he is only twelve or thirteen years old, but if he can do it at all he can do as much as a man in a day, for the horse determines the pace. Both hands are needed on the handles, however, so the operator loops the lines around his back and has to twist his body left and right to apply pressure on

the horse's bit. It sounds more difficult than it is. If either the boy
or the horse is experienced, cultivating is a simple job and, to my
mind at least, far more satisfying than hoeing.

One day Marvin was cultivating the corn south of the woods,
Dad was cultivating beans in the opposite corner of the farm, and
Nelvin and I, too young for this work, were engaged in a favorite
pastime: building shacks of sticks and leaves in the woods. Decid-
ing to take a break, Marvin parked the cultivator and his horse,
Pearl, at the edge of the field and came to see what we were up to
in the woods. It must have looked all right to him, for very soon all
three of us were deep into the design and construction of a new and
improved leaf-and-stick shack.

Pearl was normally a patient beast, but she became bored with
the delay and decided to strike out for home. Unseen by us she
started down the corn row; the cultivator flipped over; she mowed
corn all the way to the end. For a full quarter of a mile Pearl never
deviated, and thus very neatly and precisely flattened two entire
rows of corn, every blessed hill. She might have reversed course at
that point, as she had been doing all morning, and mowed another
set of rows; but she didn't. She took a right turn, got to the lane,
took a left, and made straight for the stable. Having arrived there,
she had to become resourceful to get in: some stupid contraption
seemed to be dragging behind her, something that just wouldn't fit
through the door. As was her wont, Pearl just backed off and
calmly took a couple of hard lunges until she had wiped off the of-
fending thing, widening the door somewhat in the process. Horses
are not gentle creatures, so she left pieces of her harness there, too.

Meanwhile, back at the shack in the woods, we three were
having a great time. But eventually we decided to lay off architec-
ture and return to farming. Let's see now—where was Pearl again?
All we could find in the cornfield was a very eloquent trail of evidence, leading inexorably to the barn door. At the door, various
bits of harness, doorjamb, and cultivator told us all we needed to
know and much more than we wanted to. Pearl was in her proper

stall munching hay, not a care in the world. Oh, to be a horse! Nelvin and I helped Marvin pick up the pieces, but when Dad came in from his corner of the farm, we quietly absented ourselves from the proceedings.

Plowing is regularly followed by harrowing, which is aimed at breaking up the sod chunks, leveling the field, loosening the soil, and preparing it for planting. Each field is harrowed at least twice before the seed is put in. When the seed was grain, which my father always broadcast by hand because he didn't own a grain drill and liked sowing by hand, then the field was worked a third time to "harrow the seed under." Harrowing does not require much skill. It lacks the precision and definiteness of plowing, and doesn't have the historic symbolism of plowing, either. Harrowing is banal enough so that it's hard to perform badly; and nobody ever devised a service of Blessing the Harrow. Even for horses it is easy work, but I presume horses with dignity are bored by it. The horse-drawn harrow was pretty well standardized centuries ago: it has four steel runners and several dozen spring-steel tines, each two and a half inches wide, which can be adjusted for depth. With this elementary contraption and a team of horses, a young man can, on his very first dash across the field, do the job just about as well as anyone ever will.

However, there is one serious mistake that can be made with a harrow.

When you reverse direction at the edge of the field, you can make too sharp a U-turn, and the results can be spectacular. Many a farm boy has grown to manhood, I'll bet, without knowing exactly what would happen if he were to make that mistake. I am not so innocent. On a normal turnaround the harrow simply slides around on the ground, the outside runner doing a semicircle as it revolves around the inside runner, which pivots in place. How-

ever, the harrow is designed to flex or fold at the center—like a
face-down open book—to accommodate itself to uneven ground;
and if you turn too sharply the harrow rides too heavily on its inside runner, rises and flexes at the center, and drags the outside
runner underneath it. (Push a face-down open book against something: it will rise up, snap closed, and flip over. So will a harrow!)
At this point the harrower must react with lightning speed to keep
the harrow from folding and flipping like a book. As with many
farm jobs, the driver suddenly needs four hands: two to grip the
reins to straighten out the horses, and two to yank the harrow back
into its normal flat position.

The day I lost my innocence I dropped a line while making a
desperate lunge for the tipping harrow. The horses cranked around
in too sharp a turn, and the harrow rode up on its edge, started to
flip, and frightened the horses. At that we all rapidly descended
into a state of churning chaos. Panicked, the horses went into a
brisk circling maneuver, kicking over the traces, snorting, then
jumping, dragging the harrow in bouncing circles—a crazy dervish
dance that scared me witless. Tugging at the one line I still held
and shouting, I tried to keep out of the path of the spinning cy-
clone of horseflesh, field dust, and flying harrow. How would I ever
stop this ghastly dance? No way. I could not stop it.

It just stopped. Precisely at that moment an angel appeared at
my side. He was oddly disguised as a truck driver who had seen a
boy in trouble in a field, stopped, alighted, and strode over. He
calmly helped me untangle horses, harrow, and harness. "The fun-
niest things can happen with horses," he said. That's exactly what
he said! I was staggering from terror and adrenaline overdose, and
he thought this was *funny*? Evidently, angels have a weird perspective on reality. The harrow, having been through some very un-
harrowlike maneuvers, had a, well, funny shape. But what was so
funny about that? Even the horses, Pearl and Barney, were trembling, their great heaving sweating bodies shaking like quaking as-
pen leaves; they did not seem amused to me. It would take me years

to find the funniness. I thanked the obliging stranger, who disappeared into a cloud (dust, I suppose), I rehitched the horses to what had been a harrow, compensating as well as I could for a cracked evener and two broken tugs, and then we crawled together back to the stable. I unharnessed the horses, fed them some hay for consolation, gave a very watered-down report to my mother to pass on to my father when he came home from town with the grain he had gone to get ground, and then slunk off to the orchard to have a private service of Cursing the Harrow. Obviously, I had no future whatever as a farmer, probably not much of a future at all. I had no idea how my father would react to the disaster.

Dad stood on the porch and called me from my retreat. I came slowly to within earshot, dragging my chains.

"There's still time to finish that harrowing if you get right at it." He turned away.

I took a few steps nearer. "Want me to go back out there?"

"Yeah," over the shoulder.

"D'you see the harrow?"

"That it?" he said, pointing.

"Was," I said.

We focused exclusively on the task at hand. With a crowbar, maul, hammer, and plank, we reshaped the harrow, which was made of magnificently unbreakable spring steel; with binder twine and baling wire and a spare strap and some rivets we repaired the harness; we substituted a spare evener for the splintered one; and then he harnessed one horse while I harnessed the other. We were father and son again, farming again, repairing damage. Because no alternative presented itself, harrow and horses and I were soon heading back to the field of anxiety.

For the rest of the day I made very wide turns and, little by little, I slew the nemesis. And chopped it up. And harrowed it under.

❧ 21 ❧

The Long Arm of John Calvin

We were brought up religiously. Therefore our common life was hallowed with an uncommon sense of order and purpose.

My parents believed (in words they never heard) that "There's a divinity that shapes our ends,/Rough-hew them how we will." Our sense of self and world and God was formed by a certain rich interplay between immediate material facts on the one hand and a variety of transcendent symbols on the other. It's as if we moved in two realms.

The immediate order consisted of a small community of mixed farms in a climate of restrained, obedient Protestant piety. Beyond this circle, anything with scale—Cities, Biblical History, Global Wars, Dominions, Powers, Glories, Art, Crime, Foreign Missions, the Future, Catholicism, Wealth, Science, God's Providence—was exotic, sustained in quite another order, known by sign or testimony or impinging upon us like allegory from another realm. The line between the immediate and the transcendent, as between two kinds of reality, was sharply drawn, such as it cannot possibly be drawn today in the age of mass communication; so we engaged the remote, the noble, and the terrible in perfect safety from afar, through the veil of religion and imagination—whereby it all remained decently distant and benign. Our physical life, rough-hewn, rested securely on one side of the line, and our imaginative life thrived on the other, shaped by divinity.

Twice on Sunday we went to church, and each service was at least an hour and a half long, very formal. No one but the minister ever spoke, and nothing unexpected ever happened. The singing was strong, heartfelt, fast; the preaching tended to be bookish, doctrinal, lengthy. All children always attended all services, and it was tedious to sit still through the long prayer and the long sermon that were the main features of the long service. I hope I sometimes had the sense to dislike it. For a time my mother had a Fidget-Control Ruling: "You may turn around three times in church, not more." I usually saved one of those until after the sermon: someone might drop a hymnbook during the last song and it would be unbearable not to be able to turn around and stare. Anyway, religion had a lot to do with obedience.

As small children we had to find remedies for tedium. A useful trick was to watch the big Regulator clock and see how long you could keep a peppermint going in your mouth. I learned to keep one throughout an entire sermon, something like forty-five minutes, by tucking the mint into the southeast corner of my mouth and disciplining my tongue to look the other way no matter how strong the temptation. Self-discipline was also an important part of our religion.

When we really grew weary of sermons, we added and subtracted the posted hymn numbers or leaned back and counted the tin squares in the ceiling. Then we turned to stalking flies—of which there was an ample supply and at which we developed brisk and ample skills—by baiting a sweaty fist with a piece of peppermint and waiting for the wary fly to step into the parlor of our palm. Flies are suspicious creatures, very ceremonial too, and they'll kick up a pompous fuss over that mint. Old Mr. Fly would circle around, run in, back out, bounce, sniff, do headstands, and scratch his wings with his back toenails. That tickled the daylights out of my palm, but I sat there, a grim little pilgrim, suffering patiently and never twitching a muscle, while that stupid fly did his aerobics and devotions before trotting in to munch the mint. I could work up a pretty good passion for smashing a fly like that. I snapped shut my hand! Zap! I'd have to pick up the lost thread of the sermon in the long summary at the end while toting up the body count of flies at my feet. I don't suppose it's likely that I ever had the grace to thank God for the distraction of the flies; but I hope so.

Our church's ties were to the Christian Reformed denomination, whose origins lay in a mid-nineteenth-century separation from the Reformed Church in America. The denomination was young but already chastened by theological controversy, and full of selective and solemn memories harking back through Dutch Calvinism to Reformation Geneva. Dutch, orthodox, serious about education, its internal denominational lines were tightly drawn and carefully nourished, and a sense of Christian community thrived among the four to five hundred churches of the denomination—many separated by thousands of miles—from Paterson to Pasadena. On the other hand, there was little openness in those days toward the immediately surrounding neighborhood. That was the world; we were the church. We thought a lot about foreign missions, less about neighborhood missions.

Wherever the Christian Reformed immigrants settled in clusters, they started churches and later Christian day schools, whether in California, Iowa, Michigan, New Jersey, or one of half a dozen other states. That sharpened the exclusiveness of those communities, and for a hundred years (1850–1950) one could go to any of those very widely separated nuclear clusters of Hollanders and find the same patterns—whether in politics, theology, the mating dance, amusements, hymn sings, family rites, educational ideals, or even the names of people. All the scattered communities of Hollanders had the same historical memories.

Pastors of the Christian Reformed churches had all studied at the same place, Calvin College and Seminary in Grand Rapids, Michigan, founded in the late nineteenth century by Calvinist immigrant pastors—men who acted for exactly the same reasons as those recorded by the Calvinist immigrant pastors who founded Harvard College in 1636: "to advance learning, and perpetuate it to posterity, dreading to leave an illiterate ministry to the churches when our present ministers shall lie in the dust." Christian Reformed pastors without exception had studied Greek and Hebrew and had absorbed a formidable amount of theology. Their sermons were systematic explications of scriptural texts.

So glib and automatic is today's celebration of diversity and individuality that to describe this religious/ethnic culture seems already to be criticizing it. True, it had the liabilities of insularity and ethnic uniformity, and it had a certain tedious theological superiority complex. But it admits of no easy judgment. As a shaper of character and family structures it had extraordinary resources, such as seem conspicuously wanting in the social chaos of today's world.

That culture was predominantly rural, and the aggressive side of the American career-cash-and-success ethic was slow to penetrate it. Barriers held that ethic at bay for generations: a colonial immigrant mentality, Calvinistic otherworldliness, the Dutch language, the Depression. Its own work ethic focused not on virtue and diligence being rewarded but on their being religiously required. Motives for actions counted more than consequences. Duty, responsibility, gratitude, and obedience (and hence shame and guilt) were the vital concepts of that ethic. In that culture's best image of itself, success was a seductive and empty concept, liable to be filled with vain values; therefore, life's enterprise was not to seek that but to find one's vocation, one's calling, the proper avenue for the use of God-given talents. In such a world avarice was probably a less available temptation than spiritual pride.

My generation—those whose grandparents were immigrants and whose parents were bilingual—picked up the last inklings of this colonial Calvinist outlook. Coincidentally, it was almost perfectly suited to the culture of the family farm.

Mealtime at our home was a structured affair, though I suppose it sometimes seemed a chaotic yammer to our parents. Three times a day (twice on school days) we assembled, gave thanks to God, ate a full meal, and concluded with Bible reading and prayer. This was not peculiar to us; it was normal. At about age five each of us got a Bible and in it we followed along as my father read, each of us then reading one verse at the end of the selected portion. Thus we absorbed the Bible; thus we learned to read—more or less—even before school; thus we were guaranteed better acquaintance with the adventures of Abraham, Isaac, and Jacob than with those of Dick, Jane, and Spot. It would be hard to regret that.

Ours to be reared with the diction and cadences of the King James version of the Bible in our ears, its "peradventure," "thou," "verily," "whosoever," and "wherefore," its "cometh" and "goeth" and all the memorable rhythms and poetry of its prose. Elizabethan English contrasted and merged with the salty, slang-laden homespun grammar of the second-language English of most adults; and with an arsenal of Dutch words that never could be translated. "He done everything good," my father might say, and my mother might correct that to "He did everything good," though "He did everything well" seemed favored by teachers, and "Verily, he doeth all things well" by the Bible.

We marched straight through the Bible in our mealtime reading, a chapter at a time: long arid stretches of Leviticus, doleful prophetic lamentations, soaring poetry, psalms of cursing, parables of Jesus, hymns of devotion; also, and unforgettably, the wonderfully labyrinthine genealogies of the Old Testament, the King James universe of the begot and the begat, arrayed in all their elaborately hyphenated and unpronounceably polysyllabic glory. We took it all in, chapter by chapter, week in, week out, year in, year out. We never read any other book in this resolute way; and certainly nothing else that we read had such wonders combined with such obscurities. It was a fair way to learn a lot about what is in the Bible but a poor way to study it; different parts of the Bible require different kinds of approaches, but ours never varied.

Our stance toward the text was invariably reverent, even devotional, including the vast cumbrous portions of the Old Testament; and that made it seem somewhat less inscrutable. Or rather, it didn't bother us a whole lot that we understood so much so dimly. We knew the things of the spirit were otherworldly, that we could catch but a glimmer of their remote majesty. The Bible itself said as much: "My thoughts are not your thoughts, neither are my ways your ways, saith the Lord." *That* we understood. Shouldn't we expect God's word to be unfathomable? We were mystics but we didn't know it.

There was no real problem with understanding the New Testament, which I think we read more than the Old Testament anyway. Except for the last book (Revelation) it is straightforward, and we were never in the slightest doubt about its central message of God's redeeming love for His world, including us. That fact made it possible to assimilate the Old Testament even if we couldn't digest it. Regarded from the New Testament, all the tumult and histrionics in the Old Testament—emitting surpassing poetry and epic narrative along the way—seemed somehow the appropriate sort of social turbulence God might have stirred up among recalcitrant men and women while shifting the pieces of His cosmic drama into place. Of course, it wasn't exactly clear how all the dry stuff from Deuteronomy or Habakkuk fitted in, but evidently it did, or at least had, and we caught glimpses of it here and there. Whatever was mystifying was a sacred mystery still.

Immersion in Scripture was inseparable from our other practices, including regular attendance at church, Sunday school (summer), catechism classes (fall, winter, spring), and later, Christian High School. Discipline of the heart and head seemed to go easily together: in Sunday school we memorized for recitation a verse of a hymn and a verse from the Bible each week; in catechism classes we memorized set answers to set questions of Christian doctrine. The regular Bible reading and prayer at home undoubtedly nurtured certain spiritual habits, a capacity for reverence (and hence irreverence) among them. It aimed to kindle also an inner piety that would allow us to feel at ease bowing in humility and gratitude before the Lord of the Universe.

Ours was a rather muscular Calvinism, emotionally somewhat reticent, perhaps even lacking in warmth; it was not the sweaty fundamentalism one easily associates with groups wherein religion is so prominent. But some of what we in this community of churches did in the name of religion was adverse to the higher sentiments. We often confused mores with morals, as when we imposed a very strict taboo on women smoking. And mores got mistaken for religion: all dancing was regarded as flatly unchristian, movie attendance was forbidden, and card playing (Rook and Flinch usually excepted) disapproved of. A more serious breach, such as pregnancy outside of marriage, required confession to the ruling Consistory of the Church of "sinning against the Seventh Commandment," and the confession was announced to the entire congregation. And so on. Selectively condemning some activities (through an inherited list of "worldly pleasures") and simultaneously overlooking more subtle slippages (lovelessness, exploitation, gluttony, pride, spite, avarice) produced some peculiar stresses. It intensified but didn't focus the vague sense of guilt that always hovered in our background. From such or similar contortions of the spirit Mencken fashioned his famous quip about Puritanism: it is the haunting suspicion that someone somewhere might be happy.

Of course in Calvinism you start out guilty; but it was discouraging to be reminded, or to observe, that you are probably going downhill from there. Historically, Calvinism is the expression of an agonized conscience, said Santayana, and we felt it festering all the way to McBain. Although the theological concept of "orthodoxy" got the larger press and was officially at stage center, the dominant motif of our spiritual climate was something else. It was religious duty, surrounded by its various forms and minions—obedience, fidelity, responsibility, dedication. Almost everything radiated from that intense center.

It may seem a rare notion nowadays that the currents of religious life may be properly channeled not only in terms of prayer and worship, or in the highly personalized and subjective forms of "the Lord's will" so beloved by fundamentalists, but also in more generalized forms of objective religious duties. Yet the *Westminster Shorter Catechism*, a classic seventeenth-century Calvinist document, *begins* there: "What is the chief end of man? Answer: To know God and enjoy him forever." Duty—to enjoy. Whatever else it is, that is not a simplistic notion. Another classic document, the *Heidelberg Catechism*, was closer to our mentality and was one of our denominational creeds. It begins thus: "Question: What is your only comfort in life and death? Answer: That I . . . am not my own, but belong to my faithful Savior, Jesus Christ."

The traditional way to make and keep these thoughts available through the generations was to have youths commit them to memory. However, we who were required to memorize and recite such answers often had little interest in them. Inevitably there were times when the whole doctrinal yarn seemed terribly profound and simplistic, wonderful and hateful all at once. Chief end? Duty? Comfort? We were adolescents, prey to swiftly alternating moods of moroseness and high spirits, caught up in the mystifying tangles of suppressed sexual energy, guilt, idealism, rebellion, religious fervor, laziness. We had enough puritanism bred into us to spoil some fun, but not enough to find comfort in doctrine.

Hymn writers declare that God moves in a mysterious way—a proposition hard to doubt, in view of the evidence. The hope for the next generation was that somehow the imperatives of conscience and Scripture would ripen into religious habits of the heart. And usually it worked out that way. The great background symbols of the faith—Paradise, Fall, Salvation—and the cosmic drama of the Bible, its sweeping allegories of sin and redemption, its quiet intimations of hidden glories to be revealed, somehow those things sank into our souls to stay there. In most cases it wasn't just a matter of appropriating the story in a vacuum; rather, in some mysterious way, it had already usurped our imagination as *the* story at work throughout all history.

On the whole, I believe that rearing children in that particular climate was relatively simple. Simple—not necessarily easy. Parents had a commonly understood and quite precise idea of what they were doing, how they were to do it, and what they were up against. Their theology told them that it was the perversity of human nature that they were up against, and that it was the grace of God and prayers to Him that were their allies; certainly they never supposed that they were merely dealing with an all-absolving abstraction called Society. They had never heard of such a convenient repository of unacknowledged guilt. To them sin was far more real than Society. Every day we asked for divine forgiveness, even on our good days. (Calvinists cover their bets.) Of course, we were exposed to a very, very small range of the world's goods and evils. But certain moral and religious signposts were clearly marked and we knew where we were—even though the next generation had to change some of the signs. Families were intact, divorce was unknown, serious crime was unknown, sin was well known, and youth was held in a network of forms and formulas that seemed as durable as any government. If parents did not overtly indoctrinate on matters of morals and religion, it was because they did not need to: models and guides were before our eyes and didn't have to be always in our ears.

On our eighty acres our own parents avoided the extremes: we were not made victims of virtue (on a farm there are so many and such varied activities that cannot plausibly be disapproved of); nor were we so bullied by indulgence that there were no useful forms of misbehavior left to us. We had room to maneuver, to be creative, even though some prohibitions were a little eccentric. We did not ride our one bike on Sunday: that was thought to be the kind of discipline that would strengthen spiritual sinews. Such an environment, stern and kindly, practically guaranteed that some of our preferred forms of transgression would be elevated into rites.

Smoking, for example.

"Smoking cigarettes when young may stunt your growth." Such was the gist of the received wisdom—received because it had been said for a generation and because anybody could point to presumed examples. Short men, heavy smokers. But the appeal of smoking was wafted our way with every community breath, reinforced by the advertising of that day: "I'd walk a mile for a Camel." That was not a benighted idea; that was a masculine idea. So there came a time when a boy sneaked off somewhere with a friend and tried smoking corn silk or hay chaff, eventually a hand-rolled tobacco cigarette, and on up to a Camel.

Nelvin and I made our smoking debut with cousin Bob in his father's barn, which is not a recommended place for boys to play with matches. But we entertained ourselves in high style for a few hours with an old pipe that Bob had liberated and hay chaff from the barn floor. We'd take a couple of quick, hot puffs and hand the pipe around, cementing our conspiracy. How seductive the incense from this strange new religion of masculinity—the smoldering chaff and the sweet, smoky smell of forbiddenness. Under the circumstances, it was dangerous, careless, and eventually somewhat sickening too, but those seemed minor details at the time.

Having tasted the pleasures of sin I was soon emboldened to try smoking by myself. I had no pipe and so I learned that if you roll dry chaff into cigarette paper and light it, you will inhale as much chaff as smoke. Frustrated, I considered giving abstinence and virtue a chance, but downed the impulse with aplomb and elected to switch smoking brands instead: I upgraded my act to corn silk. I happened to be in the chicken coop at the time and once more my guardian angel swooped in to keep me from burning the place down. The experiment was interesting, worth repeating later behind a corn shock (I had been warned by my angel to stay clear of buildings), but it didn't deliver the ecstasy it had seemed to promise. By the time I was old enough—say, twelve—to try a Camel, I had already pretty well given up on surreptitious smoking. (Later, in college, I took to the pipe and stayed with it for some decades.)

If I was timid about these forays into the great Masculine Unknown, it was because I had a vivid memory of Marvin's first public smoking adventure. With Dad's permission he had lit up a cigar one Sunday noon after dinner and puffed away right there in the living room—to the wide-eyed wonder of us all. Here was this brother of ours, more than four years my senior but a boy still, and presto! At the stroke of a match and a cloud of smoke he was transformed into a tough cigar-chomping adult right there in the heart of the family. However, by the time he had fully inhaled the heady clouds of masculinity, had gotten the requisite local notoriety, and had taken personal stock of his newfound manhood, he had also absorbed a chest and stomach full of heavy cigar smoke. Soon he became very, very pale and then very, very ill.

My big smoking brother sat down. Then he groaned and lay down, then went outside and promptly came in again, paler still, sighing with spasms of agony or self-pity. He lay down again and rolled on the floor—a man no more was he. I was very impressed. And very baffled. Did manhood require that one simply learn to accept such awful duress and come to enjoy it? My father appeared to like pipe and cigar smoking. Presently we all went off to church, to worship God and kill flies, and left Marvin there to nurse his woes by himself. I have no clear knowledge of what our parents thought about the episode, but I have dark suspicions, the blackest of which is that the event went approximately as intended. Many teenagers of the time became heavy cigarette smokers, but not us. No camel put its nose very far under our tent. And we all grew tall and lean.

❧ 22 ❧

High School: Mainly Extracurricular

On our eighty acres the tumbleweeds rolled mainly east. There came a certain day at season's end when, as if by prearrangement, they cut loose and went off together like birds migrating. It was the dry west wind of September that did it, swooping down to release the summer's tumbleweed crop from the roadside ditch and sending it rolling in cohorts across the meadow or tripping like ballet dancers across the broad stage of the bean field.

Such a day was my first day of high school. Walking home I took a shortcut through the southwest bean field, where my father was working alone, methodically turning over the bunches of recently pulled field beans so they could dry. We would haul them into the barn the next day after school. Tumbleweeds rolled past him, heading for the pond, but some were waylaid by the barbed-wire fence, which caught and held them, impaled. I see them now—remembering how the wind had coerced them into a line at the fence, how they leaned into it, nervously trembling on the barbs in the breeze, straining to get through. I carried a book in my hand; my father had a fork in his.

"Hi, Dad."

Something in his demeanor made me check the impulse to start bubbling about high school.

"There's work here to do, you know," he said. "School stuff is one thing, but we've got crops to get in." He looked at my book. I looked at the beans and at the tumbleweeds. We looked at each other. We looked away.

A fleeting, memorable moment. Only two sentences uttered. On that first day of high school I had peered over the fence to glimpse larger fields in which I was eager to ramble, while my father, bend-ing his back alone in the field through the heat of the day, had glimpsed the sacrifice he was making. Meeting tuition bills was one part of it; losing help with the farm crops was another. Marvin had a job; Nelvin and I were back to school; he was working alone. Yet he ardently wanted us to go to high school. So his feelings were undoubtedly conflicted. He himself had left school in the seventh grade to work on his father's farm; I do not know that he ever regretted putting down his books to pick up the reins, but he remembered it. Sometimes I remembered it too.

I walked toward the barn and past the tumbleweeds at the fence. They were jumping up and down with the wind on their back, trying to climb the barrier and get away. Some rolled up the backs of other tumbleweeds, got nearly to the top, fell back, then caught another warm gust and leapt to the top of the fence, rolled over, and bounced away. Some rolled and tumbled all the way to the edge of our eighty, where they just hopped the low fence and pushed on, spreading seed to other fields, other farms. I got a fork from the barn and returned to the field to help with the beans.

During the winter of my second year in high school I took a job doing the farm chores for one of our neighbors who was unable to do his own. My four-day-week routine was short on leisure, short on study time, but long on responsibility, and I liked that. From the school bus I walked home the last two miles, changed clothes, and hurried across the fields to Harold's place. Cows of that era remained stationary in the stable throughout the winter, fastened side by side in stanchions, a long gutter extending behind the row of cows. First I cleaned the stables, then I threw down hay from the mow, straw from the stack, and ensilage from the silo. A delicacy for cattle, ensilage consists of chopped-up green corn stalks packed into the silo where they ferment and develop a deep golden aroma, rich and sour, like tobacco cured with rum. I fed all the stock and then started the milking machine. It didn't take long to milk a dozen or fifteen cows, two at a time, washing the udders first with a disinfectant solution. Then I fed the calves, hoisted the milk cans into the cooler, stuffed the mangers with hay, bedded the cattle with straw, and said good night to the animals. Two and a half hours. I stayed overnight and repeated the process the next morning. Then I trotted home just in time for breakfast, changed clothes, and walked off to meet the school bus. In such a scenario school homework was not even considered.

For most rural families, busy with farm work and daily chores, the idea of schoolwork at home just didn't fit in. Were there not hours enough during the day for books? Arrangements for home studying were improbable in any case. We were typical in having just two heated and kerosene-lighted rooms, kitchen and living room, neither suited to study. And, indeed, it was *we* who were not suited to study, so the idea that schoolwork did not belong at home fitted my own inclinations. Maybe that troubling book I carried home on my first day was my textbook for world history, and maybe it was but a pulpy novel. I don't know. I believe that for the next four years, excepting exam times, I successfully fought off most temptations to take work home.

Ours was a Christian high school, still a young and struggling institution when I entered, in the late forties: three teachers, eighty students, and the building itself was a recycled three-story residence from the era of McBain's lumber barons. Considering the community's resources, the school's very existence was remarkable, a heroic adventure of faith for the people of those eight rural Christian Reformed churches. Most of the early school board members, my father among them, did not have a high school education themselves.

The inspiration for the high school did not emerge from a critique of the public schools, except for the fact that they were by definition secular. It came from internal sources, from tradition and church and faith. The ideal of Christian day schools, the conviction that all learning should be in an explicitly Christian setting, derived from the Netherlands of seventy-five years earlier. In starting their Michigan schools, these Dutch Calvinists were doing what came naturally; and they would have done it, I think, regardless of the existence or condition of the public schools. In our larger community several Christian grade schools had been set up—none of them near enough for us—and by about 1940 a Christian high school seemed the proper culmination of those efforts. My parents were early and ardent supporters, though this came at some cost to them.

I had supposed that they might feel, as some others did, that they simply could not afford to put all their children through a Christian high school. It would have been all right with me to stay with my friends in the public school. But in fact my parents' commitment to a Christian high school education for all of us was absolute—a commitment I came to admire and value. Therefore we five siblings all followed the same path: McBain Rural Agricultural School through the eighth grade, and then across town to Northern Michigan Christian High School.

If our high school education was academically shaky, it was solid in other respects: friendships, values, teachers, attitudes toward God and humankind, an environment to reinforce and not subvert the standards of our homes. Although a few courses served us well in subsequent years, mental discipline, study habits, and serious learning of any kind all lay in the future; for us who headed that way, the first year of college was catch-up. For my own pleasure and satisfaction, I did memorize large chunks of poetry, and I read piles of books, as many of us did, but few of them were good books. Like most others, I took high school studies seriously for brief and selective moments, such as the hour before a semester exam.

Our small high school began to outgrow the cozy old mansion, and that triggered a building program. First one classroom, then several more, then a gymnasium, and once the four high walls and bare floor of a gym were planned, an irresistible logic took command.

We were headed for extracurricular activities. Before the cement was hard somebody had said, "Hey, let's field a basketball team," and before a wiser voice could breathe, "Omygoshthatwillbeadisaster," we were penciled into the league schedule. So the chemistry teacher was recruited to coach, a businessman paid for suits, somebody bought a basketball, and we chose a name: Northern Christian Comets. We had momentum; all we lacked was a team.

Most of the striplings who turned out for our team were good at handling a pitchfork but had never handled a basketball; nor, indeed, had they ever seen a basketball game. Nelvin (a junior) and I (a senior), former students at the McBain School, had a slight edge, for we had played basketball in junior high. But that was three and four years earlier. We had not been stars then and we did not resemble comets now. Still, it was easy for us to make the starting lineup of *this* varsity team.

We worked out on what we had, a concrete floor; a permanent hardwood floor was scheduled for the next year. Our early practice sessions were such stuff as nightmares are made of.

"You mean if you want to run with the ball, you have to bounce it too?"

"No. I mean yes. Not 'bounce'—'dribble.'" Coach Kooy tried to learn patience while the team tried to learn basketball.

"You mean you can't dribble with both hands?"

"No, and you're not supposed to put the ball in your opponents' basket, either."

Eventually something like a team emerged, our scrimmages improved, and we began to look toward the regular games, the first of which was to be against our opposite numbers from the other side of town, the Ramblers of McBain Public High. About this meeting, Nelvin and I had deep forebodings. Did our teachers really plan to send *us* against that veteran varsity team, against boys who had been playing together for five years? Apparently they did so intend, thinking . . . what? Simply that we had to start somewhere? That we'd make a good showing? That we would promptly begin a march to a championship? Nelvin and I suspected that we knew something those in authority didn't know. Only yesterday we had played with these fellows, who were now the opposing varsity Ramblers. We knew how good our team of Christian Comets was. We knew very well, in fact, that we were in for, well, the time of our life. We dreaded it, and we wouldn't have missed it for the world.

So we drew near to the fateful evening, January 9, when the Northern Christian Comets were to blaze across the skies in glory. There were people who believed that, even people who had seen us practice, though it is hard to know how they managed it. Ah, yes—their ardor alone would propel us into orbit. At the McBain School gym all the bleachers were jammed. Before the game I walked out to meet the referees and the opposing captain, who was my friend Ed from grade-school days. He was friendly, and no bigger than I was. Maybe, just maybe, I reported back to my teammates, we could really handle them. Let's do it! I knew that was preposterous, but I believed it nevertheless. Adrenaline can do that to your brain.

Our team had never even walked on a wooden basketball floor. To us the floor seemed to be made of rubber. Everything was accelerated, exaggerated far beyond anything we had anticipated. A concrete surface such as we had practiced on is solid, without resilience, unforgiving, dead; hardwood has elasticity, bounce. Our opponents leapt and cut like jackrabbits; they passed and shot before we left the floor; they pranced around us in circles. Almost at will they won the toss-ups and swept the rebounds. An inspired photo in the school yearbook captures the gist: "Jump, Jager, Jump," pleads the caption. Nelvin is playing center, and in this shot of the opening toss-up the opposing center is high in the air about to tip off the ball; Nelvin is still crouched, getting ready to jump. Alas, he does not realize how high one can leap on this hardwood floor, and his timing is way off. All of us were way off, to say nothing of our nearly total lack of basketball experience. We were hopelessly, outrageously outclassed.

All the edgy rivalry between the two schools burst into the open; half the crowd yelled for blood, and they got it. In buckets. We were methodically slaughtered, drawn and quartered, and dragged through the gore until the final whistle, our opponents gleefully setting records that may be unsurpassed to this day. The final score was 71 to 14, numbers unheard of in that day. The drubbing was so terrible that it was exhilarating in an odd sort of way. Nothing could ever hurt us again. The age of chivalry was not yet: they simply fed the Christians to the lions while the crowd roared.

Decades and decades went by. Over the years there evolved a strong and friendly, almost benign rivalry between the McBain Ramblers and the Northern Christian Comets. Eventually came something like a coda for that initial humiliation, when the Comets were nearly wiped out before being projected on their long journey among the stars. In the spring of 1987, the spring of Halley's comet, thirty-six years after our first sputtering, the Comets were in orbit, winning the state of Michigan Class D basketball championship. Some of their most ardent and loyal boosters came from the ranks of the McBain Ramblers and their fans. So far as I know, there was no one to offer a word in memory of the cheerful savagery of those good old days when the Comets were nearly extinguished at birth.

Another form of extracurricular education during my last year centered on the school yearbook. One task was to secure advertisements for the book, and the arrangement with the printer, the Walsworth Company, was this: they would send a representative to assist us, the student staff, as we visited business establishments in Cadillac and Lake City. I expected the company to deploy a portly gentleman, driving an old flivver; together we would drop in at the store and, while we high schoolers hovered in the background munching candy bars for lunch and providing authenticity, the company salesman would secure an ad for our book. That's what we thought.

On the appointed day and precisely at 8:00 A.M., a sleek 1950 Pontiac, dark maroon, with sun visor, fender skirts, and huge chromium hood ornaments eased into the school yard. Any self-respecting high school lad of that era could identify on sight every car on the road—model, year, good points, bad points. We didn't know many bad points about a new Pontiac De Lux. Five pairs of appreciative eyes caressed the contours of the car, but when the driver stepped out our rolling eyeballs came to instant sharp focus.

"Good morning," she said, spilling radiant smiles, "I'm from Walsworth. My name is Victoria Schimmel." She had a soft and silken accent, hitherto unheard in McBain, I think, for it seemed to have been honed in Dixie. And she was beautiful, dazzling.

We stood around her car, exchanging greetings, and we felt exactly like the five farm kids we were. It was the season of the rising sap, and from some distant city this extraordinary creature had just drifted by in this gorgeous boat to escort us—*us!* She talked with the school principal for a moment while we communicated in the silent language of elbows in ribs and facial contortions, trying to assimilate first impressions: her name, her voice, profession, appearance, car. The day took on new luster.

"We'll head for Cadillac first, okay?" That voice again, that smile. As yearbook business manager I had to take the lead on logistical matters, the first of which was to resolve the ambivalence some of us felt about both wanting and not wanting to ride in the privileged position. How choose among my friends? Certainly it was by default that I got the spot in the middle of the front seat.

The maroon Pontiac floated us off toward Cadillac. We could have used a quick detour down Main Street in McBain, where we might have been recognized, but I didn't know how to propose that. Victoria chatted amiably about the wonderful kids at a high school she had just visited in Traverse City, while we lapsed into enthralled silence. I gathered my courage and asked, "How long have you been doing this for Walsworth?"

"Oh, a long time, it seems—since last summer. Here, you can have this, okay?" She handed me an engraved business card. Sure enough, she was for real; the Walsworth card said as much. In a burst of altruism I asked for cards for the rest of my team.

"Oh sure. Spread them around, okay?" We passed the cards around and studied them. *Victoria Schimmel.* It was the sort of name we had never met, and would not forget. By the time we approached Cadillac we realized that we five were the sales force, that she was hostess and chauffeur only, an ex officio member of the working team.

We glided up to the Northwood Hotel. "Tell you what," she said. "This noon we'll all have lunch here in the Dining Room; I'll meet y'all in the lobby at twelve o'clock, okay?" I think it was the way she smiled and said "Okay?" that put us (well, me at least) at her mercy. She could have said, "At noon you will lie down in the gutter at my feet and eat dirt, okay?" and we would have done it. Dining Room? We had never been in a dining room more ambitious than a grill or a soda fountain in McBain. We did not have meals in restaurants.

"Ron, where shall I let you off?"

Under the inspiration of her gaze, my fertile brain instantly concocted a full day's strategy and compressed it into one creative sentence: "Well, I think we'll . . . let's see . . . we'll start on Main Street. Okay?"

We formed two teams and went to work like professionals. The printed evidence tells me that we sold ten ads that morning—a superb performance, if I do say so—but I remember nothing whatever of it. At noon we gathered again in the lobby of the Northwood Hotel. Victoria Schimmel followed the maître d' to a large white-clothed table in the center of the room. At each place there were huge bulky blue napkins, rows of flatware such as we had never seen, two or more of everything, huge tumblers upside down, small side plates, stoneware cups and saucers of magnificent proportions; in the center of the table were covered baskets and a bowl of bright flowers. I had never seen anything quite like that, but then I had never been in a genuine restaurant, either. Spread before us was everything one could think of, except what I was accustomed to on a kitchen table—namely, plates and food.

Each of us sat down behind one of these exhibits of equipment, each of which seemed to say in a loud voice, "Don't touch." I became aware that it was utterly impossible to figure out what to do with my hands: I seemed to have six pairs of them and no convenient pockets to stow them into. I noticed that Victoria, at my left, had rings on her fingers. She had her napkin in her hands, but I did not know what she was going to do with it. I watched without looking. So, this was dining out in Cadillac. What was to happen next? My head was stuffed with an uncertain mixture of exhilaration and sheer unsuppressible awkwardness. Shades of a first date. But this was not a date; this was merely my first restaurant, my first business luncheon, my first . . . lots of things. Victoria caught my eye and held it for a second. Was she sending me the reassurance that I required and disdained? She *knew* how vulnerable we were? Then she suddenly said that Mr. Bruce, a friend of hers, would soon be in to join us for lunch—"Okay?" We all nodded and said "Okay." Victoria was a fountain of surprises.

Enter Mr. Bruce, talking. "Hi there, sales folks!" he said, as if he had been waiting all morning to see us. He put a hand on my shoulder: "Have a good morning, did you? Made lotsa money, I hope. Say, Cadillac's a swell town, isn't it?"

"Yeah, 's okay," we said.

"Man, I could live around here. Fish, hunt. Ya know? You guys do any of that?" He sat down, his breezy entrance condensing all the tension in the air.

Then with one proprietary sweep of his left hand, Mr. Bruce expertly collected his seven pieces of flatware and piled them up neatly on his left, like a stack of kindling. What a gesture! He plunked his napkin on his lap, stacked two side dishes, put his right elbow on the table, and swept a glance around him, gathering all our eyes.

"Speakin' of moola," he said, "d'you ever hear about the three kids who were bragging about how much dough their dads made? First kid said, 'My dad's a lawyer; he just fills out some forms and he gets fifty bucks for that.' Next kid says, 'My dad's a doctor; he just yanks out somebody's tonsils and he gets a hundred bucks.' Next kid says, 'That ain't nothin'. My dad's a minister; he preaches one little sermon and it takes two deacons to carry away all the money.' Ha! Ha! Ha!"

Mr. Bruce kept the stories coming, and they kept improving; in five minutes our giddiness had been expelled in giggles. When the waiter came I was so relaxed that I dared to order broiled trout, which I enjoyed, even though I didn't know what to with that slice of lemon until it was too late. Victoria had trout too.

I kept her card in my yearbook for a long time.

23

Potatoes by the Book

From childhood I believed my vocation was farming. I directed my ambition not so much toward what I could achieve in crops or cash or livestock but toward the notion—presumptuous, certainly— that I was going to do it right, the way farming was meant to be done. Headstrong but unable to fault my father's basic values, or his calling, I picked on his technique. He should be more progressive, modern, scientific; he should fertilize more, rotate crops more carefully, plan better, breed differently, select seed more scientifically. Whatever. I grew up with those ideas, but they were fed by my reading, and by Marvin, who fed me stuff to read, and by my own playing at farming with rabbits, geese, and bees.

In my second year in high school I learned that by writing to our congressman I could get a free copy of the agriculture yearbook, published by the United States Department of Agriculture. Here was an easier way to acquire a good book than by pumping water for it, so I wrote to Congressman Engel and promptly received *Grass: Yearbook of Agriculture*, 1948, 892 pages, an extraordinary book. Now and then I see it listed in a used-book catalog and invariably identified as a "classic." The same goes for the bigger and even more interesting one I acquired in the same way the next year, *Trees*, 1949. It turns out that there is now a consensus that the agriculture yearbooks of that era were easily the best ones produced, and I was just lucky to start in at the right time.

Indeed, the decade of the forties, the years of my teens, was a most unusual period for agricultural literature generally, though I didn't realize it at the time. A textbook I used in a high school agriculture course has achieved a permanent place in the canon: *A Practical Guide to Successful Farming* (Wallace and Moreland), a 1,001-page summary of the farming lore of the time, still eagerly sought by used-book dealers and studied by agricultural historians. That was also the decade of Louis Bromfield's famous report on his Ohio farm-restoration experiment, *Malabar Farm*. But the most talked-about book of the era was Edward H. Faulkner's controversial *Plowman's Folly* (1943), which Marvin ordered from Sears, Roebuck and which fueled in our house the first discussions that I recall about the theory of farming. The book's thesis, impressively laid out with lots of scientific data, that plowing—in particular, burying a heavy sod—should be abandoned for rototilling, that is, mixing the chopped-up sod with the topsoil, has had a continuing influence on farming practice.

Since our family ethos was somewhat skewed toward books, it

was natural that when we of the younger generation thought about farming, we thought of farming by the book. Or rather, farming by the pamphlet, for we ordered reams of pamphlets on all kinds of rural topics, from potatoes to parsnips, through the United States Department of Agriculture and the Michigan Extension Service. They were always cheap and often free, and they gave us a lot to think about. Often the authors of the pamphlets assumed not only that we had a tractor but that we had more farm implements than we in fact did. But they also convinced me that carefully selecting breeding stock and seed stock was one of the most important principles on the farm. My reading reinforced my impression that on our eighty acres we were not exactly up-to-date.

My father's farming orientation—as was painfully evident to me—was not toward machines or toward ideas out of books. Not machines, because it wasn't really necessary: he had sons to help with the work. A manure spreader would have saved labor, but we *could* do it by hand; same for a milking machine, a corn binder, a grain drill, and other implements. Many of these tasks, especially milking and sowing grain, he simply enjoyed doing by hand more than he ever could have enjoyed managing a machine. And with extra hands available, the scale of our operations didn't warrant the larger tools or the tractor to pull them. Farming with horses as he did reflected a rational set of choices, though I doubt that my father's regular reaffirmation of it was ever wholly rational. I wasn't assailing it on strictly rational grounds, either: ideology was my forte. And I simply took it for granted that when I farmed with a tractor I would move twice as fast with tools twice as large and thus cover fields of twice the size in half the time.

Our differing ways of viewing the world showed up plainly in the Great Potato Experiment.

Occasionally we had a year when Indian summer disintegrated into rainstorms before we had the potatoes harvested. On wet ground a potato digger will not function: the mud piles up in front of the blade, which is supposed to run smoothly under the potatoes, lift them up, shake out the soil, and drop the potatoes on the surface. Under ideal conditions a potato digger is a remarkably simple and effective machine; in mud it's terrible. That year there was a low area of about an acre in the potato field northeast of the orchard that we concluded would never dry out sufficiently to allow the digger on it. We would dig that acre by hand, one hill at a time. Having finished high school, Marvin had taken a job on the section gang of the local railroad and was not available for potato digging; therefore, my father and I would dig the potatoes and Nelvin would pick them up. As we began, Dad observed that if we had a tractor-drawn digger we would have had to harvest the entire hillside by hand as well, since horses can go places, such as on a wet hillside with a potato digger, where a tractor cannot. I treated this insight with silence.

We went to work with four-tined forks, the task made more difficult by the clay soil—damp, rubbery, tough. Some potatoes were locked into chunks of clay, and we had to break them out by slapping at the clods with the tines. But we found good potatoes buried there and that gave us something to talk about. When we found a really good hill, we counted the potatoes in it.

"Dad, we should save the best hills for seed."

He didn't look up or slow down. "Yeah, maybe so. Be a lot of trouble, I guess."

"Might pay, though."

"Not too likely, I don't think."

Farmers used small potatoes for seed. It would be a squandering of both effort and potatoes to plant large potatoes; and a potato planter, whether hand-held as in our case, or large and tractor-drawn, is not made to accommodate large potatoes. Therefore, the standard practice was to save seed potatoes from what was left over from the grading and selling of the main crop—culls to be cut up, and seconds to be used as is. Culls are bruised or scabby or misshapen; seconds are small potatoes.

"Look at this hill. Fourteen Number Ones, and five seconds. We should save it," I said. A Number One potato is one that will not fall through a two-inch potato-grader mesh.

"And here's one with . . . let's see . . . six, call it seven seconds. Nothing else." Seconds are the ones that fall through the mesh. We were estimating sizes here, but much experience had made Dad good at it.

I tried again. "We should save the good hills for seed."

"Wouldn't be enough of them, I s'pose."

"How many bushels do we need?"

"Quite a few."

My father had a tendency to think that one seed potato was pretty much like another. He *knew* as well as anyone that looks didn't constitute the whole genetic story, but the knowledge made him uncomfortable, since he didn't really know what to do about it. And he didn't always like my questions, which were sometimes impolitic.

"Dad, if we plant seconds we're using the poorest potatoes for seed. That's dumb."

"Not exactly. If the seconds come from hills with lots of Number Ones, it's all the same, the way I hear it."

"Okay, but what about the seconds that come from hills with mostly seconds? Like that one—seven seconds! Plant those and we'll get seven more hills of seconds, right?"

"They might do better next year."

"Yeah, *might!*"

Farmers are optimists, and they have to be. My harsh theory was that their optimism made them complacent when they should be scientific.

"Plant seconds every year, your seed gets worse and worse; it just runs out. That's all there is to it. Crops get poorer and poorer."

I was preaching the textbook sermon, exasperated, stating what I took to be the merest common sense. Why was my father fighting it? Apparently, he simply didn't *want* to accept it. We'd had the same discussion about cattle breeding, which had ended in stalemate. And about rabbits, when I had gone off to buy Flemish Giants. And about chickens, when he had done the more or less scientific thing and bought chicks from productive bloodlines. The signals were mixed.

Now he said, "We plant the same wheat year after year, and I have better wheat crops now than I did fifteen years ago—'course that could be the soil, too. But why didn't the wheat run out?"

That one was easy, and I suspected he knew it; he was just warming to the argument. "Well, with wheat you *don't* screen out the small kernels and plant them, like we do with potatoes. Besides, this summer didn't you save wheat seed from the front field, which was so good, instead of from the back forty?"

My father farmed approximately as he believed his ancestors had farmed, and that included the inherited feeling, however vague, that somehow, somewhere, the deep questions about stock breeding and seed selection would resolve themselves. They were beyond us. They were in the safe hands of nature or God or both. But this intuition did not leave my father without argument to confront my dogmatic impatience.

"If potato seed will run out doing it my way, the way we always did it, why hasn't it run out already long ago? How many centuries has this been going on? Where do these big potatoes come from? Run-out seed?"

It began to look more like a draw, and I went back to digging potatoes out of the clay.

The only thing that keeps potato digging interesting is the slight sense of expectancy about what the next hill will produce. It occurred to me now that a horse-drawn potato digger, a great labor-saving implement regarded as indispensable by all farmers, automatically mixed all the potatoes in the row together, so it never let us see the produce of the individual hills. Digging by hand with a fork blatantly exposed the production of each individual hill. Something to think about.

"Did your dad have a potato digger?"

"No, we dug by hand."

"Did your grampa dig potatoes by hand?"

"Guess so."

"How did you pick out seed potatoes in those days?"

"I don't just know."

"Did they select the good hills? I don't suppose they selected the *bad* hills, did they?" Seeing a sudden opening I pressed harder: "Did they have potato *graders* in those days?" My father didn't know.

"So now potato diggers mix all the spuds together—from good hills and bad hills—and then the grader comes along and sorts out all the seconds and leaves *them* on the farm for seed! You call that good farming?" My argument was so strong that I thought I could afford the sarcasm.

My father straightened up, put his fork in the ground, and rested his toe on the heel of the tines, glancing off toward the orchard. "So I guess what you're saying is that potato diggers, graders, tractors, and modern machines make for bad farming! Never heard you say that before! How'd you get on that side of the fence?" He shot a spurt of tobacco juice at a round stone next to a crate. Perfect hit. He had me.

We went back to the clay and dug out more potatoes. We worked quietly, noting the good hills with a nod and a smile, not counting for a while.

Dad got a big one. "There's fifteen or sixteen Number Ones," he said, pointing with his fork.

"We should save it for seed," I suggested.

Then Dad abruptly let me know that he thought it was a really good idea, that he was eager to experiment with it and was glad I had brought it up. We would save some good hills and plant them next spring in separate rows to see if they really were better. He let me know all this by catching my eye and simply saying, "Well, we could try it once."

We dug more potatoes. By unspoken agreement we left the potatoes from the best hills in special little piles on the side. But that afternoon we saved all potatoes from hills with twelve or more Number Ones, and when we had two bushels of them we agreed it was enough.

Those two bushels stood in the corner of the basement next to the fruit cellar all winter, and the next spring we cut the largest of those potatoes into halves, thirds, and quarters and took them, including all the seconds, to the new field along with the regular seed from the grading. It was a long and narrow field, and down the middle of it, side by side, Dad and I planted two rows of selected seed potatoes, almost all the way from the orchard to the woods, a quarter of a mile.

Surprise! Ten days later those two rows came up ahead of the other rows. And that was just the beginning. From the day they first appeared and throughout the entire summer, those two rows stood out from all the rest: the plants were unmistakably bigger, greener, healthier. We could see it from the house. My sharpest memory of the experiment, and the image round which the entire episode gathers, is of my father talking to someone in the yard and inviting him to bend and peer eastward under the orchard trees to the potato field beyond and confirm this remarkable thing for himself. Unfailingly the visitor *could* see that, yes, there were two rows that were different. "Same kind of potatoes," said Dad, "all Sebagos. But the two rows are handpicked seed." Was that pride I was overhearing in his voice?

My father enjoyed the experiment, as I came to understand, because he saw it as a remarkably neat trick, like getting maple syrup out of trees or rabbits out of brush piles. To him the whole experience was apparently a kind of farmer's sport, belonging more to leisure, perhaps, than to farming as an economic enterprise. To me it was more science than sport. But I was even more amazed than he that my eager pamphleteering about seed stock seemed so stunningly confirmed. Our plan to see whether the selected seed would make a difference in the final harvest was upstaged by this unexpected difference in the size of the plants. But here, I thought, was a demonstration of farming by the book; these kinds of principles had merely to be applied and extended to the whole farm operation. We weren't at all surprised that the fall harvest confirmed the summer appearance: those two rows did yield a heavier crop— enough to count the difference in bushels.

Scientific farming overwhelmingly vindicated!

Now what?

The first step was easy: in the fall we took our seed potatoes from those two favored rows. But we didn't select the seed; it was run-of-the-field. The alternative would have been to dig them all by hand and again select out the best hills, and we had no time for that. So whether the improvement in our seed made a real difference the second year couldn't be directly proved, for we had no control group for comparison, as in the first year. It was a matter of faith. I had plenty of that. I was certain that since our seed had been better this second year, our crop was better whether we could prove it or not. Dad was not so sure. "Maybe the benefit of good seed lasts only one year," he said cheerfully.

Amazing! We were back to square one.

To me the whole potato episode—such a clean and successful experiment!—was thoroughly subversive, and I had meant it to be. Yet my father never let that happen, for it was never fully serious to him, just very interesting.

But whether its upshot was sporting, as he thought, or scientifically important, as I thought, it was the logistics of the matter that stopped us both cold. Within our framework, we couldn't figure out how to institutionalize raising potatoes by the book. Who selected our seed potatoes thereafter? Not us. It was done by our crude machines, the digger and the grader.

We were back to the old arguments. And when we agreed, it was not because my father accepted my viewpoint; it was because he accommodated it. The difference between us was two rows of potatoes and one generation.

❧ 24 ❧

Sports Afield

In our family sixteen was the age that divided the men who hunted from the boys who didn't.

On the farms around McBain we grew up in an atmosphere made heavy each autumn with the sensual and imaginative associations of hunting. We pursued small game, primarily rabbit, but also pheasant, partridge, squirrel, and occasionally duck. Big-game hunting meant the white-tailed deer. Hunting seemed the most natural thing in the world; we did it for enjoyment and for food, a form of harvesting more stimulating than gathering field crops. By the time a boy first went abroad with a firearm, he had already mastered many of the techniques of hunting and the essentials of its code, and he was probably already steeped in sporting doctrine. I had often gone hunting with my father before I was old enough to handle a gun of my own; from Marvin I learned to pore over stories and articles in *Outdoor Life, Field and Stream, Fur-Fish-Game,* and *Sports Afield,* and then I helped to infect Nelvin with the same tastes. Heads buried in these pages, we might fantasize about big-game hunting in distant exotic regions and dream about gritty sportsmanship and its trophies, about the wily habits of the game animals and how we might outwit them.

Hunting had its local mystique as well, also nourished by literature (if that's the word) and fancy: field lore, firearms, adventure, trophies, providership, machismo, gamesmanship—imaginative elements far too potent and hazy for me ever to sort out. The sensual components were very direct: the pungent, heady aroma of gunpowder, the sizzle of birch bark on campfires, the ambience of the forest, the feel of the shotgun in hand, the metallic click of its magazine, the sweet taste of game at mealtime, the sight of a good dog working a warm track, the music of a distant baying beagle, companionship afield, and, alternatively, the dispassionate pleasures of solitude, serene communion with God and nature or with Nature and its gods. To have drunk at these waters is to have savored one of the great privileges of life.

For high school boys, hunting provided a format for such forms of misbehavior as we could muster.

There was the bright January school day when my friend Rich and I were sauntering down McBain's Main Street during the noon lunch hour. Being imaginative young men, we became aware that here was a perfect day to exercise the dog. In fact, quite suddenly that became a matter of much greater urgency than the pending chemistry test. We agreed that Rich should come to my home for the night, so that we could go hunting right after school. In another minute we had concluded that this proposal was so good that we ought to implement it immediately. Before the chemistry test. No need even to go back to school, for the day was already half gone.

As a first step Rich would call home to get a pass for the night. During that brief call I noticed rather more frowns, uh-huhs, and throat clearings than I had expected.

"What'd she say?"

"Said it was okay for the night." Pause. "She might've smelled a rat." Pause. "She said, 'Don't you skip school, though.'"

Here was a huge black cloud suddenly thrown across the sun, followed by nearly two seconds of deep and dark brooding, after which Rich shrugged and brightened. "Well, sure, but that's just the standard line anyway."

Evidently it was time for some creative thinking, and Rich was already at it full speed. If his subsequent collection of elegant insights were to be laid out in linear fashion, they would be to this effect: Yes, "don't skip" was of course his parents' position on school; he already knew that before he had called. They were parents, after all. So this evidently wasn't really a special prohibition for today but just the familiar status quo, so to speak. There was really no news; nothing had changed since we had first formed the plan eight minutes ago. Rich looked at me. "What d'you think?"

What I thought was that he was very ingenious indeed. I saw no need to rehearse his logic to look for weak spots. As for my own further thoughts, fully sketched out they would have looked like this: I could not recall that my parents had ever instituted an official prohibition on skipping school to go hunting. An oversight, perhaps. True, they hadn't told us not to eat hay, either. Or not to smash school windows. Or steal cars. Or rob banks. But in particular, so far as I could recall, they had never said, Don't skip school to go hunting. So today's plan (though possibly undesired in some obscure way, for all I knew) did not in fact involve my breaking a specific commandment.

Having thus woven our insights together and having stretched a loophole or two to slip our consciences through, we concluded that, phone call notwithstanding, we were pretty much in the same position.

"So?"

"So let's go."

For all I know, the seeds of subsequent careers may have sprung from that brief curbstone exercise in sophistry—Rich became a clinical psychologist, I an academic philosopher—but of these arcane disciplines we had not yet heard. What we had heard, what was ringing in our ears, was my dog Chips in full cry on a hot rabbit trail. As is evident, we were conscientious youths, and once we had decided that the only proper use of the afternoon was to repair swiftly to the woods with dog and gun, we did not wish to be guilty of the sins of sloth and idleness by standing around on street corners engaging in frivolous conversation. We felt obliged to head immediately for my place, and we did so.

We had intended to hitchhike, but we had to walk the five miles home, since no aiders and abetters of truants stopped to pick us up. By then the sun had gone into hiding behind clouds, but there was no turning back. My father was working elsewhere and not available for complicity; and my mother was not nearly so keen about our plans as was my dog, Chips, who indeed showed his usual sound judgment about hunting, namely, "Let's." "You can trust a dog on these things," said Rich.

So we did. Shouldering our guns we marched off toward Stick Crick, two and a half miles away, despite the now overcast and threatening sky. Eventually, Chips got a rabbit going there, and that led us farther away than we had intended. Waiting for the rabbit to appear got us thoroughly chilled, so we walked some more; and we walked again after it had started snowing and we had wasted our last match trying to start a fire. Then Chips gave up on the rabbit and came back to us.

We got home at dark, estimating that we had walked nearly twenty miles since noon. We admitted to being hungry but not to being tired. What almost made us tired, though, was the fact that Nelvin brought home word from school that the chemistry test had been a snap. Still, we thought that someone had to uphold certain honorable traditions and that we had done that, despite its inconvenience to us and the lack of public approval and suitable reward. We slept the sleep of the just.

There was the year of the wet December, when creeks turned to rivers, and riverbanks to mud. Marvin and I and our two friends, the brothers Wes and Rich, were hunting in the "Armour Land," a large and brushy cutover timber tract of uncertain ownership to which we often resorted for berry picking and hunting. Jackrabbit, we called our quarry there, but the books called it the varying hare.

Unlike the cottontail, which will hole up when it is tired of being pursued, these jackrabbits didn't mind exercising a dog— leading a beagle in a two-mile circle, casually outrunning him at will, backtracking to confuse him. Such was the sport of hares. Nevertheless, Chips had been having a good day and we had several hares in the bag. But now it was nearly dusk and I was having difficulty calling Chips off a warm track. When I finally got near him, it turned out that he was on the other side of the swollen river. Had he crossed on ice floes in pursuit of his prey? Where? Had the hare led him across a fallen log—perhaps hoping to drown him? How could I get him back? I ordered Chips to come over to me; each time, he paused, barked, and stared back at me as if he thought I had gone berserk. Anger didn't work and neither did commands, so I changed my tune. Despite my newly calm entreaties, Chips would not plunge into the frigid waves and swim across to join me; and despite his plight, I was not about to plunge in and wade across to him. We went sloshing back and forth along the banks, each on a side, searching for some combination of rocks and fallen trees that could bridge the route back to me. No luck. Faking cheerfulness, I called encouragement, and Chips now simpered frustration in reply. Or was that cowardice? The daylight was dying out of the woods and presently I could not even see him, or he me. Meanwhile, my companions had assembled at the car and were leaning on the horn, an urgent signal for me to rejoin them. Alas. Nothing to do now but to scramble forlornly through the puckerbrush toward the car, guided thither by the horn. It was getting very dark and I was very miserable. This was not the way the story ran in the magazines. How I loathed hunting—a wretched, dismal, and stupid sport. The reception I got only heaped guilt upon my frustration and worry.

"Where'n the dickens *were* you? We've been waitin' an hour."

"Chips is on the other side of the river and can't get back across."

"Well, call 'em. Can't he swim?"

"S'pose so; but I couldn't talk him into it." I was now thoroughly crushed. No need to stomp me any flatter.

We four young Nimrods of the sporting fields stood there in the gloom and just stared at one another. We needed someone to blame for something, if only to clear our heads. Marvin broke the silence with a definitive analysis. "Dumb dog," he said.

Having established our data base, we were free to be creative. "Guess he'll have to find his way home by himself," said Wes.

"Dogs in books find their way home," said Rich.

Wes snickered. "Yeah, and if they don't, they don't get into books."

Farms, hills, roads, and dozens of fences intervened between the Armour Land and our eighty acres, and that seemed to me to add up to more obstacles than the easy miles of open terrain the dogs of literature traveled when they were homeward bound. Chips was not Lassie, and he was only a couple of years away from puppyhood. Anyway, wouldn't he eventually have to cross the river to get home? How would a dog do an end run on a river unbridged for miles?

Marvin thought Chips might possibly make it home. Wes now thought it doubtful. I thought it extremely doubtful. Rich thought we needed a plan. We grumbled and worried and muttered as the moon rose on our futile meditations. Then we picked up the unmistakable baying of Chips far off to the west. Was he on the trail again, across the river and into the trees? Calling for us? When the baying stopped, we called. When the calling stopped, we went off into the woods and whistled. Nothing availed. "Dumb dog," said Wes. We were back to square one.

"Won't he eventually track us back to this spot?" Marvin wondered.

Rich shivered and took up the idea: "He'd come back here if we waited long enough."

Rich was thinking aloud, not making proposals, and there was no telling if his idea was a tautology or an insight. In any case, we could not wait for Chips, for two sets of parents were already waiting for us.

Marvin made a breakthrough: "If he gets back to this spot, he'll stay right here and wait—*if* he has some excuse to do it." Marvin had read more sporting magazines than any of us.

What we had to do was to provide Chips with that excuse. Food? A piece of rabbit? No, said Marvin; something he would recognize by smell as ours. We had it! A shirt, a jacket—something to suggest that we had not abandoned him. Leave a message.

I removed my hunting jacket and my shirt; then I spread the shirt out on the snow beside a stump. Opinions were divided about the outcome: Chips would be home by morning; he would try to recross the river and freeze or drown; he would turn up in somebody's yard; he would never be seen again; he would try to follow the car out of the Armour Land and become utterly lost on the road. Or he would come back to this very spot and wait. By this time I didn't know what I thought, but I was willing to bet my shirt on the plan. As added inducement I took off my cap and put it down beside my shirt. *Wait here for me, Chips. I'll return.*

At home that night we rehearsed the details of the occasion when Chips's predecessor, Rover, had gotten lost near the Clam River and found his way home by morning. Not much consolation to be eked out there. That was less than three miles away and, besides, that was Rover, swampwise veteran of many a wild and rugged race; Chips was an irrepressible juvenile delinquent and astray in a far larger and far more distant wilderness. Dad said Chips would have plenty of strength left to get home by morning. I simply tried to picture a scene in which Chips would somehow ford the icy river, find my message, and sit down on my shirt and wait there for me. A lot to ask of an allegedly dumb dog.

No dog greeted us at the dooryard the next morning. "Give him time to get home if he's coming," said Dad, who never, ever acted precipitously, "or time to get across the river if he is going to wait for you." It was almost noon when I drove alone into the Armour

Land, parked the car, and hurried over to inspect the place where I had left the message. Shirt and cap were there, somewhat disheveled. I took that as good news. Fresh dog tracks were everywhere. Better news. Chips was nowhere in sight. Terrible news. My heart sank. "He didn't believe me," I sighed half aloud. "He didn't trust me. He didn't wait." I tried to whistle and couldn't—my lips were trembling. Why, why hadn't I returned earlier?

"Chips!" I then called as loudly as I could manage it. "I'm here, Chips! Chips!"

A yelp of recognition broke from nowhere, and a hundred yards down the lumber road Chips appeared, heading right toward me full tilt, faster than he had ever pursued a rabbit. Straight into my open arms he flew, and set about licking every inch of my face. When we had finished our hugging and smooching, I realized that the ecstatic Chips had dribbled all over my pant legs. At least I think it was Chips's doing. No matter, the reunion was better than catching all the rabbits in the Armour Land, and it turned the whole world around. What a great sport was hunting, what a fringe benefit to have a beagle who could read and follow instructions! There was no dog like my dog.

Our hunting performances varied from complete failure to spectacular success. Now and then everything seemed to go right. My eighteenth birthday fell on a Saturday and with it fell a light coating of soft white snow, perfect for tracking. Chores and breakfast out of the way, Chips and I headed for the woods to celebrate the day by looking for rabbits. Within a few hours, Chips had nosed out three cottontails, tracked each one perfectly to bring it within range; and I bagged them. By noon we were back again, and I brought my trophies to the house and laid them out on the porch for the family to admire. Then I took them to the barn (my mother butchered chickens but not game animals) and dressed them out with my jackknife and delivered the meat to my mother. I was eighteen now and, like any man, a provider.

By the time lunch was over I had decided that this was the day to go for the bag limit. Was there any better way to spend a birthday afternoon than hunting? I knew of none. Chips was willing, and so we went directly back to the woods. Before dark we were home again—tired young man, tired young dog, two more cottontails. I had reached the bag limit: five shots, five rabbits. I remember giving thanks that night for the privilege of having so exemplary a day, and of being able to make so solid a contribution to the family larder. It was the only time I got five rabbits in a day.

During that winter Chips and I brought home about twenty-five rabbits; my father brought home at least as many, and my brothers added uncounted others as well. In years like that, rabbit meat was a winter staple. It was always prepared the same way: first soaked for several hours in slightly salted water, then boiled until nearly done, then fried in an iron skillet with butter, lard, and seasoning. That's the entire recipe. Some things in life are simple.

Hunting had a free and easy rationale, naturally come by, cementing bonds between generations; it also had a high place among the rites of initiation. Tractors, cars, girls, guns—such were the vessels of those rites, each with its incomparable allures and threats.

It is true that the sport was often unsuccessful or physically uncomfortable, true that it sometimes left us wet or cold, but it was never without its deeper pleasures. If hunting had its critics, they held their peace in our community. My brothers and I, our cousins, our neighbors, our friends—we came to manhood in an environment steeped in the ideas, in the sights, smells, sounds, and ceremonies of hunting; and we cultivated them and we added to them and formed friendships among them. To know those things was to love them; and much of what was attractive there is still valid and still vivid across the years. My present ambivalence about hunting—next chapter—is entirely retrospective.

In November, when small-game hunting shifted to deer hunting, all the ritual elements were deepened and ennobled.

Rites of Deer Hunting

Incomparably the best, the most graceful, the most beautiful among the game animals familiar to us was the white-tailed deer. It followed automatically that deer hunting was the noblest form of outdoorsmanship. And deer hunting was the only form of vacation my father ever willingly took.

Hunting may be at its best with companions, but it may also be savored for its solitariness. For me deer hunting perfectly combined the pleasures of solitude in the woods with the pleasures of camaraderie at regular intervals, such as around noontime camp fires. I'm sure my father knew well before I did that long drafts of the total silence of the forest, measured and slow, were nourishment to the soul. To a young person inexperienced in these things, the woods is an alien place, haunted with unseen presences such as to make one uneasy. Farm boys early overcame this. Partly from my experience of hunting I first came to admire the poets of nature. "There is a pleasure in the pathless woods, . . . there is society where none intrudes." When I came across words like those of Byron in high school, I felt that they were not abstract and highfalutin but that they touched upon something deep and wise. They may not express the typical sentiments of adolescence—only one of its temporary extremes—but they are not foreign to a hunter.

November 15, the annual opening day of deer season, was flagged from afar on the farm calendar. Even schools accommodated themselves to deer hunting, giving an automatic pass to those who went. My father tried to have the fall plowing done by then but didn't always succeed—in which case the plowing waited; for in November, as he was fond of putting it, he had to tend to "Uncle Sam's cattle."

For every boy of our inclinations there came eventually his First Day of Deer Hunting. For us it was age sixteen.

On the opening day of my first deer season I went with my father and Marvin to the area we knew as the Plains, known also for its huckleberries, "jackrabbits," and white-tailed deer. Marvin had a proper red-checked hunting coat, but for Dad and me Mother had sewed swatches of red flannel to our jackets. On that first and unforgotten morning we drove to the woods while it was still dark, and stole quietly, by guttering moonlight, to our preselected places. It was not deer hunting itself that required such covert action as being in the woods before daylight, but tradition demanded it. On other days we might go at other, more convenient times, but something decreed that on the first day of the season unusual stealth was required, so the schedule had to be unreasonable. The cows were milked early, the farm animals fed off schedule, all nature bearing witness that this was no normal day. Most religions, I suppose, have rituals of obeisance to some such abstract value of uncertain rationale. We settled into our positions while it was still dark.

Standing alone before the dawn that first day—a boy inserted into the world on a man's terms—I felt blissfully absorbed into the vast serenity of the Plains. Nothing was happening among the silent trees in the quiet, quiet woods, the forest no less hallowed today for being so deep and damp and chill. Tranquillity without boundaries held everything in its palm but relinquished it now and then to a vague and distant tramp, tramp, muffled as through damp leaves, of another hunter or, as I fancied, perhaps a solitary black bear. Gradually, I became aware of a strange radiance that seemed not to come from the sky, which was sullen gray at best, but to emanate from the woods, from the trees themselves. Totally alone as I was in this universe of calm, I did not feel the least bit uneasy or lonely—just exhilarated. Dad would be off somewhere a few hundred yards to my right, Marvin far to my left. Silence everywhere. Everything in place. Eyes straining in every direction. Waiting, waiting for the sun to light up the landscape and reclaim the world.

The day seeped slowly into the woods, and with it a hoarfrost appeared everywhere, first gray, then lighter, then white as bleached wool. The early luminosity that had puzzled me in the unlighted forest had indeed come from the trees, from the shapely, furry hoarfrost, custom-fitted to every twig in sight. In the new half-light a white blotch on my left resolved itself into a wondrously vivid and exaggerated spiderweb, perfectly engineered, face-high, simulating newly spun yarn of purest white. Or a frozen sunbeam. Evidently the forest itself had been dressed before dawn in early-winter finery to usher me into this day of all days.

On the ground, moisture had toughened fallen leaves, silencing them, so I knew a deer could caper quite unheard through the brushy clearing where I kept watch. Consequently, the early challenge would be on my eyes, to see before being seen, to see what I could not hear. Initially, all I could discern were the soft and pure layers of hoarfrost embracing bushes, branches, and shrubs as far as the eye could see. Each sprig dipped in dazzling white.

I had no expectation that my first day would match Marvin's first day of a few years earlier. That was 1945—the war was just over and it was still impossible to buy shells. Whatever ammunition anyone had was what he had left over from earlier years, what somebody had gotten for him on the black market, or what he had himself loaded from raw materials—spent shell, powder, lead, and cap. What Dad had left over to offer Marvin for his first day of deer hunting was just three shotgun shells: one "Double O" buckshot and two slugs. On the afternoon before opening day, Marvin had expended one of those slugs on target practice; he had wanted to know exactly how far a twelve-gauge slug would drop at seventy-five paces. Using one of those three shells to test his sights seemed to me to be an act of extraordinary poise and confidence. Then he had gone off to the woods the next day with two shells, and by noon he was back with an eight-point buck and one shell left. That stellar performance was a little too perfect to serve as a model for me.

My father never took practice shots with his deer rifle, never "sighted the gun in," since using ammunition for practice did not fit his idea of stewardship. When occasion arose, which was rare enough, he just fired a shot as best he could. Although he had hunted since his youth, harvesting a score or two of rabbits each year with his shotgun, he had invested a dozen years in deer hunting before he first brought home venison. That didn't bother him; and there were comparatively few deer in those days, anyway. Experience in Michigan and elsewhere shows clearly that the more intensively the land is farmed with the mixed crops of the traditional family farm, the less congenial is the land for deer; and vice versa. When Missaukee County shifted to fallow land and to corn and hay cropping for dairying during the last generation, the deer herd multiplied rapidly. There were virtually no deer in southern Lower Michigan in the thirties and forties, and our part of the state was bucks-only hunting territory. The odds against success at deer hunting were something like ten to one. However, sporting instincts do not require feeding by success or even by its likelihood—only by its possibility.

Daylight now, and behind me somewhere, gunfire. How far? A mile? Half a mile? My hands moved instantly and tightened on my twelve-gauge shotgun, thumb and finger on hammer and trigger. How warm and congenial a companion, that gun. Weapons: what fascination, what power. A spear is but an extension of my arm, an arrow is but a better spear, a bullet but a better arrow. Time passed.

Only the pounding of my own heart could be heard, and I listened to it subside slowly, slowly, like faraway footsteps retreating. Then absolute silence rolled in once more and spread itself everywhere among the trees, over the frosted shrubs and the damp leaves. I was the only person in the universe again.

Thoughts drift. There had been another time, four or five years earlier, when I had been "deer hunting" with Dad—unarmed, but along for company and for a glimpse inside the arcane world of the hunter. On that occasion we had walked until we were thoroughly warm and then we sat down on a log—side by side in total silence for what seemed hours and hours. We said nothing. Just once when a rustle of leaves caught our ears, Dad whispered "squirrel," whereupon a squirrel emerged from a brush pile to stare at us, then to jump and stare again, then to curse us fervently and flee. We smiled with pleasure at such eloquence. I watched Dad watch the woods for any sign of movement and I tried to do the same. A partridge landed nearby, strutted around eating lunch, and then strode off, full of dignity and aplomb and beechnuts. It hadn't seen us or hadn't cared. A lone chickadee dropped by. It kept daring itself to perch on the end of Dad's gun barrel. Then we went home. So this was deer hunting? It was somewhat confusing—gratifying and also disappointing and boring and yet exhilarating. Strange logic of trophies: we had been lying in wait for a victim that, captured, would have become a prize. We might have seen deer, but we didn't; we might have missed the pleasures of very small things, but we didn't. I do not suppose a lesson was consciously intended, but the one I learned was something about the simple satisfactions of quiet observation, something about the way periods of absolute stillness heighten powers of observation.

My mind drifts back to my own clearing, where the sun has sprinkled the hoarfrosted landscape with diamonds, and I settled down to study the woods. During the hours of that first morning I scoured every nook and contour of the woodscape around me, alert to every flicker of movement. Not a chickadee stirred but I saw it. Then slight breezes began to chop up the fragile skeins of hoary yarn, dropping fragments that broke as they fell and disappeared.

Although the weather was getting warmer, I, immobile as a stump, was emphatically getting colder. It was a first and stern lesson in how very cold one can become standing stock-still on a moderate fall day. My solution would be to walk for a while to restore the circulation to my stiffened legs. I would be as silent as an Indian.

Not silent enough. I stepped on a branch, which snapped, and then I saw the deer. Like magic she just appeared fifty yards away, an elegant doe who leapt a small knoll, waved a hurried white-tailed good-bye, and vanished. It took about three seconds. Snap of branch to fare-thee-well, three priceless seconds! In that brief moment I took a mental picture that remains unfaded to this day: she clears the little knoll, gray against the shining hoarfrost, full of grace and glory, forever young and far too strong to die.

At the noontime rendezvous Marvin had a fire going, and Dad came up just as I did. He had seen no deer, he said, but he'd heard one, and he had seen lots of places for them. Marvin had spotted three—far away and going farther, he said. Around the fire we bantered and joked, an escape valve for a quiet, suppressed ecstasy. We spread cold fingers toward warm flames, inhaled the fragrant, smoky air, opened the sandwiches and coffee, laid out plans for the afternoon. The trees around us were spangled with diamonds.

There would be days and years to come when I would see lots of deer, lots of action, and be with friends who shot a deer, eventually get one myself—days of high adventure and nights of tall tales. But on this one particular day, my first, not very much happened at all: a day of intensity if not of adventure, a day of simple graces impossible to forget. I recollect that three men stood tall around a certain noontime fire, and all the world was ablaze with meaning.

On the long-abandoned farmlands of my property in the New Hampshire countryside, white-tailed deer wander, eating now and then from my garden, walking at night across the yard; and throughout the winter months I find in the woods innumerable tracks of varying hare. I study the animals' habits and whereabouts, take note of what they eat, and observe also that sometimes the hares are themselves eaten by coyotes. Now and then I find a place where a hare has died at the beak and claws of an owl.

I haven't eaten any New Hampshire hare myself, though I fancy I should certainly enjoy it now after more than thirty years—the dinner, if not the harvesting. I am less certain that my wife would, for she did not acquire this taste in youth, and the same goes for my teenage son. The thought of venison roast or loin steak does not set their juices flowing as it does mine. And certainly neither of them yearns for a fried-rabbit dinner or encourages me to procure the ingredients for one. And theirs is not sentimentality toward the hares, for I have seen that they do not deplore the hunting coyotes and the owls. But if I went hunting hare, I do not think that they would cheer for me.

The attractions of hunting, its complex lore and its simple charms, its intense sensual and imaginative associations, its deep attachment to the mythos of rural America, are all undoubtedly grounded in universal human impulses, and, accordingly, the pleasures of hunting have very long roots. But they are learned pleasures still, and they may in time also become unlearned. For them to become unlearned, hunting need not lose its attractions, only its rationale.

Today my son and I "hunt" together, after our fashion, almost as much as my father and I did; and my son started at a younger age than I. But we do not bear arms.

It is true that he is missing something that might have been, and he knows that but he does not feel it. I miss something too; but I have found that the pleasures of tracking and observation overlap with many of those of hunting, though some of them are of a different order, too. There is a shift of gravity, from the mystique of man-the-hunter to the lure of nature-the-mysterious. The forest and uplands lose none of their sparkle, and new networks of affection flourish where old ones fade away.

To the Original Calling, Farewell

> Life can only be understood backwards.
> But it must be lived forwards.
> —SøREN KIERKEGAARD

I am leafing through old copies of the *Cadillac Evening News*. October 14, 1944, front page:

> A new type of farmer who is more business-like and who turns more to mechanized, scientific agriculture will develop after the war, Ernest L. Anthony, dean of agriculture at Michigan State College, predicted in an address to the Michigan feedmen's conference. Farming tomorrow will be a business.

Do you hear what I hear? I hear America singing.

So after the war, farming became mechanized and scientific, just as the dean had said; it became a business. To accommodate the achievements of this business after four decades, Congress had to write a new chapter in the Bankruptcy Code.

I am leafing through copies of the *Michigan Farmer*. December 1986—an article titled "New Hope for the Family Farm." It speaks of "shock and desperation in the countryside" and says that lenders are "foreclosing and liquidating" farmers' assets "in record numbers." It says that farmers "are losing their homes, livelihoods and dreams with no place to go."

> There is now an alternative, available exclusively to farmers, that will permit them to keep their farms and have their debt reduced to manageable levels. Congress recently amended the Bankruptcy Statutes to create a remedy for distressed family farmers. The remedy is Chapter 12.

Two years later came the Agricultural Credit Act of 1988: in the spirit of Chapter 12, it established a new appeals agency, barred creditors from taking farmers' homes, and gave small farmers the first option to buy back their farms in cases of foreclosure.

That wasn't exactly what the dean had in mind when he recommended making farming a business. Mysterious are the ways of progress.

Was it evident in the years immediately following the end of World War II that the way of life to which we were accustomed might change drastically? We read what the dean said, but I do not think we fully caught the signs of change. We knew we would grow up; we did not imagine the rural culture we knew would be entirely supplanted by another kind of farming, one that would eventually wind its way around to the bitter consolations of Chapter 12 of the Bankruptcy Code.

"Men do not like hard work," says Emerson, "but every man has an exceptional respect for tillage, and a feeling that this is the original calling of his race." Precisely. How easy it was to tell myself as I entered my last year of high school in 1950 that I intended to be a farmer. That was a reasoned intention, but it was also an affirmation of the life I then knew, my assent to the proposition, strongly felt but unexpressed, that farming was the original and the noblest calling of the race.

I could not have known, but my own "exceptional respect for tillage" had put me on a mental trajectory that would have carried me—if undeflected—straight into the heart of agribusinessland. By the time I was old enough to be exasperated with my father's conservative ways, I could see that the path to bigger and better farming would lead through college. As a practical matter that meant Michigan State College (now University), in East Lansing. But by the time I had completed my high school years, college loomed as more than just a means: it seemed a full-time, though temporary, calling in itself. So if a college education in its own right was the thing to focus on next, why *that* college? Why not one more in line with our cultural background, one where I already had friends? So I went to Calvin College, in Grand Rapids, as did all my siblings, a college to which many rural youths went and from which almost none returned to the farm.

If my own long-standing plans were now suspended, somehow I still assumed that while my back was temporarily turned, things would go on as before on the farms of Missaukee County. They didn't. Not even on our eighty acres.

That communal arrangement of small-scale mixed husbandry with all its nicely interlocked odds and ends, its balance of land and hand labor and horsepower and livestock and cash crops and wood-lot and tools and family and neighborhood—had it not shown itself eminently workable over succeeding generations? And was it not a perfect enactment of America's recurring agrarian dream? Strenuous and bleak it was at times, and there were those who couldn't wait to escape it for the presumed comforts and pleasures of the city, but that way of life seemed to most people of its own time to be intrinsically secure, a permanent achievement, durable and enduring, maybe inevitable, like the land itself.

In fact, it wasn't at all inevitable and it wasn't lasting.

It had gained a certain social plateau and had fashioned a certain intricate economy—organic, cunning, hovering near to the land, strongly banked against internal breakdowns. The husbandry had been designed on the spot; it was communally and economically manageable, and it was in harmony with what the land itself, still unexpended, could sustain over the long haul. Jefferson would have approved. For half a century or so the regular interplay of many small elements was the secret of its resilience. No one could invent from scratch such fine-tuned social and economic arrangements, any more than one could invent in the abstract a human language and breathe into it a public life. Some social and economic systems, like languages, find their proper habitat, adapt to it, and grow vigorously like the flowers of the field.

Like the flowers of the field—which have their day and cease to be.

For the only thing more remarkable than the inner coherence of the rural network that we knew so well was its final and utter vulnerability. Suddenly it was in jeopardy, unexpected and profound, to the state of the larger world and to the ideological crosscurrents that, just at mid-century, whispered through the farmland with their unsettling rumors of bigger and better and more, rumors amplified from all the land-grant colleges of America's Middle West. Michigan State's dean spoke for a whole company of wise men. "A new type of farmer," they said, and the progressive farmers hearkened to their word. And the experts and the machinery manufacturers all agreed: "Farming tomorrow will be a business." Consequently, new machines and new ideas and new chemicals, and new hybrids, and new expectations—subversive without meaning it, ironic without even knowing it—simply pulled the local system apart like a house of hay. The seemingly endless story in which we lived turned out to be but a brief, bracketed episode, not much more than half a century long, a story quickly told. It became clear that our mode of farm life, with all its intricate simplicities, did not form an isolated Missaukee County enclave at all; it too was an organic part of the vast commercial and speculative American system. That had been true all along, but for some time it had been possible not to notice.

For the quarter century between 1925 and 1950, through depression and war, through good times and hard times and inflationary times—unsettled times—the rooted assumptions of that rural life remained firm. How ironic that in the next quarter century, 1950 to 1975—relatively stable times—those same firm assumptions were all uprooted. Farming did not disappear around McBain, and neither did the community, but almost all the small farms of mixed crops and varied livestock did. Hundreds of fields that had been productive through two world wars and a depression were abandoned or left fallow through a government soil-bank program, or reclaimed by the woods or planted to evergreens. And in short order those farmers who first chose to specialize in hogs or hens or beans or potatoes began to give way to those who specialized in dairying.

Today, most of the Missaukee County farms that are not fallow or reforested are parts of very large dairy farms. And hardly anyone knows the taste of homemade butter.

Looking back, the plot seems inexorable, like that of a Greek tragedy, its end implicit in its beginning, its destiny presaged but not understood by a chorus of agricultural deans, who only sang America's own song. Since that rural culture was invaded by so many novelties, one can point almost at random and find elements involved in the subversion. Science was part of it—hybrids, pesticides. Technology was part of it—bigger, newer, stronger machines. Fantasy was part of it—the mystique of progress and machines and modernity. And economics was deeply implicated.

The only economics that we knew had always been more immersed in value judgments than in cash. Today's economy posits that manufactured goods are cheap and replaceable, and that time is costly. That's an exact reversal of values in little more than a generation. "More time than money" was a cliché that energized that older world, a statement of value and not of despair.

In the landscapes revisited in this book, time and many raw materials were abundant, inexpensive; most manufactured goods were rare and costly. Often we thought of a new purchase as a last resort. So we straightened bent nails; we mended leaky pails; we patched the old gunnysacks; and my father did not buy a new scythe handle—he resorted to the woodlot and made one from a crooked elm sapling. Almost without exception, whatever was wooden was grown and hand-fashioned and not bought, and whatever was metal was thought of as repairable. The time involved hardly mattered. Indeed, did we not grow up thinking that farm implements were simply not used up at all? How could you wear out a mower or a cultivator? Parts wore out, yes—mower knives and cultivator shovels and plow points—and those we patched or replaced; but the thing itself endured through the generations, like the stones on the hillside.

I suspect that our family carried these presumptions further into practice than some of our neighbors, for deeply ingrained attitudes of my parents were involved. Their native conservative outlook was strongly reinforced by the Depression, when there was simply no money for anything but the barest necessities; and it was reinforced again by the war, when many things thought necessary were not available at all. Still, it was an attitude well suited to the economy of that time and circumstance.

Like farmers of all ages, those of that era too were at the mercy of the market and of nature. Until recently, these were somehow vaguely worthy adversaries, implacable though they be. When the farmer prevailed against them there was a sense not just of triumph but of professional achievement, success with honor, hard labor rewarded. Though fitful, both nature and the market were made up of familiar components, near at hand. One learned to work around them, and the discipline of learning accorded a dignity to the process.

One year in the late forties, on the morning after Labor Day, we awoke to a landscape white as snow: a vicious frost was killing everything, even leaves on trees. Corn and beans died unripe; potatoes, at the height of their growing season. One day everything had been lush and green and growing, the next day the corn stood bleached in the afternoon sun, the beans drooped brown, the potato vines lay black in their rows—sights to sicken brave hearts. That year we just fed the corn stalks to the cows, husking out only a few shriveled ears. We had to buy corn for the chickens, and my parents did not pay off the farm mortgage as they had hoped; they barely paid the interest. Such are the caprices with which the farmers contended, forces completely out of control but familiar as nightfall. The farmers of that day responded, as farmers had for centuries and centuries, with the weapons they had, mainly persistence, patience, and more work. They learned to lean against the blast, and learned to live with small potatoes—there might be a bumper crop next year. Disappointed they were, and sometimes shattered, but not aggrieved: even the Bible concedes that the rain falls and the storm beats on the just and the unjust alike.

The vagaries of the market were a more complex thing, also out of control, but they had seemed to make some sense, as an adversary ought. The market had something to do—so it was alleged—with the habits of city housewives at the grocery, with the size of the crop, and with people's taste for pork and butter and eggs. Some years my father stored the potato crop in the cellar for the winter instead of selling from the field in the fall: the winter or spring price would be better. One spring there was no price at all. The abundant harvest that had depressed the price in the fall had outlasted the winter and nobody was buying. Came late spring and it was time to plant the new crop even though the old crop was still in storage. In July Dad carried all the potatoes up out of the cellar, bushel by bushel, and dumped them out. Some we cooked up as mashed potatoes for the pigs. Too young to help or even to know what was going on, I was old enough to aggravate the problem with questions.

"Why are you doing that?" I pestered. "What's wrong with our potatoes? What are you going to do next?"

Dad said something about throwing out the potatoes because of the Depression. But he had just planted potatoes! I did not comprehend this at all, though I was sure he did and that sufficed. Things were basically understandable, but depressions were confusing to a child. So we farmed under the shadow of the whims of the weather and the markets—and under the rays of Providence, mysterious but kindly still.

Today's farmer, laboring too under the shadow of the weather—and of Chapter 12 of the Bankruptcy Code—is also at the mercy of the market, but perhaps not quite in the old sense. The baffles he confronts are not so simple as the variable demand for potatoes and bread in Detroit groceries; they concern things less humane, more remote, more frustrating, as far out of his reach as the climate and as recondite as the Depression was to me. What sets the market? Abstractions: the world competitiveness of the U.S. dollar, the shape of the debt crisis in the third world, mismanagements of the agricultural bureaucracy in the Soviet Union, world interest rates, oil prices in the Persian Gulf, the size of the national debt, politically volatile subsidy interventions of the U.S. government.

So far as comprehension and reasonable response are concerned, he might as well deal with a sudden early frost or he might as well be a child and deal with the Depression.

If the style of yesterday's farmer ran mainly to persistence and toil, tinged with the kind of stoical pride that sometimes looked like meekness, the posture of today's farmer is far more embattled. He combats nature with machines and chemicals, and the market with politics. He is in business, after all, just as the dean said. When he fails, there are few voices to remind him that failures too come with the territory, and many voices to tell him that someone somewhere is at fault and that someone somewhere owes him recompense. He is a family farmer, after all. Offered the bleak relief of a new and improved Bankruptcy Code, he finds that it tastes like rancid butter. It's easy to feel aggrieved and hard to tell just what one is up against. When he prevails, it may seem more akin to good fortune at the lottery or the stock market than to the rewards of self-respect and labor such as the older farmers often felt.

My parents would not claim to have foreseen the world that was to be. But sometime in the mid-fifties, with four of their offspring in college and the fifth entering high school and evincing little enthusiasm for farming, they read the signs of the times. My father looked at the prospects of Michigan farming—looked without reproach—and guessed that perhaps there was not much of a place there for him. He was too young to retire, but he saw with a sidelong glance that farming was bent on passing him by. For a decade he had heard the sounds approaching. If depression and war were no longer baying at his heels, progress was. This time he decided to move over and let it pass—a sensible judgment, I believe, made slowly, thoughtfully, and without trauma.

A step at a time he stepped aside. One year he sold the pigs, the next year the horses, then the cows, and then he rented out the back forty. The next year the grain bins were empty, and he sold most of the chickens. One day on a visit home from graduate school in the late fifties, I found the stables vacated and the barn empty. It was late July and the smell of corn pollen hung in the air, but it was not our corn. Young cattle had taken up residency to keep the pastures down. My father was now employed as a carpenter and not noticeably saddened by the change. He had left farming while he was successful at it: without debt, without wealth, without obligations, and perhaps without regret.

If he was relieved to be free at last of the eternal rhythm of morning and night milking and the daily rounds of chicken feeding and manure hauling, we of the next generation did not greatly regret the change, either. We were preoccupied. We had all had long schooling in accepting the course of human events, and we were not now disposed to try to stop history in its tracks by throwing our own careers across its path. Nor were we disposed to feel qualms over leaving the family tradition. All our ancestors, as far back as memories and records go (less than two centuries), were people of the land, but none of my father's four sons followed him into farming. Never was there any shadow of reproach upon us for that. If anything, Dad may have underestimated whatever was noble in his calling.

Our parents had desired for us the education they had not had, and they were prepared to accept the consequences, unanticipated though they were. But all historical experience shows that the city recruits from the countryside. Although they would have been pleased to see one of us assume the farm, they had the grace to believe that we were pursuing more valuable callings in remoter places. And we for our part were confident that they would not sell the farm and would not themselves leave the land except for reasons of emergency. So it was not forever and forever farewell; a part of ourselves would remain in place to be revisited. We had all learned the spiritual uses of fellowship with the land and with green and growing things, and it was unlikely that those impulses would ever wither away.

Although our farewells to the original calling—those of both generations—were well made on the whole, and were not absolute or conducted in remorse, I would not overlook the prodigious changes that swept across the rural landscape, or neglect even the humblest surface symbols of those transformations.

It was during that crucial decade of transition, the fifties, that the corn and bean planters, the potato planters, the little hand-held clover seeder, and the potato duster were hung up on nails on the wall of the garage, along with the corn knives and the beet toppers—tools whose memory inevitably touches a lyrical vein in the American story. And in the barn, the big barley fork, the grain scoop, the three-tined pitchforks, and the four-tined manure forks were put aside. They had all had thirty or forty years of daily use, and some of them had used up a handle or two and some of them had worn down their tines. The rural revolution that was afoot, the devious path toward the rendezvous with Chapter 12, did not at first replace *men* by machines; it replaced hand tools by machines. And that was precisely why it appeared desirable, why it was welcomed, and why it was insidious.

It is now a fixed part of America's larger rural memory that not only hand tools but many larger farm implements as well went into permanent retirement at about that same time. A younger generation may be unaware that on many old farmsteads you can find them still—peer over a hill and see them, but maybe not recognize them. Hard by the fencerow or in the grassy hollow by the orchard they wait, undecaying remnants of horse-drawn farm implements: mowers, binders, plows, cultivators, harrows, potato diggers, culti-packers, wagons, dump rakes. Congregations of venerable relics. No war-driven scrap drives conscripted the old iron in those tools, and when they were no longer useful to the farm they had farmed, they no longer had value to anybody. They merge with the background American mythos.

But as I drive again across the flatlands of Michigan, over the straight roads, past the prosperous-*looking* dairy farms, the fallow fields, the long horizons, here and there I shall spot again that retired plow mounted on a little pedestal in the front yard of a semi-suburban home. It bears a little awkwardly, it seems to me, its swift promotion from necessity and utility to a place in history and ceremony. True, the plow has an honored seniority within the ranks of farm implements now dispossessed (the goddess of agriculture is often represented as seated upon a plow), but on the clipped lawn the old plow seems self-conscious, almost embarrassed, a lone alumnus of a forgotten culture.

Even the dump rake participates in the old mystique, appearing now and then at a town celebration in a public parade, tines a bit rusty and ajangle and aclatter; in that honored and unnatural setting we can admire, perhaps for the first time, its weirdly ungainly elegance. In contrast, the potato digger is just a homely and grubby thing. A plow has class, a dump rake has style, but a potato digger has neither, and it does not earn a second glance. And here lies the horse-drawn harrow, which will never be put on parade either and, indeed, is not much of an aesthetic object; it rests and rusts in tranquillity beneath the uncut grass. Yet the old harrow is still tense with wonderfully resilient steel in its teeth, metal still sturdy enough for years and years of chewing sod.

Indeed, almost none of the steel in these venerable farm implements has lost its temper—which is somehow a pleasant and vaguely reassuring thought. It's as if something still hints of a world that is gone but whose character and values were intense and tough and well composed.